Taking a Big Picture Look
@
Technology, Learning, and the Community College

Edited by
Mark David Milliron
&
Cindy L. Miles

League for Innovation in the Community College
2000

Published with support from Oracle Corporation
www.oracle.com

TABLE OF CONTENTS

ACKNOWLEDGMENTS

Any publication is the result of the contributions of many people. All involved will attest that this *Big Picture* book was indeed a *big* project, one that began with the blessing, support, and direction of our dear friend and League President Emeritus, Terry O'Banion. Thank you Terry for all you've done to help us step back and view the community college landscape through the eyes of learners.

We must also thank the contributing authors for their patience and hard work in bringing the book together. We often joked that this was the project that would not die–and it was the good spirits and deep convictions of these authors that helped keep it alive. Finally, we need to thank League staff members for their work on this team effort, particularly Gerardo de los Santos, Nancy Italia, Edward Leach, Stella Perez, and Pam Schuetz, who helped shape and improve our thinking and writing about these important issues. Finally, we need to say a special thank you to one more League team member, Cynthia Wilson, whose dedication, talent, and editing and writing skills helped bring the Big Picture into final focus. We couldn't have done it without you. What a blessing it is to work with such a *talented* group of colleagues during so vibrant a time in the community college movement.

INTRODUCTION

Mark David Milliron
Cindy L. Miles

For more than 32 years, the League for Innovation in the Community College has been exploring the major forces shaping the community college movement and pioneering innovative solutions to the educational challenges these institutions encounter. In 1998, when the editors of *Change* honored our former President and CEO, Terry O'Banion, as one of the top ten idea champions in higher education, they pointed out that in his tenure he had helped transform the League into "the most dynamic organization in the community college world," one that takes seriously its mission to catalyze positive change in two-year institutions nationally and internationally.

Taking a Big Picture Look @ Technology, Learning, and the Community College is another of the League's ambitious explorations of the most powerful trends facing community college educators. Given the omnipresence of technology and its influence on the way we work, play, and learn, it is not surprising that stepping back to take a "big picture" look at technology, learning, and the community college became a colossal undertaking. Each lens through which we looked at the intersection between the Technology and Learning Revolutions and community colleges brought to light a complex array of issues, stories, and research, each of which might merit a full focus of study.

Ultimately we endeavored to portray these trends with meaningful breadth and depth by including perspectives from across the community college spectrum: teaching and learning, student services, leadership, developmental education, staff development, distance learning, marketing, and enterprise management. This resulting volume is the culmination of more than three years of work with some of the most talented and dedicated community college educators in our business, each of whom contributed significant insight and effort to this collective exploration of how the whirlwinds of technology and learning are sweeping through our institutions.

As you peruse the following chapter overviews, you will find that we have incorporated a range of methodological approaches, including primary research, practical applications, case studies, and essays, to give the topics of inquiry a larger context. Whether you are an administrator, faculty member, classified staff member, student, trustee, policymaker, or observer of higher education, we believe you will find information of interest in the chapters that follow.

In the end, we think you will find this panorama of perspectives on the confluence of technology and learning to be engaging and challenging. It is our greatest hope, however, that you find this book a useful resource in your own work with community colleges to improve the learning and lives of the millions of students touched by our institutions each day.

CHAPTER 1
Seven Signs on the Road Ahead for Community Colleges
Mark David Milliron, President and Chief Executive Officer
Cindy L. Miles, Vice President and Chief Operating Officer
League for Innovation in the Community College (CA)

> At the dawn of a new century, community colleges face transformational challenges and opportunities as they celebrate their 100th anniversary in the higher education community. The authors use data from a three-year study of more than 700 institutions to explore key trends influencing community colleges, and to give particular focus to the effects and potential of the Learning and Technology Revolutions in helping community colleges meet the range of challenges on the road ahead.

CHAPTER 2
Maintaining the Technology Edge: Leadership Lessons for an Uncertain Future
Paul A. Elsner, Chancellor Emeritus
Maricopa Community Colleges (AZ)

> The Maricopa County Community College district has long been seen as a pioneer in the use of information technology in higher education. In this chapter, the author, who served as chancellor, visionary, and change champion of the district for more than twenty years, reviews lessons learned from Maricopa experiences, offers competing visions of the future of technology, and predicts the implications of those visions for community colleges.

CHAPTER 3
Administrators' Roles in the Adoption of Technology by Faculty:
Inside the Traditional Classroom and Beyond
Alice Wildes Villadsen, President
Brookhaven College (TX)
Mary Kay Kickels, Vice President for Academic Affairs
Moraine Valley Community College (IL)
Sunil Chand, Executive Vice President for Academic and Student Affairs
Cuyahoga Community College (OH)

In today's world, the rapid pace of change and the growing need for education make the community college faculty member's ability to adopt and adapt to technologies increasingly critical. This chapter reports on a national study of methods community college administrators are using to encourage and fund faculty use and acceptance of innovation, change, and technology. Numerous strategies demonstrate how leaders from department chairs to senior administrators are helping lead their colleges through change and improve student and organizational learning along the way.

CHAPTER 4
Technology, Learning, and Community (TLC):
Perspectives from Teaching Excellence Award Recipients
Mark David Milliron, President and Chief Executive Officer
Cindy L. Miles, Vice President and Chief Operating Officer
League for Innovation in the Community College (CA)

Although the unprecedented number of tools available for engaging, inspiring, and connecting learners makes this is an exciting time for faculty, an abundance of apprehension and controversy surrounds discussions of ways teachers can make best use of available resources. Reporting on a national research project involving almost 2,000 award-winning community college faculty, the authors of this chapter explore the variety of ways these faculty use information technology to inspire learning in and out of the classroom while maintaining the sense of community that is the hallmark of the community college.

CHAPTER 5
Cyber-Counseling, Virtual Registration, and Student Self-Service: Student Services in the Information Age
Carol Cross, Director
Edudigm (NC)

During the last fifteen years, information technologies ranging from student information systems for managing enrollments to computer assessments for informing advising and placement have transformed the traditional community college student services department. In this chapter, the author takes a broad look at information technology's role in serving students in the community college and synthesizes strategies from colleges that are making good use of today's technology in student service programs.

CHAPTER 6
Keeping Up to Speed When You're Moving Too Fast Already: Information Technology Staff Development Programs and User Support
Lynn Sullivan Taber, Associate Professor, College of Education
University of South Florida (FL)

User support and instructional integration are the key issues facing community colleges struggling with information technology. This chapter explores research on the modes and models in information technology staff development to help provide solutions to the sticky issue of keeping staff up to speed in this time of rapid change.

CHAPTER 7
Into the Breach: A National Study of Computers and the "At Risk"
Laurence F. Johnson, President
Fox Valley Technical College (WI)

As community colleges have become more adept at using computer-based methods, these approaches have been increasingly applied to address the needs of students who come to community colleges lacking basic skills. Computer-based methods of delivering basic skills instruction at several community colleges were examined in this study to determine patterns and guidelines for success. In this chapter, the study is described, several essential attributes of successful programs are identified, and a useful set of suggestions for practitioners is presented.

CHAPTER 8
The Evolution of Distance Education
Judy Lever-Duffy, Professor, Business and Computer Information Systems
Miami-Dade Community College (FL)

From telecourses to classes on the Web, alternative learning opportunities are more common than ever for today's community college student. In this chapter, the author tracks the development of distance learning in the community college and explores its role in today's and tomorrow's instructional programs.

CHAPTER 9
On the Moving Rock We Stand: Technology and Transition
Steven Lee Johnson, Provost, Clearwater Campus
Conferlete Carney, Vice President for Technology
St. Petersburg Junior College (FL)

The rapid pace of change of the Information Age places challenging demands on leadership. Major technology projects are very difficult to manage, both from a technology management point of view and from a total college management point of view. As technology changes are integrated within colleges, they create widespread changes in culture, policies, practices, and other essential college characteristics. In this chapter, the authors explore key factors and issues related to approaching major technology transitions effectively.

CHAPTER 10
Selling the Sizzle: Marketing Community Colleges Through Information Technology
Lawrence G. Miller, President and Chief Executive Officer
Miller and Associates (TN)
Paul Fuchcar, Administrator of Development
Erlanger Health System (TN)
David T. Harrison, Dean, Business Technologies Division
Sinclair Community College (OH)

> In the competitive educational environment, community colleges must position themselves through marketing to recruit students, to secure funding, and to enhance the institution's image. This chapter looks at using research, marketing strategies, and technology-driven approaches to marketing in the Information Age.

CHAPTER 11
Internet Vision: Unleashing the Power of the Internet in the Higher Education Enterprise
Mark David Milliron, President and Chief Executive Officer
League for Innovation in the Community College (CA)

> The Internet has moved from minor use to a major part of daily lives of administrators, faculty, and staff in only five short years, and now holds the promise of bringing long-separated people, processes, and systems together to transform higher education. From distance education to in-class instruction, degree programs to workforce development, business office operations to student services, developing an Internet Vision has become essential for leadership in the Information Age. This chapter explores how the Internet is leveraged by the best companies worldwide, how it is being applied in higher education, and the implications for higher education constituents.

CHAPTER 1

SEVEN SIGNS ON THE ROAD
AHEAD FOR COMMUNITY COLLEGES

Mark David Milliron and Cindy L. Miles

As we enter the new millennium, we approach the celebration of the 100th anniversary of the community college as a member of the higher education community. Joliet Junior College in Illinois, the recognized pioneer of public two-year schools (Phillippe, 1997; Vaughn, 1995), opened its doors in 1901 and sparked new thinking about the paths available for students across the United States. The spark met with the proper fuel in America: the land grant colleges of the 19th century. These institutions began the shift from aristocracy to meritocracy in higher education. They offered more "applied" curricula–such as business, architecture, and engineering–and made these programs available to a much broader set of students based on achievement. Still, most avenues were closed to women, minorities, and those from rural areas or less affluent backgrounds.

The advancement of junior and technical colleges, which subsequently developed into what is now known as the community college movement, cleared the path toward dramatic democratic educational opportunities, bringing down barriers for millions of students over the course of the 20th Century. Currently, more than ten million American citizens are enrolled in community college programs each year, representing close to half of all undergraduates. Overall, 46 percent of all African American students, 55 percent of all Hispanic students, 55 percent of Asian/Pacific Islander students, and 55 percent of all Native American students in higher education attend community colleges (American Association of Community Colleges, 1999). In California, three out of four students in public postsecondary education are enrolled in a community college (California Public Postsecondary Enrollment Projections, 1999). Moreover, adult education of all kinds is burgeoning, as more than 40 percent of the adult American population (76 million people) now participates in one or more types of formal, workplace, or continuing education, many provided by local community colleges. This represents an increase in adult education of 32 percent since 1991 (McClenney, 1998). From humble beginnings in 1901 to more than 1,500 campuses nationwide, serving millions of students with a strong commitment to access for all, community colleges have stormed onto the 4,000 year-old higher education scene (Davis & Wessel, 1998; Phillippe, 1997; Vaughn, 1995).

The rapid maturation of this distinctly American social invention has coincided with massive societal change. As junior and technical colleges opened their doors during the first part of this century, they were enlisted to help move the U.S. from an agrarian-based economy to an industrial giant. During the late 1960s and early 1970s, when the shift toward an information-based economy began, our institutions grew at a rate of almost one new college a week. Over the last two decades, community colleges have embraced technology and technology training as powerful tools and essential program areas. Indeed, in the 1990s we saw key national leaders, from the president of the United States to the CEOs of Microsoft, Oracle, and 3Com, visiting community colleges across the nation and pointing to our role in moving America along the "road ahead" into the Information Age (Davis & Wessel, 1998; Gates, 1996).

Now, as community colleges move into a second century and strive to help America meet the challenges of the Information Age, we hear predictions such as those from Peter Drucker who claims that "in the next 50 years, schools and universities will change more and more drastically than they have since they assumed their present form more than 300 years ago when they organized themselves around the printed book" (Drucker, 1992, p. 97). Since change has been so common in our short history on the higher education scene, we should not be afraid of such views of the future. We can envision a place where access to information and the power to manipulate it offer learning options never before known, instructional capabilities unimagined, and tools for decision-making that exceed all expectations. Nevertheless, it is becoming increasingly evident that realizing these exciting powers will not be easy. Many students and educators already feel as though progress is so rapid that they are running as fast as they can and are still unable to keep up. Will traveling on the road ahead be any different?

This chapter explores the road ahead for the community college as it enters its second century and provides some possible directions for educators. In the first section, seven key trends driving the current change will be explored, with a special focus on two key change agents: the

Learning Revolution and technology transitions. Discussions of these trends will be intertwined with the results of a series of national surveys, focus groups, and interviews involving hundreds of community college educators and dozens of site visits conducted by the League for Innovation in the Community College (the League) between 1997 and 2000. The closing section synthesizes these findings and suggests strategies for taking steps on the road ahead. Placing these trends and strategies in a broader context may provide useful direction for those embarking on this journey, those committed to using their resources and talents to make a difference in student learning in the 21st Century community college.

Methodology for Study

In 1997, the League began a long-term trend study to examine the major forces influencing community colleges as they enter a new century. Multiple approaches are involved in the analysis to provide rich, reliable data from multiple perspectives. First, key issue clusters were drawn from a review of recent research, conference programs, and higher education publications, identified by using Miles and Huberman's (1994) cluster analysis techniques. Seven key trends were identified that are influencing curriculum, enrollments, funding, pedagogy, administrative decisions, institutional practices, and public perceptions of community and technical colleges across North America and steering travelers on the community college road in significant directions. Next, these clusters have been tested for validity and importance via two national surveys of community college leaders as part of the League's quarterly CEO survey service entitled, "What Do CEOs Want to Know About...?". This survey population includes the CEOs of the League's board member institutions and members of the League's Alliance for Community College Innovation (Alliance) colleges. (A current listing of these colleges is available online at www.league.org.) The first survey was conducted in 1997 (League membership at that time totaled 523 colleges); a follow-up survey was conducted in early 2000 of the CEOs of the League's current 705 member colleges.

The argument can be made that the CEOs of these institutions differ from a broader random sampling of community college CEOs because of their expressed interest in fostering innovation and change. Indeed, the published purpose of the Alliance states: "The League is an international association dedicated to catalyzing the potential of the community college movement. League Alliance member institutions from around the world join forces each year with our board member institutions, corporate partners, and association colleagues to stimulate innovation, experimentation, and institutional transformation through League Web services, conferences, institutes, publications and projects" (Alliance Brochure, 2000). The stated goal of "catalyzing potential" makes this population ideal for exploring future trends. Arguably, these leaders have their eyes pointed down the road ahead and are likely to be more sensitive to powerful trends that may influence the community college. Other surveys of this population show it to be more diverse in terms of gender and ethnicity than the national cohort of CEOs (Milliron & Doty, 1998). The average age of CEOs responding to the 1997 survey was 54, their average tenure as CEO was 9.1 years, and the overall response rate was 62 percent (n=324). CEOs responding to the 2000 follow-up survey had a mean age of 55, an average tenure as CEO of 9.4 years; the response rate for the more extensive 2000 survey was still 47 percent (n=331).

The 1997 survey featured 21 questions that explored key issues identified in the review of conference programs and education literature (see Appendix A). In addition, the survey prompted the CEOs to offer other ideas or trends for us to consider. The survey items were posed as one overarching question–"Do you believe that in the next three to five years at your institution:"–followed by statements such as "general enrollment will increase." Our goal was to have leaders respond based on what they believed to be happening at their own institutions. The CEOs' responses were recorded on a variation of a standard, seven-point Likert scale that used the following response keys:

YES! **Yes** yes ? no **No** **NO!**

This response scale has been demonstrated to differentiate levels of intensity well and to intuitively appeal to respondents (Cheney & Tompkins 1987; Milliron, 1995). Several questions were negatively phrased to help avoid pattern responses.

The 2000 follow-up survey featured many of the same items from the original survey, but added and revised questions for a total of 36 core items (see Appendix B). New questions and revisions to previous items were developed from responses to the original survey as well as from further review of the literature and feedback from presentation of the

1997 survey findings in a special edition *Leadership Abstracts* (Milliron & Leach, 1997) and in almost 50 keynote speeches, conference presentations, college convocations, workshops, and focus groups conducted by the authors across North America and Canada over the last three years. Responses from educators to the 1997 study findings have validated and expanded our understanding of the factors currently affecting community colleges and expected to shape the rapidly changing two-year college landscape.

This chapter does not capture every issue that community college educators will face in the coming years. The League's community college trend study is ongoing, and at this writing, analysis of findings from the 2000 survey is still under way. Moreover, the pace of change is increasing and neither the researchers nor the community college practitioners participating in the study are infallible or clairvoyant. As Boettcher and Conrad (1999) observe, even Bill Gates, Microsoft CEO and technology guru, did not include the impact of the Internet and the Web in his 1995 book *The Road Ahead*, but corrected this omission in an updated 1996 edition. Similarly, we strive to remain open to new possibilities and ideas that should be included in our research framework and welcome the reader's comments and feedback to strengthen this work in progress. Still, we believe that the following typology and data offer a valid snapshot of the issues at play in the community college world today, a solid look at the road ahead, and guideposts of special interest to institutions striving to use learning and technology to meet the upcoming challenges and capitalize on the opportunities of the Information Age.

Seven Signs for Travelers on the Road Ahead

After conducting the review of literature, formulating the issue clusters, and conducting the 1997 CEO survey, the researchers divided the data into seven key trends driving change in community colleges: (1) the Learning Revolution, (2) technology transitions, (3) enrollment pressures, (4) turnover waves, (5) partnership programs, (6) at-risk access, and (7) accountability mandates. We address the first two–Learning Revolution and technology transitions–in more depth than the others, as our study findings indicate that these two factors may provide the necessary integration power for managing the challenges of the other five.

The Learning Revolution

O'Banion (1997a; 1997b; 1997c) and Barr and Tagg (1995) document and describe what is being called a Learning Revolution spreading throughout North American higher education and beyond. O'Banion (1997b) suggests that this revolution is the culmination of a series of educational reforms started by the work of the 1983 report, *A Nation At Risk*, which called for action against a "rising tide of mediocrity" in American K-12 schools. In the higher education sector, the rhetoric of these reform movements has evolved through several iterations over the last fifteen years, with a great deal of activity aimed at what O'Banion calls "trimming the branches of a dying tree" or futile efforts to fix our outmoded educational systems and processes. These reform efforts have now reached a turning point at which educators are calling for more fundamental change, change based on *placing learning first*, that is, returning to a central focus on learning in every policy, program, and practice in higher education.

Learning has always been an unstated "given" in higher education. However, being "unstated" may have created what organizational theorists call goal displacement–the consequence of an organization losing sight of its key goals and becoming bureaucratic to the point of actually impeding its core mission. Indeed, as Robert Barr, director of institutional research at Palomar College, observed, the word "learning" was almost never mentioned in the college mission statements of 107 community colleges in the California Community College system.

As the Learning Revolution progresses, a lack of focus on learning could be very costly for higher education. Oblinger and Rush (1997) note, "[a] multibillion dollar learning industry is growing while higher education debates the issues" (p. 12). McClenney (1998) points to the University of Phoenix–an institution with a stated commitment to anytime, anywhere learning, which has grown from 3,000 students a decade ago to 70,000 students on 100 campuses in 32 states–and notes that "within little more than five years, postsecondary proprietary education has been transformed from a sleepy sector of the economy to a $3.5 billion-a-year business, making education one of the hottest emerging growth sectors of the U.S. economy." New, fast-moving educational competitors are responding to demands from students, communities, legislators, and businesses for more effective, flexible, and quality learning experiences.

Increasingly, community colleges are recognizing that the traditional time-bound, place-bound, role-bond, efficiency-bound structures of higher education are in the way. Students and faculty want to be freed from fifty-minute classes, thirty-person classrooms, strictly defined relationships, and restrictive bureaucracies. Too often, our current community college system can be characterized as an industrial factory model operating on an agrarian calendar trying to meet the needs of an information-based society. This anachronistic system is not meeting the needs of 21st Century students. Improving and expanding learning in as many different, innovative, and meaningful ways as possible is essential for learners who continue to walk through the community college's open door.

Community college CEOs responding to our surveys echo this growing emphasis on learning and transforming their colleges into more responsive, learning-centered institutions. More than 97 percent of the respondents in 1997 predicted that their institutions will become more "learning centered," and 93 percent of the CEOs participating in the 2000 survey answered with an even more specific expectation that their institutions will adopt strategies from the learning-centered education movement in the next three to five years (Figure 1A).

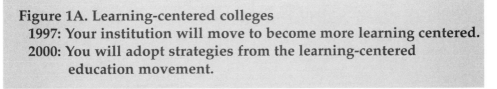

Figure 1A. Learning-centered colleges
1997: Your institution will move to become more learning centered.
2000: You will adopt strategies from the learning-centered
education movement.

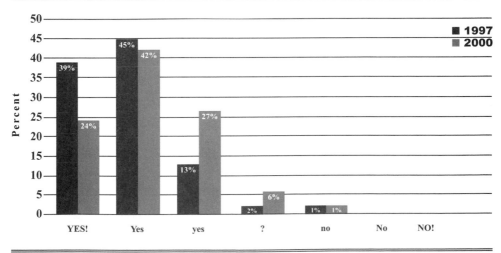

O'Banion (1997b) outlines the ends toward which these institutions are moving in his article, "The Purpose, Process, and Product of the Learning Revolution in the Community College":

> Learning-centered colleges are institutions where: (1) programs and services create substantive change in individual learners; (2) learners are engaged as full partners in the learning process, assuming primary responsibility for their own choices; (3) there are as many options for learning as possible; (4) learners are assisted in forming and participating in collaborative learning activities; (5) the role of the learning facilitator is defined by the needs of the learner; (6) all college employees identify with their role in supporting learning; and (7) success is measured by documented, improved, and expanded learning for learners. (p. 2)

In keeping with the third characteristic of learning-centered colleges–increased options for learning–more than 98 percent of CEOs responding to the 1997 survey predicted increases in the available times, places, and methods of learning in their institutions. Respondents to the 2000 survey were unanimous in their expectation that this trend toward diversity of learning opportunities in community colleges will continue (Figure 1B).

Figure 1B. Options for learning (times, places, and methods) will increase.

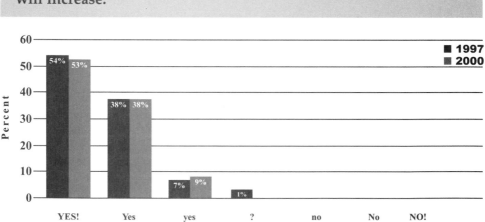

To meet the demands of the new millennium–aptly called the Knowledge or Learning Age–a number of community colleges are returning to their roots by actively making all their decisions, planning, and activities more learning-centered. They are guided in this journey home by embedding two key questions in the culture of the institution: *Does this action improve and expand learning?* and *How do we know this action improves and expands learning?* (O'Banion, 1997a). The vision statement of Palomar College (CA), one of the leading colleges in the Learning Revolution, exemplifies such an approach and "captures the essence of what it means to be learning centered" (O'Banion, 1999):

> Our new vision statement reflects a subtle but nonetheless profound shift in how we think of the college and what we do. We have shifted from an identification with process to an identification with results. We are no longer content with merely providing quality instruction. We will judge ourselves henceforth on the quality of student learning we produce. And further, we will judge ourselves by our ability to produce ever greater and more sophisticated student learning and meaningful educational success with each passing year, each exiting student, and each graduating class.

Across the country, community colleges like Palomar are enacting the principles of the Learning Revolution in recognition that this movement has the potential to transform community college education. When combined with the persuasive forces of the Technology Revolution concurrently sweeping across the higher education landscape, the learning-centered community college's programs and services take on powerful new shapes and forms.

Technology Transitions

Even the most cursory look at the explosion of literature, conferences, products, services, new businesses, and websites focused on the technology revolution in education over the last five to ten years leaves no doubt that information technology is transforming the educational enterprise. Davis and Meyer (1999) describe the whirlwind of technology-driven transition changing the world in which we live and work as *BLUR*. Marked by almost instantaneous communication and computation, connection of everybody and everything, and the explosive growth of intangible values like service and information, *BLUR* is creating a new economy based on speed, connectivity, and intangibles. They explain that changes are "blurring the rules and redefining our businesses and our lives...[and] destroying solutions, such as mass production, segmented pricing, and standardized jobs, that worked for the relatively slow, unconnected industrial world" (pp.6-7). Education has been slower than other sectors to experience this blurring of rules and redefining of practices, but community colleges are increasingly feeling the *BLUR* of the Technology Revolution on higher education.

Most educational writers addressing the question of the effect of information technology on higher education's future forecast substantial change (Holmes, 1999). Predictions range from the obsolescence of higher education institutions to a shift from provider-centered education to learner-centered systems made possible by information technology. On one point, however, they all agree: higher education *will* change. Much of the recent flurry surrounds Internet-based education programs, and every week another e-college, virtual university, mega-university, educational consortium, or corporate university makes the news. Chapter 11, "Internet Vision," specifically addresses how community colleges can benefit from the transformational power of Internet technologies. The first chapter's exploration of the major trends affecting community colleges at the turn of a new century concerns itself with more general considerations of how community colleges are interacting with technology throughout the institution.

For the last three years, the League's annual Conference on Information Technology (CIT) has attracted more than 3,500 participants from across the educational enterprise–administrators, staff, faculty, and technologists–making it the largest community college conference of any kind. This level of interest in the use of technology to improve teaching and learning, student services, and institutional management is one indicator of the power of the technology transition in higher education. Shifts in the focus of discussion surrounding the use of information technology (IT) in education over the last fifteen years help shed light on the current changes under way. The initial CIT program included sessions that dealt predominantly with issues surrounding administrative computing and infrastructure. One of the major instructional debates in the early years was whether or not students should be encouraged to "compose on the keyboard" in writing classes. The argument opposing use of the word processor was that some sort of crucial mental process is activated only by putting pen to paper.

Educational technology discussions no longer center on whether or not IT should be used, but rather on the many ways it can be effectively used and how we can best integrate and support technology to enhance the teaching and learning process. K.C. Green's Campus Computing Project (www.campuscomputing.net), the largest continuing study of the use of information technology in higher education, surveys more than 600 two-and four-year public and private colleges and universities each year to determine key issues and trends affecting campus planning, policy, and activities regarding technology. The 1999 Campus Computing Survey found the infusion of information technology into instruction to be the single most pressing concern confronting U.S. colleges over the next two to three years (Green, 1999). Analysis of more than 450 presentation proposals for the League's most recent information technology conferences reinforces this finding, with submissions on the use of technology in teaching and learning outnumbering all other technology considerations by a ratio of 9 to 1. By all indications, the use of technology to improve and expand instructional options will continue to be a key issue on the road ahead for community colleges. CEOs responding to our original survey agreed almost unanimously (Figure 1C).

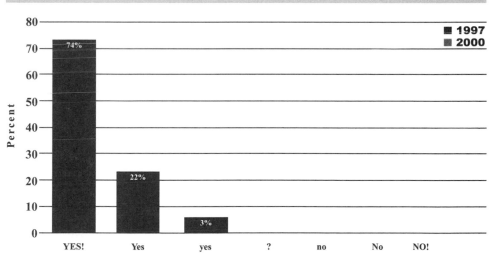

Figure 1C. The trend toward the use of information technology in instruction will increase.

In the 2000 survey we explored the issue of instructional integration further by asking about the movement toward integrating the growing number of online learning applications with college's student information systems–not an easy task–and 91 percent of the CEOs indicated their colleges will be building such technology linkages in the next few years (Figure 1D).

Figure 1D. Steps will be taken to integrate your various online learning applications with your student information system.

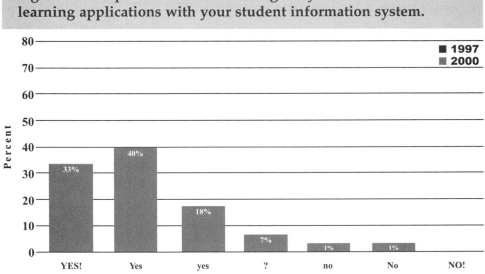

From the more standard use of presentational technologies like video data projectors and presentation software, to more interactive technologies such as computer-aided instruction and the World Wide Web, faculty have powerful new tools available to improve student learning. Moreover, students have more access to both information and instructional options than they have ever had before. One clear example of this is in the area of asynchronous learning. Open entry/open exit labs, interactive tutorial materials, threaded discussions, bulletin-board services, chat rooms, net meetings, and a host of other technologies are giving students and faculty the ability to break away from the time-bound and place-bound model of education, in essence, enabling them to learn on demand. A recent U.S. Department of Education survey found a 72 percent increase in the number of post-secondary distance education programs from 1995 to 1998 (Carnevale, 2000).

Ironically, most of the new technology-enabled options are still referred to as "distance learning," even though many of them are used on campus or within traditional classrooms and despite the fact that most of these serve to bring learning opportunities closer and make them more convenient. Steven W. Gilbert (2000), President of the TLT Group, the Teaching, Learning, and Technology Affiliate of the American Association for Higher Education, balks at the narrow notion of distance or online education and suggests a broader alternative view of "connected education" in which "individual learners, teachers, and related support professionals connect better to information, ideas, and each other via effective combinations of pedagogy and technology–both old and new, on-campus and online" Terminology notwithstanding, our survey found that few community college CEOs expect distance learning options to decrease in the coming years (Figure 1E).

Figure 1E. Distance learning offerings will decrease.

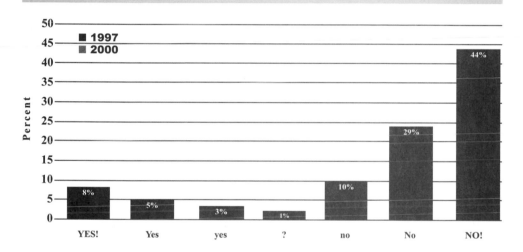

Several challenges come with the growing technology-enhanced educational options. The first, already confronting many community colleges, is what Gilbert (1996, 1997, 2000) calls the "support service crisis," in which the supply of resources available to provide adequate support for faculty, staff, administrators, and students using technology across the institution is simply inadequate to meet rising expectations. It is not surprising that the 1999 Campus Computing Survey found "providing adequate user support" to be the second most important IT issue confronting colleges–second only to "integration of technology into instruction"–and outstripping even the challenge of "financing the replacement of aging hardware and software." What is most striking about these findings is that the data come largely from college technology officers who might be expected to focus on network or infrastructure concerns, but even these "techies" identify the human factors as critical areas of concern (Green, 2000). As Green underscores, "the real technology challenges in education (and elsewhere) involve people, not products," and much of this challenge relates to training.

With students demanding more sophisticated options, faculty more aware of and interested in applying the new teaching and learning tools, and employers seeking graduates who are highly trained in new technology, community colleges are finding it almost impossible to keep their own faculty and staff up to speed. The training infrastructure necessary to support technology use throughout the institution is not in place at most community colleges, and college leaders suggest this will continue to be an important challenge in the years to come (Figure 1F).

Figure 1F. Training faculty in the use of information technology will become an essential part of ongoing staff development.

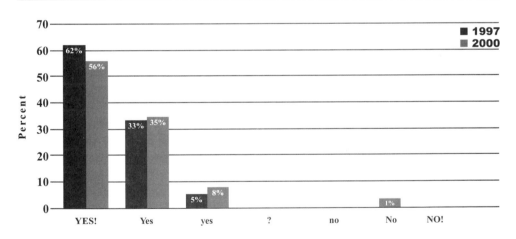

Beyond technology applications for teaching and learning, community college student services, institutional research and planning, and administrative divisions will also be challenged to make use of the powerful information technology tools available. Escalating public demands for fiscal accountability and increasing attention to student retention and success exacerbate the need for increasingly sophisticated data collection and analysis systems. This observation was shared by 93 percent of the 1997 survey respondents who agreed that obtaining and maintaining quality information systems will become increasingly important (Figure 1G).

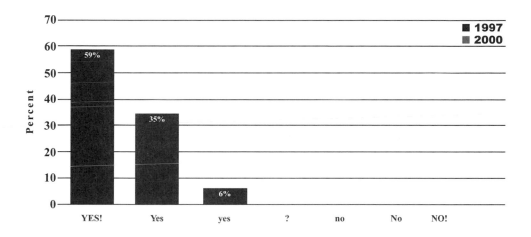

Figure 1G. Obtaining and maintaining information systems to collect outcomes data (performance measures) will become increasingly important.

Companies such as Datatel, SCT, PeopleSoft, and Oracle recognize the growing demand for integrated data systems that bring together financial, human resource, outcomes research, and student information, and are aggressively moving into the community college market. This market movement is validated by almost 80 percent of the presidents responding to the 2000 survey who indicate they will replace at least part of their student information system, human resources system, or finance system within the next three to five years.

Our research suggests that paying for all these technology tools for instruction, student information, research, student services, and administration will tax even the most entrepreneurial CEOs. CEOs surveyed in 1997 almost universally (97 percent) predicted that IT costs would emerge as a key issue for policymakers; three years later, 84 percent still see the trend toward greater scrutiny of IT costs increasing in upcoming years (Figure 1H).

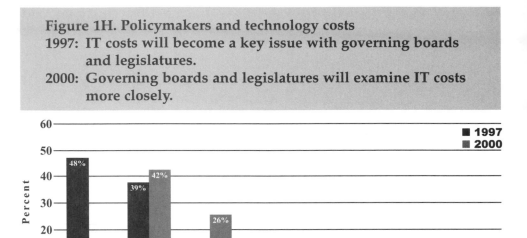

Figure 1H. Policymakers and technology costs
1997: IT costs will become a key issue with governing boards and legislatures.
2000: Governing boards and legislatures will examine IT costs more closely.

Study participants as well as researchers in the field stress that IT costs must be considered in light of the broader institutional priorities rather than in simple economic terms. Graves (1998) contends that paying for IT means having a strategy that doesn't just "bolt on" the least expensive technology to existing instructional processes, but supports strategies that transform and empower an educational enterprise. He argues that leaders must view technology as an investment rather than a cost, an investment in creating a more learning-centered environment that meets student learning needs:

> Higher education executives cannot awaken too soon to the need to view information technology as a strategic investment rather than a cost. Most academic executives are aware that the problems facing their institutions do not beg short-term solutions, but few have seriously challenged the culture of traditional instruction. . . . If academic leaders hesitate to act as partners to create a national educational fabric, viable alternatives to the present model of institution-based education will present themselves, and higher education as an institution may be hard-pressed to compete. (p.34)

More and more, technology is being viewed not only as an investment, but also as an essential element of student learning. Most observers now agree that students need information technology skills to participate in modern discourse, contribute to the national and international economies, and provide for their families (Davis & Wessel, 1998). Community college leaders responding to our 2000 survey almost unanimously agreed that technology basics are becoming a new education requirement of most academic programs (Figure 1I).

Figure 1I. Information technology literacy will become a requirement in most academic programs.

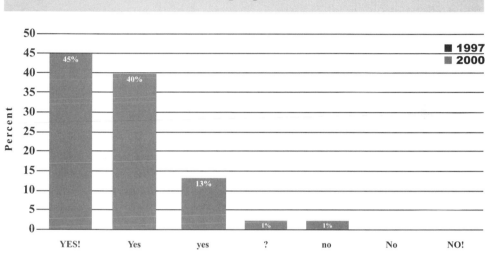

Technology presents a two-fold opportunity for community colleges: IT enables our institutions to offer more learning options while enabling students to develop vital IT skills they need in their continuing studies and in the workplace. Technology is means and end, medium and message. Johnson (1997) points out the associated double challenge for community college leaders:

> Community college students are becoming more accustomed to information technology, and they expect [and need] the associated innovations to be a part of their educational experiences . . . . The dual challenge of today's community college leader, then, is to develop the kind of organization that can flexibly adapt to the Information Age and its rapid change, while simultaneously maintaining a laser focus on the core mission–learning. (p.2)

Despite the great promise of technology, our interactions with community college educators across the continent suggest that many educators perceive the Technology Revolution as stressful, disruptive, and even destructive. Our observations suggest that technology advocates will have to face the thoughtful and increasingly well-supported arguments about the potentially damaging effects of technology. Ed Hollowell (1997), a doctor at the Harvard Medical School, is a national spokesperson on the topic of maintaining the human touch in the Information Age. His comments often center on the need for human connection in this age of fast-paced communication and high-impact multimedia, and he points out that although we have more contacts than ever before, we have less satisfying interactions than ever, since so many of our contacts are superficial. In his practice as a psychiatrist, he finds that the majority of his clients suffer from a lack of connectedness, a lack of meaningful contact with friends, family, and social institutions. More than ever before, Hollowell contends, our challenge in the Information Age is to maintain the human touch, to ensure that people connect with people on deep and multiple levels. His comments echo the writings of a growing number of theologians, philosophers, and educational researchers who have explored the impact of information technology upon the human physiology and upon the human spirit (e.g., Gilbert, 2000; Healy, 1994; Mander, 1992). More than three-fourths of the CEOs responding to the 2000 survey say their colleges will be developing programs specifically focused on helping students and employees deal with stress related to change and technology.

One of Hollowell's best stories about maintaining human contact in the Information Age is that of a physics professor who demonstrates the property of "fullness" to his class. The professor places as many large rocks from a bucket into a clear cylindrical container as will fit and asks the class if the container is full. The class examines the cylinder with rocks up to its brim and answers, "Yes." The professor responds by taking out a bucket of gravel and pouring it into the container. The gravel settles into the cracks among the big rocks, and the class ruffles a bit at having missed the obvious. He asks again, "Now, is it full?" The class offers a more tentative affirmation. Again the professor lifts a bucket from under the counter and pours its contents of sand into the container. The class watches as the sand sifts down through the crevices among the stones and rises up to the top of the cylinder. The professor again queries the class, and the students respond that surely this time it is full. But, again he reaches down and this time brings up a bucket of water, which he slowly pours into the container until water fills all the tiniest air pockets and bubbles up to the cylinder's brim. The professor stands the four empty buckets in a row beside the cylinder and smiles out at the class, "You see, we can fit all these into one space. But the trick is to remember to put the big things in first."

Hollowell's parable about keeping our priorities in order as we approach the variety of exciting technologies reminds us to "put in the big things first." He reminds us to maintain high quality human contact and to preserve our relationships with whatever we determine to be meaningful. Without a focus on the "big things," the minutiae can take over. The water and sand–e-mail, voice-mail, threaded discussions, and websites–might overtake the space meant for the big rocks in the container, such as family, friendships, community, and, most important to this discussion, learning.

As educators, we know this intuitively. We do not hear our students declare how a software program, network infrastructure, website, or new PC changed their lives and inspired them on their educational journeys. Students save this praise for faculty, counselors, peers, and family members who break through to them and make a difference in their lives. With this recognition, Hollowell asserts, we can overcome the negative aspects of technology and human development. Put simply, he argues that we must cultivate the human side of the learning process and engage technology to improve learning within more thoughtful frameworks of broader human concern and connection.

Enrollment Pressures

As we work to build learning-centered, technology-enabled institutions for the future, one of the key issues we will have to address is how best to serve the students who are projected to flood through the open door. As the baby boom echo–the children of the last huge wave of new students that entered the community college from 1965 to 1975–hits college and as the demands of a knowledge-based economy call for workers to upgrade skills continually, enrollments are projected to burgeon.

Data from the National Center for Educational Statistics (NCES) *Projections of Education Statistics Report* (1998) show that the 18- to 24-year-old population is projected to increase almost 20 percent by the year 2008. A 1995 report for the California Higher Education Policy Center calls this phenomenon *TIDAL WAVE II* (Breneman, Estrada, & Hayward), and this trend is expected to be particularly acute in New York, Florida, Texas, Arizona, and California. California's community college student body is projected to increase by almost 30 percent, from 1.4 million in 1996–which already strained faculty, staff, and facilities–to 1.9 million in 2008 (California Public Postsecondary Enrollment Projections, 1999). Overall, higher education enrollment is projected to increase from 13.9 million in 1995 to 16.1 million by 2007, and as high as 20 million by 2010 (McClenney, 1998). In our survey, 90 percent of the CEOs in 1997 and 93 percent in 2000 anticipated increases in enrollment at their institutions in the next three to five years (Figure 1J).

Figure 1J. General enrollment will increase.

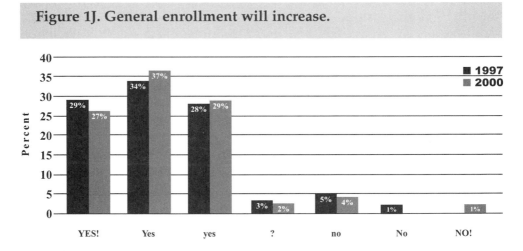

Community colleges will be hard pressed to accommodate this second enrollment surge, particularly when combined with increased calls for the expansion of workforce training and continuing education (Zeiss, 1997). NCES (1998) reports that more than 76 million people of the United States–more than 40 percent of the adult population–is now involved in some sort of adult education, with more than half of these individuals focusing on workforce training or occupational upgrade. McClenney (1998) puts these projections in a broader perspective:

Lest we begin to think of these market shifts as a problem, let us hasten to remember that we helped to create this monster. In the 1960s we touted lifelong learning. In the 1970s we touted the learning society. In the 1980s and 1990s we touted the learning organization. Toward the millennium we are excited about creating the learning college. Levine and Cureton point out that the current market is what happens when 65 percent of all high school graduates go on to college, when higher education is open to the nation's population across a life span, and when higher education is democratized. (p.1)

Not only will enrollment numbers change, but so too will the demographic makeup of the student population. Community colleges have traditionally enrolled greater proportions of minority students than other segments of higher education, and the percentage of minority students coming to the community college is expected to continue to rise, another trend echoed by the CEOs in our survey (Figure 1K). Currently, community colleges enroll 46 percent of all African American students,

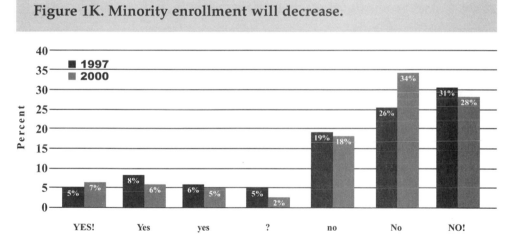

Figure 1K. Minority enrollment will decrease.

55 percent of all Hispanic students, 46 percent of all Asian/Pacific Islander students, and 55 percent of all Native American students in higher education (American Association of Community Colleges, 1999). By the year 2015, minority enrollments in community colleges are projected to increase by approximately 12 percent, while the white student population will decrease by approximately 8 percent (de los Santos Jr. & de los Santos,

2000). Not surprisingly, the same states that are slated to see the greatest enrollment increases–Florida, New York, Texas, and California–will also see the highest increases in minority enrollment. With increased immigration, higher birthrates in minority populations, and loftier expectations for the children of second- and third-generation minority college attendees, the changes in the community college student body will continue to challenge college faculty and staff to work effectively with a more diverse clientele.

Another interesting enrollment trend in many community colleges is that fully 25 percent of all incoming students already have bachelor's degrees, and these students are enrolling in community colleges to upgrade their workplace skills or to earn specific technical degrees. Educators from our focus groups and site visits suggest that high numbers of "multi-cycle" students are applying to competitive programs, particularly in the allied health and technology areas (Quinley & Quinley, 1998). In some cases, these programs could be completely filled with students who have already completed four-year degrees. These returning students tend to be older, savvy, highly motivated consumers who are eager to receive an education that will enhance their quality of life.

Combine large numbers of more diverse students with shrinking resources and it is not difficult to predict that the enrollment pressures of the coming years are likely to challenge the services and the core philosophy of open access in community colleges. We may hear calls to close the open door that has been the cornerstone of our egalitarian philosophy. As legislators and community leaders struggle with the policy and funding implications of meeting this new demand, the longstanding philosophy of access for all will continue to be challenged, as will our innovative spirit in the provision of learning opportunities. A more learning-centered college will have to respond with a range of learning options, such as advanced information technologies and collaborative frameworks. The comfortable factory model of the past will not provide adequate learning opportunities anymore and the buildings and behaviors of the past cannot accommodate the flood of new students coming our way.

Turnover Waves

The country song "You Picked a Fine Time to Leave Me Lucille" may be particularly appropriate at this point in community college history. Community colleges have successfully stormed onto the higher education scene and argued for our rightful and respected place in the higher education community. We are facing the challenges of becoming more learning centered; infusing information technology into our instruction, student services, and institutional management; and preparing for a second wave of massive enrollment increases. And, in the face of these powerful forces, many of the individuals who have been the longstanding visionaries and standard bearers for our institutions are walking out the door.

A recent survey of CEOs of the League's Alliance college membership revealed that one in four presidents plans to retire in the next three years and more than 40 percent expect to retire within five years (n=305, response rate=51 percent). These figures initially led us to wonder if a disproportionate number of retiring CEOs responded to this survey, but further examination revealed that our response rate and average CEO age was identical to that of our other surveys of this cohort (mean age = 54). These data validate our observations that a major senior leadership transition is taking place in community colleges. And, if the CEO retirements are not frustrating enough, the faculty that helped handle the first tidal wave are also exiting. In California alone, one-third of the 15,000 full-time faculty are over 55 years of age, and 55 percent are over 50. Almost 85 percent of our 1997 survey respondents agreed that more faculty will retire in the next ten years than have retired in the last twenty years, and 76 percent of our 2000 respondents said more faculty would retire in the next three to five years than in the last ten. In 1997, 64 percent of those surveyed expected significant employee turnover in the next three to five years; by 2000 that figure had grown to 70 percent (Figure 1L).

Faculty turnover will have significant ramifications for the culture of community colleges. The current cohort of faculty was hired, for the most part, during the boom years of the 1960s when a new community college was opening almost every week. These faculty have been the conduits for the core values of the community college movement for almost four

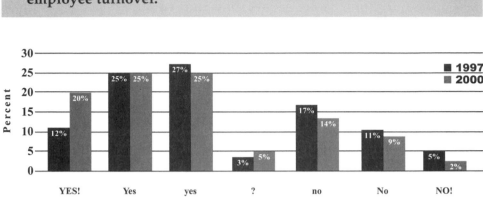

Figure 1L. Your institution will experience significant employee turnover.

decades and have helped shape our current college programs and services to meet the needs of students. These faculty helped define community colleges as premier teaching institutions. It is difficult to determine the impact their mass retirement will have on the colleges.

While conducting five focus groups with more than 200 award-winning faculty at the National Institute for Staff and Organizational Development (NISOD) International Conference on Teaching and Leadership Excellence, we repeatedly heard questions asking how the retiring faculty could pass on their legacy of care, concern, and innovation (Milliron & Miles, 1998). The focus group participants strongly felt that the new faculty coming into the community colleges should understand the history of two-year colleges and identify with their missions of access, excellence, and a strong focus on student needs. The orienting and training of new faculty will be paramount in this process, a comment that resonates strongly with CEOs responding to both 1997 and 2000 surveys (Figure 1M).

An equally pressing concern is how community colleges will develop the skills of the growing number of part-timers who increasingly are being called on to fill the gaps created by retiring faculty and budget cuts. CEOs responding to our surveys reported mixed expectations among institutions regarding increases in part-time faculty, with more than 60 percent predicting increases in use of part-time faculty in 1997 and 2000 (Figure 1N). Currently more than half of all credit hours in community colleges are delivered by part-time faculty (Roueche & Roueche, 2000).

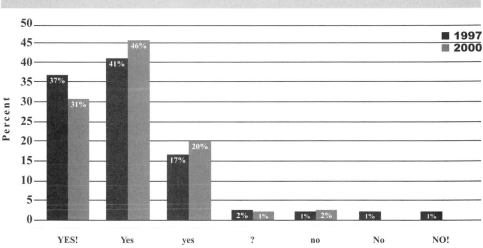

Figure 1M. Training new faculty will become an increasingly important institutional policy.

A number of college leaders have developed comprehensive selection, orientation, and support programs for integrating part-time faculty into the community college culture. Increasingly, colleges are identifying sets of desired skills and attributes that will assure that new full- and part-time faculty identify with college goals. At Sinclair Community College (OH), for example, full-time faculty who can teach in only one discipline are no longer being hired. In keeping with its learning college initiative, Sinclair targets new faculty selection as cross-disciplinary learning consultants for

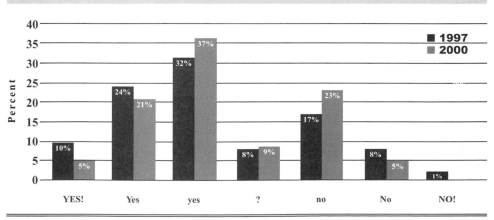

Figure 1N. The number of part-time faculty will increase.

the coming years, faculty who clearly see their role as learning facilitators. Because each hiring decision represents a potential future investment of over $1 million for each new faculty member, administrators are taking these hiring decisions very seriously.

Roueche, Roueche, & Milliron (1996) argue that to bring the new part-time faculty into the mainstream mission of a college and to strive to become more learning-centered and technology enabled, college leaders must first ask why they are using part-timers before developing recruitment, selection, orientation, development, evaluation, and integration strategies. At many community colleges, these are not easy questions to ask:

- Is the use of part-time faculty part of a broader institutional plan to improve learning, or a haphazard response to pressing needs?
- Are part-time faculty being recruited and selected with learning and technology in mind?
- Are faculty sought because they are best qualified to improve learning, or are they hired to fill slots while meeting minimum accrediting standards?
- Are part-timers oriented to value learning first and use appropriate and effective information technology?
- Is relevant professional development on learning theory and technology applications available?
- Does the evaluation process reflect these institutional priorities?
- Does the culture include part-timers in broader conversations on learning, show them respect as learning facilitators, and involve them in the community at large?
- Do the recruiting, selection, orientation, development, evaluation, and integration processes operate as a system to support learning and empower faculty with technology skills?

Many of these questions would be useful for examining selection, hiring, and integration of new full-time faculty as well.

Similarly, a number of concerns come up when addressing the replacement of leaders leaving our community colleges. In particular, institutions striving to capitalize on the Learning and Technology Revolutions are asking how we can be sure that the leaders we bring into our institutions know how to organize for learning and understand technology. O'Banion (1997b) argues that to move toward becoming learning colleges for the 21st Century, we need leaders who can help in eight key ways:

(1) building a critical coalition and involving all stakeholders; (2) creating an emerging vision of a learning-centered institution, which includes revised statements of mission and values that focus on learning; (3) fully supporting the initiative in word, deed, and dollars; (4) realigning current structures to accommodate collaboration and teamwork; (5) creating an open system of communication; (6) evaluating outcomes thoroughly; (7) committing to the long haul; and (8) celebrating changes and accomplishments. (p. 2)

These are powerful concerns, indeed, not only for a group of outgoing administrators and faculty who shaped community colleges for over three decades, but also for a new group of faculty working with new leadership who must forge a future for the youngest sector of the higher education community.

Partnership Programs

Workforce development, facilities collaboration, welfare reform, tech-prep programs, foundation development, and school-to-work initiatives are only a few of the many partnership programs that will continue to take shape as we enter the new millennium. Working well with other agencies has become a priority as the calls for greater inter-institutional cooperation from legislatures and the public become more pronounced. Our survey CEOs reported a growing sense of importance for developing and maintaining partnerships with local corporations (Figure 10). Similar high importance was reported for partnering with other educational institutions to align educational offerings. More and more, community college employees must be able to develop a sort of institutional multilingualism, quickly and easily speaking the language of the K-12, university, community, and business sectors.

With regard to the business sector, Robert McCabe's (1997) League for Innovation monograph, *The American Community College: Nexus for*

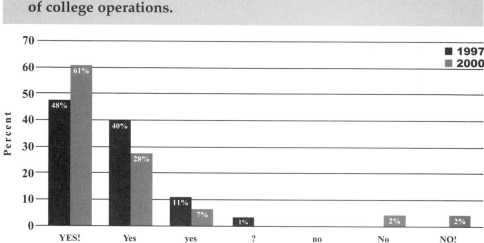

Figure 1O. Developing and maintaining partnerships with local corporations will become an increasingly important part of college operations.

Workforce Development, documents the explosion of community college workforce training. In recent years, American industry has divested itself of an estimated 50 percent of its in-house training programs, and community colleges have become central players in filling this growing gap. Workers need more training than ever before as their employers deal with the same rates of change and turnover that are challenging community colleges. CEOs participating in our surveys in 1997 and 2000 almost universally agree that workforce training and development offerings will increase in the next three to five years (Figure 1P). Zeiss (1997) points out that workforce development has the potential to transform the community college into a different kind of learning organization—one that is deeply attuned to the needs of business, industry, and the broader community. Community colleges take their workforce development roles seriously and are being recognized in this area. Zeiss' study reports that more than 95 percent of employers surveyed would recommend a community college for workforce training. His study revealed that employers feel community colleges are able to offer cost effective, customized, convenient, and high-quality training that can improve performance, upgrade skills, enrich personal and professional development, and meet the requirements of the rapidly changing workplace.

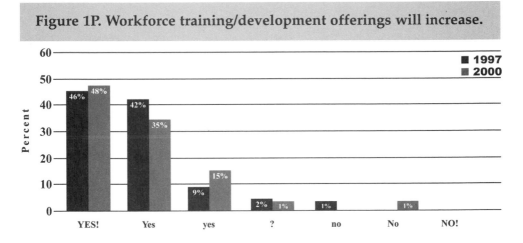

Figure 1P. Workforce training/development offerings will increase.

Ironically, when many community college CEOs are asked about the size and service of their institutions, they typically report only credit-earning curriculum students and programs. Often, however, their continuing education and workforce development divisions serve as many or more community members each year. The shadow college, as the isolated workforce development or corporate training divisions of some community colleges are referred, has emerged into the light and appears to be headed toward center stage for its contribution to learning in the community college. Workforce development program contributions are particularly notable in the technology arena. The American Association of Community College's 1998 study of "Hot Programs" found that the number one program offering for workforce development was software applications. Considering these data, it is not surprising that, in 1997, Oracle Corporation invested $50 million in its *Oracle Academic Initiative*, Microsoft invested $7 million in its *Skills 2000* project, and Cisco Systems and Novell sponsored *Network Academies* on community college campuses nationwide.

But workforce training is only one piece of the partnership puzzle. CEOs are realizing that public resources will not be sufficient to build new facilities or purchase expensive instructional equipment for capital-intensive training programs. Instructional access to private facilities, an arrangement already modeled in many technology programs, is one strategy for increasing capacity and assuring currency of practical applications. Moreover, colleges are building joint-use educational facilities with business and industry, recreational facilities with local governments, and learning resource centers with transfer institutions (Johnson, 1996; Roueche, Taber, & Roueche, 1995). Even more striking is the marked increase in outside fundraising and foundation work. While working with fundraisers and foundations is relatively new for many community college leaders, they are learning to maneuver continually drying state and local income streams. State funding has decreased by more than 10 percent in the last fifteen years, and tuition has already increased more than 20 percent in the same time period. Foundation work is becoming a necessity for many community colleges, particularly for capital improvements (Phillippe, 1997), and there appears to be room for growth in this area. In 1995, community college endowment programs totaled only $745 million, whereas public four-year institutions reported endowments of more than $20 billion (NCES, 1998).

In addition to workforce and resource development, colleges are looking to foster a range of other partnerships. For example, many institutions have elaborate tech-prep programs that closely coordinate services and curricula with local high schools. Others are integrating service learning (Exley, 1995), a curricular technique that pairs faculty and students with service organizations in the community. An AACC survey from 1996 reports that more than 31 percent of community colleges offer some sort of service learning component, and another 46 percent were interested in adding this curricular feature. Still other institutions are helping to build and staff one-stop centers, where multiple social service agencies meet the physical, psychological, financial, and educational needs of welfare recipients.

Whatever the collaboration, the partnerships forged by community colleges of the 21st Century will certainly be diverse and will surely pose new challenges and opportunities to improve learning. Again, to this end, community college leaders must step back from these engaging partnership activities and continue to ask O'Banion's (1997a) burning question: "How is this activity improving and expanding student learning?" How do we most effectively move a learning-centered college, empowered by innovative technology use, through the challenges of substantial enrollment increases, foreboding retirement waves, and enticing partnership programs while remaining true to our core purpose?

At-Risk Access

As our primary and secondary educational systems continue to face their challenges and universities deal with their burgeoning enrollments and shrinking budgets, community colleges increasingly will be asked to take on the challenges of at-risk students (McCabe & Day, 1998; Roueche & Roueche, 1993, 1999). At-risk students, usually defined as those students most at risk of dropping out because of a lack of academic or social preparation for higher education, continue to flood into community colleges, challenging educators to develop programs to identify and serve their particular needs. Nationally, between 15 and 40 percent of incoming freshmen need some form of developmental education, a statistic that has remained stable since 1989 despite more than 15 years of reform efforts since the issuing of the critical *A Nation at Risk* report (NCES, 1998; Roueche & Roueche, 1999). Many community colleges report placing between 60 and 80 percent of their incoming freshman, particularly in areas with high ESL program needs in developmental education (McCabe & Day, 1998). At-risk students bring a level of challenge to student services and instruction that other populations do not. Although their successes are often the most rewarding to witness, these students are also the most resource intensive for the organization. The CEOs studied here contend that the enrollment in basic skills and developmental education courses is likely to continue to increase in the coming years (Figure 1Q).

Roueche and Roueche (1999) contend that although there is no "quick fix" for the high degree of academic underpreparedness in higher education, experience and research point to a number of proven strategies for improving the learning outcomes of "at-risk" students: (1) initiate proactive pre-enrollment activities, (2) require orientation and early student-support structures, (3) abolish late registration, (4) mandate basic skills assessment and placement in appropriate courses, (5) eliminate dual/simultaneous enrollment in skill and regular academic courses, (6) encourage working students to take a reduced number of hours, (7) provide more comprehensive financial aid programs, (8) establish critical safety nets with faculty mentors and peer support, (9) require increased problem-solving and literacy activities in all college courses, (10) increase the impact of classroom instruction and supplement instruction with skill practice and tutoring, and (11) recruit, hire, and develop the best faculty available to work with at-risk students.

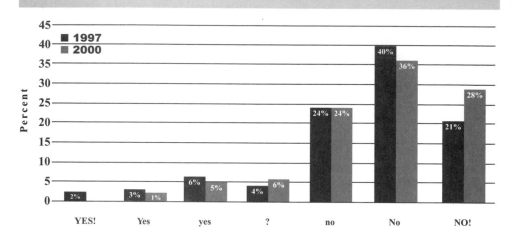

Figure 1Q. Basic skills/developmental programs will lose enrollment.

Other approaches for managing the increasing numbers of underprepared students at all levels call for more comprehensive systemic reform that involves multiple levels of education and multiple agencies of government. For example, several state legislatures are mandating the alignment of educational offerings between K-12 and higher education institutions to remedy academic deficiencies earlier in the educational pipeline. One program that demonstrates the K-16 cooperation desired by legislators is the National Science Foundation-funded Phoenix Urban Systemic Initiative, facilitated by the Maricopa Community Colleges, that seeks to align math and science curricula between K-12, community colleges, and universities in inner-city Phoenix. North Carolina's school-to-work initiative is another program that features K-16 cooperation. Almost all (99 percent) of the CEOs surveyed in 1997 and 97 percent of those responding to the 2000 survey reported that such alignments were an increasing college priority (Figure 1R).

The access issue for at-risk students will likely become more prominent in the very near future as several states are considering legislation making community colleges the sole providers of developmental education, in essence taking universities out of the remediation business (McCabe & Day, 1998). South Carolina has already passed such legislation, and several other states are considering similar

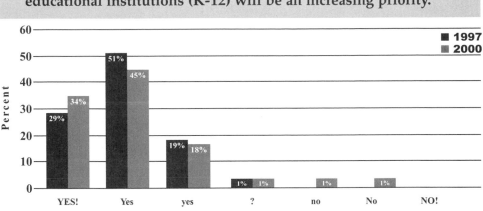

Figure 1R. Aligning educational offerings with local educational institutions (K-12) will be an increasing priority.

approaches. Clearly, the community college will continue to be the primary point of access for the at-risk student to enter higher education, and, by extension, the world of work in a knowledge-based economy. McCabe and Day (1998) argue that community college leaders will have to outfit their organizations to meet not only the on-demand market pressures from savvy, technology-enabled workplace learners, but also the continuing and complex needs of those requiring developmental education. In an Information Age in which more than 65 percent of the adult population attends college to become part of a new technically savvy middle class (Davis & Wessel, 1998), community colleges must continue to open the doors wide to those who most need learning. A wide line symbolizing the necessity of constant learning and the demands of new technology will mark the societal gap between the haves and have-nots. A learning-centered community college, formed on the foundation of democratic ideals, cannot hide from this challenge.

It would be unwise to leave the most needy students to be served solely by open labs and websites. Because of their poor information technology literacy skills and their lack of training in how to learn, these students are the least likely to make good use of these services. We must include strategies for improving learning hardiness (Milliron, 1998) and technology skills in our developmental programs and consider how we can bring at-risk cohorts up to par not only in reading, writing, and math, but also in learning and technology.

Accountability Mandates

Governors, state legislators, taxpayers, and students continue to call for greater accountability from all public agencies. As with other sectors, education has been accosted with cries for accountability, many accompanied by mandates to provide information on how and to what extent these publicly funded institutions are achieving their institutional missions, meeting the needs of their communities, and helping students succeed (Alfred, Kreider, & McClenney, 1994; Cortada, 1998). Kay McClenney (1998), Vice President of Education Commission of the States and nationally recognized educational policy advisor, paints the scene vividly:

> The inescapable reality is that policymakers and the public are through signing blank checks for higher education. We are going to be expected to perform, to document performance, and to be accountable for producing return on taxpayer and student investment. We are going to see this dynamic reflected in performance indicators, performance funding, performance contracting, and performance pay. And it is not going away, however hard we wish.

More than 87 percent of CEOs in our 1997 survey agreed that legislatures would continue to seek greater accountability from community colleges. In 2000 we inverted the item to avoid pattern responses, and 97 percent of the CEOs responded NO to the prompt "Legislators will call for less accountability from colleges" (Figure 1S).

In *Embracing the Tiger: The Effectiveness Debate and the Community College*, Roueche, Johnson, Roueche, and Associates (1997a) document the growing trend toward accountability mandates and predict even stronger measures in the very near future. The authors point out that accountability measures increasingly strike at two of the key necessities of community colleges: accreditation and funding. Accrediting associations are demanding that institutional effectiveness measurement systems be implemented before granting accreditation. Several states, including Tennessee, Texas, Florida, and South Carolina have implemented performance-based funding, arguably the strongest accountability mandate. In these systems, data must be collected to document student outcomes (e.g., retention, graduation) with future funding tied to a college's performance on these key

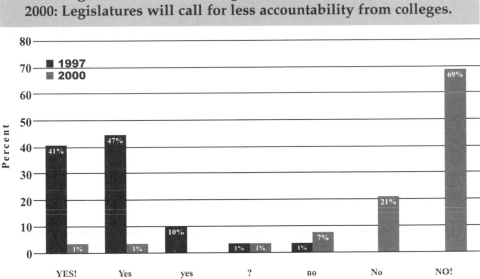

Figure 1S. Legislatures and accountability
1997: Legislatures will call for greater accountability from colleges.
2000: Legislatures will call for less accountability from colleges.

indices. Currently, more than 40 states require some form of outcomes evidence, and the newly passed 2000 U.S. Government Performance Act now requires performance data for all federal funding. Eighty-eight percent of the CEOs surveyed in 1997 predicted that their funding would be tied to some type of performance indicators in the next three to five years, a figure that grew to 93 percent among the CEOs survey in 2000 (Figure 1T).

Two of the key challenges surrounding accountability mandates are (1) influencing the indices that will be used to measure performance and (2) collecting the complex data necessary to report on effectiveness. Roueche, Johnson, and Roueche (1997b) contend that community college leaders must take the time to advocate their unique position and mission in higher education, to "describe who they are, rather than be measured by the standards of others." To advocate effectively, however, community college leaders must also be able to collect good data on which to base decisions and report effectiveness, a sentiment echoed by 99 percent of community college CEOs. Institutional data systems must be able to reflect and explore the diversity of mission and the transitory nature of community college populations and programs. Without this complexity,

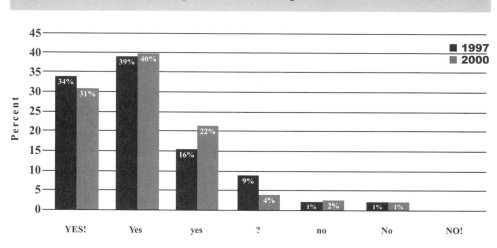

Figure 1T. Your funding will be tied to performance indicators.

particularly in performance-based funding states, community colleges could be relegated to chasing simplistic outcome measures like graduation rates at the expense of other equally important learning outcomes.

Taking Steps on the Road Ahead

We pause to look down the road ahead and see signs pointing to a Learning Revolution, technology transitions, enrollment pressures, turnover waves, partnership programs, at-risk access, and accountability. The central question arises: What can today's community college educator do to help his or her organization successfully travel this road? The uncertainty and controversy surrounding any one of these issues can ravage a community college, fragment its faculty, divide its leadership, and confuse its students.

Fortunately, taking steps on the road ahead appears to promise exciting opportunities as well as challenges. Nevertheless, those educators eager to remain safe and stationary may feel they have been born at the wrong point in history. Change, growth, and learning are our constants, and rapid change is a phrase that has become all but redundant. Institutions able to create a sense of institutional stability seem to do so by focusing on their core missions and on concepts that help integrate change into a framework that is simple to communicate, has direction, and makes a difference. Learning is an integrating concept, and our observations as well as data lead us to believe that the confluence of learning and technology will enable community colleges to take on the challenges outlined in this chapter more effectively and elegantly. This can only happen if we establish a strong collective sense of direction as we move ahead and if we remain flexible enough to make course corrections based on an evaluation of whether the direction taken is moving the organization awry.

Steven W. Gilbert's (1997, 2000) Teaching, Learning, and Technology Roundtable (TLTR) program provides one example of an effort that is working toward congruence around improving learning and using technology (www.tltgroup.org). TLTRs bring together a broad, representative, crossfunctional group of individuals within an institution to discuss core teaching and learning issues and, as Gilbert puts it, "oh by the way, technology." Through regular focused meetings, a TLTR can help institutions make better-informed decisions, sustain collaborative change, and develop better strategies for using technology to improve teaching and learning. Group members explore core teaching and learning issues first and then work toward agreement about how technology can expand campus efforts at improving learning. Gilbert challenges each college group to develop its own "vision worth working toward." With more than 400 colleges and universities engaging in this program, the TLTR process is making a substantive contribution to helping institutions take important steps toward improving teaching and learning with information technology.

O'Banion (1998) addresses this same notion of gathering educators around a unifying vision when he advocates institutional "conversations on learning." This approach brings together all key stakeholder groups, including faculty, staff, students, administrators, community representatives, and board members, into meaningful dialogues about learning. The intent of these interactions is to foster a strong commitment to facilitating learning in all sectors of the college community. To become a true learning college, all members of the college–from the registrar, counselor, faculty, technical support staff, and cafeteria worker to the president–need to identify themselves in some way as facilitators of learning. Next steps include working together to form meaningful outcome goals and system designs that will move the institution toward becoming more learning centered, use technology to the fullest, and enable the organization to take on key challenges while meeting student needs.

Tushman and O'Reilly (1997) argue that once a sense of congruence around core goals is established and a systematic plan of action is designed, an organization must develop a sort of ambidexterity. The application of this concept in the community college world suggests that a college must be true to its mission and core goal–learning–but flexible enough to change directions if the organization appears to be moving down the wrong path. Coming to terms with the core mission of promoting learning is not the same as etching in stone the strategies for achieving that mission. In a college demonstrating healthy ambidexterity, educators are willing to ask hard questions about outcomes and activities, challenge all ideas, and face every piece of data that may not be flattering about college services. As McClenney (1998) notes, great little pockets of innovation may be flourishing in isolation on our campuses, but unless we have the courage to pull these innovators together into systems that leverage the power of collective effort toward transforming the educational enterprise, we are simply practicing the "Christmas Tree model of reform" by hanging lots of pretty ornaments on a *dead* tree. It is only with a commitment to transforming the culture of the institution from its traditional time-bound, place-bound, efficiency-bound, and role-bound systems to focus on student and organizational learning that community colleges can collectively tear down "the house that Carnegie built" and move toward building learning colleges for the 21st Century (O'Banion, 1997a).

Conclusion

As we enter a new millennium and community colleges travel down the road ahead, college leaders will encounter many changes and challenges. The Learning Revolution will likely transform education as we know it, particularly when fueled by the infusion of information technology. The power of learning centeredness as a concept to harness technology can better enable community college educators to face other key challenges they will meet along the way. Yes, enrollment pressures will mount; employee turnover will have untold impact on the culture of the community college; partnerships with local social services, corporations, and other educational organizations will become more commonplace; the challenges of the at-risk will continue to call for the best in our educational processes; and public agencies and taxpayers will increasingly clamor for accountability. Through it all, however, improving learning should be our destination and information technology our welcome companion along the path.

References

American Association of Community Colleges (1999). National Community College Snapshot. Available: www.aacc.nche.edu/allaboutcc/snapshot.htm.

Alfred, R., Kreider, P., & McClenney, K. (1994). Community Colleges: Core Indicators of Effectiveness. Preface to *A Report of the Community College Roundtable*. American Association of Community Colleges Special Report 4: Washington, DC.

Barr, R. B. & Tagg, J. (1995, November/December). "From Teaching to Learning: A New Paradigm for Undergraduate Education." *Change*, 27(6), 13-25.

Boettcher, J.V. & Conrad, R.M. (1999). *Faculty Guide for Moving Teaching and Learning to the Web*. Mission Viejo, CA: League for Innovation in the Community College.

Breneman, D. W., Estrada, L. F., & Hayward, G. C. (1995). Tidal Wave II: An Evaluation of Enrollment Projections for California Higher Education. Technical Report 95-6, California Higher Education Policy Center.

Carnevale, D. (2000, January 7). Survey Finds 72% Rise in Number of Distance-Education Programs. *Chronicle of Higher Education*. Available: www.chronicle.com/free/v46/i18/18a05701.htm

California Public Postsecondary Enrollment Projections, 1999 Series (1999). California State Department of Finance, Demographic Research Unit: Sacramento, CA.

Cheney, G., & Tompkins, P. K. (1987). "Coming to Terms with Organizational Identification and Commitment." *Central States Speech Journal*, 38, 1-15.

Cortada, J. W. (1998). Knowing How It Is All Working: The Role of Performance Measurements. In D. G. Oblinger & S. C. Rush (Eds.), *The Learning Revolution: The Challenge of Information Technology in the Academy*. Bolton, MA: Anker.

Davis, B. & Wessel, D. (1998). *Prosperity: The Coming 20-Year Boom and What It Means to You.* New York: Random House.

Davis, S. & Meyer, C. (1999). *BLUR: the speed of change in the connected economy.* New York: Time Warner.

de los Santos Jr, A. G. & de los Santos, G. E. (2000). Community Colleges Bridging the Digital Divide. *Leadership Abstracts*, 13(1).

Drucker, P. T. (1992). *Managing for the Future: The 1990s and Beyond.* New York: Penguin.

Exley, B. (1995). "Partners in Action and Learning: 1994-1995 Annual Report." Miami-Dade Community College: Miami, FL.

Gates, B., with Myhrovold, N. & Rinearson, P. (1996). *The Road Ahead.* New York: Penguin.

Gilbert, S. W. (1996, March/April). "Making the Most of a Slow Revolution."*Change*, 28(2), 10(14).

Gilbert, S. W. (1997). *Teaching, Learning, & Technology Roundtable Program: Regional TLTR Workshop–Levers for Change.* Washington, DC: American Association of Higher Education.

Gilbert, S. W. (2000). *A New Vision Worth Working Toward: Connected Education & Collaborative Change.* Available: tltgroup.org/ images/gilbert/NewVWWT2000/^NewVwwt2000—2-14-00.htm

Graves, W. H. (1998). A Strategy for IT Investments. In D.G. Oblinger & S.C. Rush (Eds.), *The Learning Revolution: The Challenge of Information Technology in the Academy.* Bolton, MA: Anker.

Green, K. C. (1999). *The 1999 National Survey of Information Technology in Higher Education.* Encino, CA: Campus Computing.

Green, K. C. (2000, February). "Machiavelli for the Millenium." *Converge*, 3(1), 76-77. Available: www.convergemag.com [August 10, 2000].

Healy, J. M. (1994). *Your Child's Growing Mind: A Practical Guide to Brain Development and Learning from Birth to Adolescence.* New York: Doubleday.

Holmes, W. (1999, October/November) "The Transformative Power of Information Technology." *Community College Journal*, 10-15.

Johnson, L. W. (Ed.). (1996). *Common Ground: Exemplary Community College and Corporate Partnerships.* Mission Viejo, CA: League for Innovation in the Community College.

Johnson, S. (1997). "Leadership in the Information Age." *Leadership Abstracts*, 10(5). Mission Viejo, CA: League for Innovation in the Community College.

League for Innovation in the Community College. (1998). *Alliance for Community College Innovation* [Brochure]. Mission Viejo, CA: Author.

Mander, J. (1992). *In Absence of the Sacred: The Failure of Technology and the Survival of the Indian Nations.* San Francisco: Sierra Club.

McCabe, R. H. (1997). *The American Community College: Nexus for Workforce Development.* Mission Viejo, CA: League for Innovation in the Community College.

McCabe, R. H., & Day, P. (1998). *Developmental Education: A Twenty-First Century Social and Economic Imperative.* Mission Viejo, CA: League for Innovation in the Community College.

McClenney, K. (1998). "Perched at the Millennium: Perspectives on Innovation, Transformation, and Tomorrow." *Leadership Abstracts*, 11(8). Mission Viejo, CA: League for Innovation in the Community College.

Miles, M. B., & Huberman, M. A. (1994). *Qualitative Data Analysis: An Expanded Sourcebook.* London: Sage.

Milliron, M. D. (1998, May). Making AAAs: Practical Strategies for Fostering Hardy Learners. Forum presentation at the National Institute for Staff and Organizational Development (NISOD) International Conference on Teaching and Leadership Excellence, Austin, TX.

Milliron, M. D. (1995). *Toward a Model of Part-Time Faculty Integration in American Community Colleges*. Dissertation, University of Texas at Austin.

Milliron M. D., & Doty, A. (1998). *What Do CEOs Want to Know About . . . Leadership Transitions?* Mission Viejo, CA: League for Innovation in the Community College.

Milliron, M. D., & Leach, E. R. (1997). "Community Colleges Winning Through Innovation: Taking on the Changes and Choices of Leadership in the Twenty-First Century." *Leadership Abstracts*, Special Edition. Mission Viejo, CA: League for Innovation in the Community College.

Milliron, M. D., & Miles, C. M. (1998). *Technology, Learning, and Community in Instruction: Perspectives from Teaching Excellence Award Recipients*. Mission Viejo, CA: League for Innovation in the Community College.

National Center for Educational Statistics (NCES). (1998). *Projections of Educational Statistics*. Washington, DC: U.S. Department of Education.

O'Banion, T. (1997a). *A Learning College for the 21st Century*. Published jointly by the American Association of Community Colleges and the American Council on Education. Phoenix, AZ: Oryx Press.

O'Banion, T. (1997b). "The Purpose, Process, and Product of the Learning Revolution in the Community College." *Leadership Abstracts*, 11(7). Mission Viejo, CA: League for Innovation in the Community College.

O'Banion, T. (1997c). "The Learning Revolution: A Guide for Community College Trustees." *Trustee Quarterly*, 1, 1-19.

O'Banion, T. (1998, May). The Learning College of the Twenty-First Century. Keynote address. National Institute for Staff and Organizational Development (NISOD) 1998 International Conference on Teaching and Leadership Excellence, Austin, TX.

O'Banion, T. (1999). "The Learning College: Both Learner and Learning Centered." *Learning Abstracts*, 2(2). Mission Viejo, CA: League for Innovation in the Community College.

Oblinger, D. G., & Rush, S. C. (Eds.). (1997). *The Learning Revolution: The Challenge of Information Technology in the Academy*. Bolton, MA: Anker.

Phillippe, K. A. (Ed.). (1997). *National Profile of Community Colleges: Trends and Statistics 1997-1998*. Washington, DC: Community College Press.

Quinley, J., & Quinley, M. (1998). "From Pipelines to Cycles: Changing the Way We Think About Learning and Learners." *Learning Abstracts*, 1(2). Mission Viejo, CA: League for Innovation in the Community College.

Roueche, J. E., Johnson, L. F., Roueche, S. D., & Associates. (1997a). *Embracing the Tiger: The Effectiveness Debate and the Community College*. Washington, DC: Community College Press.

Roueche, J. E., Johnson, L. F., & Roueche, S. D. (1997b). "Embracing the Tiger: The Institutional Effectiveness Challenge." *Leadership Abstracts*, 10(8). Mission Viejo, CA: League for Innovation in the Community College.

Roueche, J. E., & Roueche, S. D. (1993). *Between a Rock and a Hard Place: The At-Risk Student in the Open Door College*. Washington, DC: Community College Press.

Roueche, J. E., & Roueche, S. D. (1999, April/May). "Keeping the Promise: Remedial Education Revisited." *Community College Journal*, 12-16.

Roueche, J. E., & Roueche, S. D. (2000, February). What's Ahead for Community Colleges in the New Millennium. Keynote address. Innovations 2000 Conference of the League for Innovation in the Community College, Orlando, FL.

Roueche, J. E., Roueche, S. D., & Milliron, M. D. (1996). "Developing a Part-Time Faculty Support System That Makes Sense." *Academic Leadership: Journal of the National Community College Chair Academy*, 3(4).

Roueche, J. E., Taber, L., & Roueche, S. D. (1995). *The Company We Keep: Collaboration in the Community College.* Washington, DC: Community College Press.

Tushman, M. L., & O'Reilly, C. A. (1997). *Winning through Innovation: A Practical Guide to Leading Organizational Change and Renewal.* Boston, MA: Harvard Business School Press.

Vaughan, G. B. (1995). *The Community College Story: A Tale of American Innovation.* Washington, DC: Community College Press.

Zeiss, T. & Associates (1997). *Developing the World's Best Workforce: An Agenda for America's Community Colleges.* Washington, DC: Community College Press.

Appendix A

1997 What do CEOs Want to Know About. . .
Key Trends in the Community College

ALLIANCE FOR
COMMUNITY
COLLEGE
INNOVATION

What Do Presidents Want to Know About . . .
Key Trends in the Community College

A survey of and for
Alliance for Community College Innovation institutions

This survey was composed of questions exploring key trends in the community college as identified in the current national literature and conference programs. **The following survey results are drawn from the 523 presidents surveyed. The survey had a response rate of 62 percent.**

1. **Demographic Information:** 76 % Male 24% Female
   Age 54 (mean)   Tenure as President 9.4 (mean, sd=7.2)

2. **Do you believe that in the next three-to-five years at your institution:**

	YES!	Yes	yes	?	no	No	NO!
a. General enrollment will increase.	29%	34%	28%	3%	5%	1%	0%
b. Minority enrollment will decrease.	5%	8%	6%	5%	19%	26%	31%
c. Your institution will experience significant employee turnover.	12%	25%	27%	3%	17%	11%	5%
d. More full-time faculty will retire in the next ten years than did in the last twenty years.	30%	36%	19%	2%	8%	4%	1%
e. The number of party-time faculty will increase.	10%	24%	32%	8%	17%	8%	1%
f. Training new faculty will become an increasingly important institutional priority.	37%	41%	17%	2%	1%	1%	1%
g. The trend toward the use of information technology in instruction will increase.	74%	22%	3%	0%	0%	1%	0%
h. Distance learning offerings will decrease.	8%	5%	3%	1%	10%	29%	44%

	YES!	Yes	yes	?	no	No	NO!
i. Training faculty in the use of information technology will become an essential part of ongoing staff development.	62%	33%	5%	0%	0%	0%	0%
j. Obtaining and maintaining information systems to collect outcomes data (performance measures) will become increasingly important.	59%	25%	6%	0%	0%	0%	0%
k. The cost of obtaining and maintaining information technology will become a key issue with governing boards and legislatures.	48%	39%	10%	1%	2%	0%	0%
l. Developing and maintaining partnerships with local corporations will become an increasingly important part of college operations.	48%	40%	11%	1%	0%	0%	0%
m. Workforce training/development offerings will increase.	46%	42%	9%	2%	1%	0%	0%
n. Welfare reform will necessitate stronger linkages with local social services.	34%	41%	17%	3%	5%	0%	0%
o. Aligning educational offerings with local educational institutions (K-12 and university) will be an increasing priority.	29%	51%	19%	1%	0%	0%	0%
p. Basic skills/developmental programs will lose enrollment.	2%	3%	6%	4%	24%	40%	21%
q. Legislators will continue to call for greater accountability from colleges.	41%	47%	10%	1%	1%	0%	0%
r. The need for good data on which to base decisions will become increasingly important.	55%	39%	5%	1%	0%	0%	0%
s. Your funding will in some way be tied to performance indicators.	34%	39%	16%	9%	1%	1%	0%
t. Your institution will move to become more learning-centered.	39%	45%	13%	2%	1%	0%	0%
u. Options for learning (times, places, and methods) will increase.	54%	38%	7%	1%	0%	0%	0%

Appendix B

2000 What do CEOs Want to Know About. . .
Key Trends in the Community College

What Do CEOs Want to Know About . . .
KEY TRENDS IN
THE COMMUNITY COLLEGE

A Survey of and for League Alliance CEOs

This survey is a follow-up to our extensive 1997 study of key trends in the community college. Like the 1997 study, it is composed of questions exploring major trends in the community college field as identified in current national literature and conference programs.

> **These survey results are composed of the responses submitted by your fellow CEOs as part of the *Alliance* quarterly CEO survey service. The response rate for this survey was 47% (n=331).**

A. Demographic Information: Male: 78% Female: 22%
Age: 55 (mean)   Tenure as President in Years: 9.4 (mean)

B. Do you believe that in the next 3 to 5 years at your institution:

		YES!	Yes	yes	?	no	No	NO!
1.	General enrollment will increase.	27%	37%	29%	2%	4%	0%	1%
2.	Minority enrollment will decrease.	7%	6%	5%	2%	18%	34%	28%
3.	Providing access to information technology for low-income students will be an increasing institutional priority.	20%	44%	30%	4%	2%	0%	0%
4.	Incoming students will be better prepared to succeed academically than they have been in the last 3 to 5 years.	2%	12%	28%	16%	25%	12%	5%
5.	More incoming students will already hold at least a bachelor's degree (e.g., in programs such as allied health, technology).	4%	18%	46%	13%	13%	5%	1%

		YES!	Yes	yes	?	no	No	NO!
6.	Your institution will experience significant employee turnover.	20%	25%	25%	5%	14%	9%	2%
7.	Finding and retaining information technology workers will become easier.	3%	4%	8%	2%	17%	31%	35%
8.	More full-time faculty will retire in the next 3-5 years than did in the last 10 years.	25%	29%	22%	3%	14%	5%	2%
9.	The number of part-time faculty will increase.	5%	21%	37%	9%	23%	5%	0%
10.	Orienting and training new faculty will be an increasingly important institutional priority.	31%	46%	20%	1%	2%	0%	0%
11.	Training faculty in the use of information technology will be an essential part of staff development.	56%	35%	8%	0%	0%	1%	0%
12.	You will replace at least part of your Student Information System, HR System, or Finance System.	41%	24%	14%	6%	6%	6%	3%
13.	Governing boards and legislatures will examine the cost of obtaining and maintaining information technology more closely.	16%	42%	26%	7%	6%	3%	0%
14.	Steps will be taken to integrate your various online learning applications with your student information system.	33%	40%	18%	7%	1%	1%	0%
15.	E-commerce capacity (e.g., registering and paying for courses; purchasing books and supplies) will be increasingly expected by students, employees, and community members.	48%	38%	13%	1%	0%	0%	0%
16.	Information technology literacy will become a requirement in most academic programs.	45%	40%	13%	1%	1%	0%	0%
17.	Programs promoting life/work balance or mind/body wellness will be developed to help students and college employees deal with stress related to change and technology.	5%	26%	45%	15%	8%	1%	0%
18.	Developing and maintaining partnerships with local corporations will become less important.	2%	2%	0%	0%	7%	28%	61%

	YES!	Yes	yes	?	no	No	NO!
19. Welfare reform will necessitate stronger linkages with local social services.	12%	42%	35%	4%	6%	1%	0%
20. Aligning educational offerings with local educational institutions (K-12 and university) will be an increasing priority.	34%	45%	18%	1%	1%	1%	0%
21. Increasing numbers of for-profit educational providers will enter your service area.	21%	40%	27%	5%	5%	2%	0%
22. Legislators will call for less accountability from colleges.	1%	1%	0%	1%	7%	21%	69%
23. Your funding increasingly will be tied to performance indicators.	31%	40%	22%	4%	2%	1%	0%
24. External pressure to curtail affirmative action efforts will increase.	4%	12%	19%	26%	24%	12%	3%
25. You will adopt strategies from the learning-centered education movement.	24%	42%	27%	6%	1%	0%	0%
26. Options for learning (times, places, and methods) will increase.	53%	38%	9%	0%	0%	0%	0%
27. Steps will be taken to modify the general education core to meet the learning needs of the 21st century.	22%	41%	27%	6%	1%	1%	2%
28. Workforce training/development offerings will increase.	48%	25%	15%	1%	0%	1%	0%
29. Basic skills/developmental programs will lose enrollment.	0%	1%	5%	6%	24%	36%	28%
30. The number of certificate programs will increase.	23%	42%	28%	3%	3%	1%	0%
31. The number of fast track or accelerated degree programs will increase.	30%	44%	21%	4%	1%	0%	0%
32. Intercollegiate athletic programs will increase.	1%	6%	10%	21%	29%	19%	14%
33. The number of services that you outsource will decrease.	0%	3%	4%	10%	45%	30%	8%
34. New facilities will be built for campus-based programs.	17%	25%	34%	8%	12%	3%	1%

	YES!	Yes	yes	?	no	No	NO!
35. You will explore offering a 4-year degree in specific programs.	9%	13%	14%	9%	21%	14%	20%
36. Your institution will significantly increase tuition.	2%	8%	18%	9%	36%	14%	13%

C. Listed below are other key trends affecting the community college field over the next 3 to 5 years that we should consider as part of this survey:

_____

_____

_____

_____

_____

_____

_____

_____

_____

_____

CHAPTER 2

MAINTAINING THE TECHNOLOGY EDGE: LEADERSHIP LESSONS FOR AN UNCERTAIN FUTURE

Paul A. Elsner

In the latter part of the 20th Century, technology became an extraordinary metaphor for, if nothing else, the advocating of change. Entering a new century, the assumption has been that if you have a large investment in technology, and you have a lot of technology to show for that investment, you must be on the edge of change. It turns out that technology has not wholly assisted us in formulating a coherent view of a future. Technology has suggested future positioning, but it has not, for some unexplainable reason, allowed us to generate a coherent future for higher education. Technology has impressed us with its dazzling momentum and its tumultuous nature, but it has hardly given us enough breathing time to envision all of its implications.

At the dawn of a new century, community colleges face tremendous challenges in riding the wild surf of technology progress. Technology is one of the great drivers of the free market and of the Learning Revolution sweeping higher education. As traditional revenue sources shrink and competitive learning options increase, higher education is being shaken out of its traditional roles, modes of delivery, and patterns of organization. College leaders striving to maintain a technology edge must sort through rival views of the future to remain viable in the rapidly evolving education marketplace. Many of us who have been riding the technology waves for a while are beginning to realize how precarious the cutting edge can be. We are only beginning to learn our lessons from these experiences, and prominent among them is the importance of looking beyond artifact and glamour to the broader assumptions and implications connected to our use of technology.

Maricopa as Technology Pioneer and Skeptic

The Maricopa Community Colleges have enjoyed a premier reputation in technology accomplishments. For more than twenty years we have aggressively invested in and experimented with technology to improve teaching, learning, and the management of the college, and we have achieved some degree of success and acclaim. As we survey these achievements, we recognize their ephemeral nature and that we must constantly assess and renew our relationships with technology in the expanding entrepreneurial educational marketplace.

Maricopa's technology achievements include several precedents. Maricopa was the first community college district to integrate voice, video, and data in a wide-area network covering ten campuses. Maricopa developed the unique architecture of a distributive system when most other large community college districts were depending on central processing units (CPUs). Maricopa boldly built high-tech centers the size of football fields, allowing all disciplines in a college to use one central facility for teaching and learning. Maricopa perfected open-entry/open-exit instruction with the use of pervasive technology support. Maricopa passed two significant bonds, one in 1984 for $75 million and another in 1994 for $385 million. Of the latter–the largest in the history of community colleges–$130 million was dedicated to technology purchases and acquisition. Maricopa leads the nation, perhaps the world, in offering the largest alternative delivery enrollment through Rio Salado College, one of the original "colleges without walls." Currently, 149 courses are offered on the Internet, which, when combined with all other distance learning formats, contribute to enrollments of over 12,000 students in various alternative delivery courses including telecourses, teleconferencing, and World Wide Web delivery.

Maricopa continues to invest in massive and bold application software experiments such as our Learner-Centered Systems (LCS) Project, which will place more power in the hands of students. In the future, upon entering a module or a course, students will "own" their own records, know their debt service, and even know their indexing of probable career placement. In addition, Maricopa concentrates on network expansion and bandwidth capacity as it builds out the most sophisticated network in most of higher education in the United States.

Several assumptions about the changing nature of learning and the higher education market shape Maricopa's technology agenda:

1. In higher education, marketing will shift from production-driven processes to customer-controlled strategies. By this we mean that

free markets will shift power to the students. Students will have spending currency. Groups of students will eventually create alliances and purchasing cartels to offer their enrollments to the lowest bidders.

2. Because the learner is the center of everything, the Maricopa Community Colleges are concentrating on designing distributed learning technologies.

3. The integration of the Web, e-mail, video conferencing, groupware, simulations, news groups, distribution lists, chat rooms, instructional software, highly productive authoring labs, and multimedia production support, constitutes the arsenal of learning support.

4. Places such as the Maricopa Community Colleges are disadvantaged in the new marketplace in that they do not hold a monopoly on convenience. Colleges that enjoy what is called *medallion status*–brand names like Harvard and M.I.T.–can now initiate Web courses or multimedia courses and invade the convenience market. While community colleges still have a fleeting monopoly as low-cost providers by having access to public funds, the free market will probably cause the dissolution of that advantage as well.

It seems no small irony that as leading investors and apparent proponents of technology, we find ourselves among the more skeptical and tentative of those proponents. A few years ago, I gave an address at a conference of the American Association for Higher Education (AAHE) entitled "Nervous on the Edge of Technology." Typically, we find ourselves in a sea of enthusiasm for technology. Our concern is that much of this enthusiasm is unexamined. It is not unusual for the League for Innovation, for example, to draw 4,000 attendees to a technology conference. Great energy fills in the conference halls as hundreds of panelists and speakers demonstrate their wares and show their most recent triumphs. However, behind all of this enthusiasm–fueled by the vendors and marketers of technology–is an eerie absence of a reason for which we are buying the latest product applications and the general euphoria of technology.

It would be easy to make the case that most buyers of technology (and I speak mainly from the community college perspective) have been "had" by the vendors. Let me propose some reasons why this is so:

1. Vendors, both large and small, have had the corporate monopoly on releasing product development in such a way as to constantly keep the consumers in the dark-even though community colleges are spending millions in hardware acquisition and on applications software.
2. One of the industry's greatest hoaxes has been its "pushing out" of application software. Most community colleges will attest to having spent agonizing months, even years, trying to correct and adapt bad product design to real-time applications in their colleges to serve such simple functions as admissions and records and the support of learning systems.
3. The computer industry is an industry that brags about its product efficiency, but has no fundamental efficiency in the marketplace of users.
4. Often computer industries will create elaborate user groups on the assumption that the users have some sense of ownership of product development. It turns out that most commercial vendors do not have a clue what users need or want. Vendors often ignore user needs even when clear explanations and friendly overtures are made to them. The best advice, of course, is to avoid most computer industry representatives. They have not done much for you in the past and they are not likely to do much for you in the future except take your money.

Michael Emmi, CEO of SCT, an industry pace-setter, addressed the Canadian and Japanese Business Higher Education Forums in Banff, Canada on the knowledge worker. He said that two-thirds of all IT projects fail, largely as a result of too few skilled software engineers, a shortage he cited at about 750,000. Still, the challenges facing Maricopa and its sister institutions worldwide continue to force higher education leaders to turn to industry and its vendors for guidance. The tremendous changes going on in society, so intricately interlaced with technological advancements, have left leaders in the educational world unsure of the technological future.

Many Ways of Foreseeing

What are some of the competing views for the future? We have argued that higher education does not have a coherent view of the future of technology. There are, however, some views emerging without higher education's help or involvement. Each view has implications for the role of technology in community colleges. Each represents a different force that will undoubtedly be woven into the social fabric of the new millennium.

Future as Cyberfreedoms

One conceptual image of the future that is emerging is "cyberfreedoms," a model derived from the Internet. The coda for this model is, *I can communicate on my own time, under my own conditions, and with everyone, everywhere.* The editors of such publications as *Wired* best espouse this emerging social view with images of the future that are revolutionary in tone and have little use for large organizations like television networks, corporations, universities, and government–particularly the Federal Communications Commission. This model holds forth at least four implications for individuals and nations:

1. Our borders are redefined.
2. Nation states are less important.
3. The individual feels more empowered.
4. The state cannot be seen as responsible for as much.

In general, authority is being redefined in this view of societal progression. The state and the nation play a lesser role in our lives, and most autonomous, decentralized commerce is seen as self-organizing, as self-correcting, and, eventually, as an improvement. The metaphor of the Internet characterizes this new society–highly intuitive, highly self-organizing, highly empowered.

A number of years ago, Bill Strauss, coauthor of the book *13th Gen*, which explores the post-baby boomer generation and its growing influence on American culture, addressed our faculty at the annual All Faculty Convocation. Following Strauss' presentation, Vernon Smith, a 13th Generation faculty member at Rio Salado College, stood up in front of hundreds of faculty and strongly defended his generation. Vernon spoke to us about how the "13th Generation," or "Generation X," or youth sometimes referred to as "slackers," might view higher education with this manifesto:

Truth is much more subjective than one might think. People, governments, and professors have their own "spin" on truth.

Information is not found in any single source or form.

For the future, control and access to information is power.

Show me how to get and use that access.

Help me learn how to learn. Since instructors are no longer the source of information, of truth, they can take a more useful role as facilitator of learning, not the source.

Don't bore me. If you are going to stand up and lecture me from your yellowing notes, put it on a disk, and I will take it home and read it on my time. Use an electronic forum or presentation–music, video, computer-based tutorials, visual peripherals–not just lecture.

No ideas are new or unique–there is nothing new under the sun. Pooled knowledge and appropriation are not plagiarism.

Be explicit with your expectations in the classroom. I want to know all of the hoops you want me to jump through from the start.

Teach me process, not content. Don't mark down my grade on a paper for a misspelled word (a content issue). Mark down my grade for forgetting to click on the spellcheck button (a process issue).

Remember that I am strapped for time and out of money. Between the "Mcjobs," school, and play, I know where the payoff will be.

Perhaps Tony Carnavale, Public Policy and Leadership Executive for the Educational Testing Service (ETS), describes the cyberfreedoms model most succinctly: "The new activists, who are often business people, have an almost pure interest in reforming education–they have no concern about the politics of it or the cultural issues associated with modernization."

In a *Wired* article entitled "New Rules for the New Economy," Kevin Kelly (1997) describes how connectivity is the essential currency of the cyberfuture:

Everything becomes connected–billions and billions and billions of connections so the network redefines the economic premises of our lives. It drives all the new commerce, which is shorthand for connections. . . . As we implant a billion specks of our thought into everything we make, we are also connecting them up. Stationary objects are wired together. The nonstationary rest–that is, most manufactured objects–will be linked by infrared and radio, creating a wireless Web vastly larger than the wired Web. It is not necessary that each connected object transmit much data. A tiny chip plastered inside a water tank on an Australian ranch transmits only the telegraphic message of whether it is full or not. A chip on the horn of each steer beams out his pure location, nothing more than "I'm here, I'm here." The chip in the gate at the end of the road communicates only when it was last opened: "Tuesday." (pp. 141-142)

Kelly goes on to explain that this is a process of rapid evolution, and not all of this connection is going to occur overnight.

The whole shebang won't happen tomorrow, but trajectory is clear. We are connecting all to all. Every step taken that banks on cheap, rampant, and universal connection is a step in the right direction. Furthermore, the surest way to advance massive connectionism is to exploit decentralized forces–to link the distributed bottom. How do you make a better bridge? Let the parts talk to each other. How do you improve lettuce farming? Let the soil speak to the farmer's tractors. How do you make aircraft safe? Let the airplanes communicate among themselves and pick their own flight paths. In the Network Economy, embrace dumb power. (p. 142)

In the cyberfreedoms future derived from the Web, traditional boundaries become redefined, as connectivity becomes the coin of the realm. Organizations, including nations, states, and governments, become less important than individuals. And, as power moves to the level of the individual, the processes by which we solve our problems become self-organizing, self-empowered, self-connected.

Future as Collectives

A second emerging future is defined by the special interests that drive policy direction. These special interests become more important than schools, governments, or universities. The burgeoning power of such special interest collaboratives is evidenced in the Beijing Women's Conference, Rio Summit on the Environment, Cairo Population Conference, and the Singapore Conference on Thinking. A future defined by the hegemony of such collectives implies that our connections and our collaboratives drive more significant events in our lives than the authorities to which we are normally responsible. No head of government could forge as expansive a women's agenda as the Beijing Conference. Nor could the politics be as local as actual issues women face in their villages, their communities, their families, their religious environments, and in their own localities of country or community. Reflecting the pervasive power of some religious collectives, the Cairo Population Conference broke down when population control became the central agenda issue that could not be tolerated by certain Islamic countries.

More often, the future as defined by special interest collectives will find the coalescing of groups along lines that ignore conventional boundaries. As we become more globally interdependent, individuals will move about the world, fashioning business and personal bonds within the new international community. The growing worldwide eco-consciousness, which is stimulating international responses to traditionally private, national decisions about levels of pollutants and consumption of natural resources, hints at the power potential in the new collectives.

Future as Media

Still another prospective can be envisioned as a media-defined future. This future presupposes that media shapes global attitudes because of similarities and tastes in music, film, art, food, clothing, and lifestyles translated through shared media-based experiences. Today, approximately 800 million teenagers around the globe listen to the same sitar, rock n' roll, steel band, Reggae music, and video productions. Madonna, Ricky Martin, and other international entertainers set cultural standards around the world. Our multicultural world, in many ways, is increasingly monocultural through the effects of mass media. The media-based collective model of the future is more youth-centered, and its tastes, desires, interests, and perceptions are created by and reflected in television, film, video, music, and other ubiquitous media. Standards of sound and visual quality are extremely advanced. Youth demand high fidelity, high resonance, and a quality standard that determines the basis on which they will receive information.

Global acculturation to media is staggering. Increasingly, the media define our accepted limits of violence, drama, romance, heroism, and even love. Yet, few technology planners take into account the homogenizing effects of global media. No doubt, positive futures could be projected as well as the negative ones that are evident. Again, here rests the potential for building an even more coherent future for technology. If teenagers are listening to the same sitar, alternative, hip hop, steel band, and rock n' roll music, they are at the same time seeing the same signature clothing ads and resonating to the same general values of love, romance, heroism, and increasing violence. Just as Reggae and rock have fused, so have the youth cultures. This youth phenomena may have more implications than any of the alternate futures described. It has shaped massive global, commercial, economic, and market policy in the past and will continue to do so in the future. For a country like the People's Republic of China, which exports 80 percent of the global clothing market, the implications are staggering.

Finally, in considering how a collective mental view of a future can shape destiny, I turn to the example of the 1939 New York World's Fair. This fair is an excellent example of how a single event helped shape an entire era, in this case six decades of a country's values and culture. The vision proposed at the 1939 World's Fair, during a troubled and shaky time in U.S. history, was of a better standard of living, beneficial modernism, suburban optimism, unlimited consumption, and the massive commodification of American products. The promise of technology for a good life–first the automatic washing machine and dishwasher, then the microwave–changed America in profound ways we could not have foreseen. Americans drew a new national identity from the fair's utopian visions and promise of prosperity for the common man. From this new ideology, the U.S. colonized the future with a standard of technology and consumerism that has lasted more than 60 years.

Sifting Through the Futures

As new waves of technological change and competing views of the future approach, I ask only that we examine our technology revolution in more thorough ways. The 1939 World's Fair is illustrative of an extravaganza building upon a hopeful vision. It drove future decades of consumption and unprecedented material pleasure. We allowed that future to play itself out because that was what we thought we wanted. At the World's Fair, people visited massive pavilions illustrating a happy, hopeful future of freeways, automated machinery, and conveniences in the home that would allow us to draw upon new leisure and a more pleasurable existence. At the time, Europe had entered the front-end of World War II, and America clung to a hope of peace. After Poland was invaded and Nazi troops occupied Paris, there seemed little hope for America to avoid the war; certainly fascism and communism abroad were not feasible alternatives. After the war, the American people renewed their commitment to the images of peace and prosperity they saw at the 1939 World's Fair. In a sense, they colonized the future. It was the only safe place for America's imperial destiny, which was played out in the moon landing and the NASA space shuttles. There was no way to see the long-term effects of this new technological imperialism.

One cannot blame all of our social ills on a blind commitment to technological development, but we now have to live with the complexities of maintaining air quality, clean water, overcrowded cities, and unsafe neighborhoods. We have saddled ourselves with social problems that possibly could have been avoided by envisioning a different future. Too often, our technology planners do not see much beyond the euphoria and the dazzling momentum, which they mistake as progress.

At the League for Innovation Conference on Information Technology in November 1996, which attracted 3,600 participants, I presented a video-assisted speech that outlined the consequences of five decades of unprecedented expansion, development, and consumerism-all riding the crest and glories of technology. This video's closing metaphor is the depiction of the seemingly bottomless swamp of the Fresh Kills Landfill in New York, which by height and depth exceeds the elevation of Denver. Fresh Kills is the highest point of elevation among the New England seaboard's landmasses and by 2010 will reach more than six miles in height and width. This man-made mountain is testimony to the unforeseen effects of our rampant consumerism technology progress. The social critic and artist-in-residence for the New York City Sanitation Department, Marian Laderman Ukeles, is using Fresh Kills in creative ways to communicate the effects of our technology decisions. At the Marine Transfer Station in Lower Manhattan, Ukeles presents "Flow City," a multimedia collage of technological accomplishment and waste, not unlike a Jackson Pollack painting. A block-long tunnel made of recycled materials presents cross-cuts of the waste of two or three generations, from our infatuation with the acrylic world of hula hoops, old toothpaste containers, broken bottles, and bean cans to the more recent throw away society of old Apple II computers, broken television tubes, and Radio Shack modems. At the Glass Bridge we can see and hear the dumping of new waste as it arrives. As the compression chambers crush down on the technology we threw out last year, we hear a wonderful cacophony of sounds that make up the symphony of technology progress for the last several years. A Media Flow Wall with 24 television monitors shows us videos and live camera shots from Fresh Kills.

Ukeles' artistic treatment of our technological by-products is meant to be instructive for touring children. As they visit the Manhattan Transfer Station, they can see that our habits of consumption are not someone else's, but our own decisions about what we value, what we purchase, and what we throw away. Through an artist's view, they can see the past and its influence on the future.

Technology Future at Maricopa

The technology beat goes on at Maricopa. We continue marching. Although we have been described as visionary, more sobering arguments give us perspective on a more coherent future. We are only beginning to learn our lessons from these experiences, and high among them is the importance of looking beyond artifact and glamour to the broader assumptions and implications connected to our use of technology. Based on the overarching assumptions described previously, Maricopa is orienting its technology future in two strategic directions: (1) JAVA-based software architecture, and (2) distributed learning systems. Implementation activities are under way in both areas.

JAVA-Based Software Architecture

Ron Bleed (1997), Maricopa's distinguished Vice Chancellor for Information Technology outlines the rationale for adopting a JAVA platform in his comprehensive report, "Innovation Advantages for New Realities." Among the advantages Bleed outlines are ease of adaptation, flexibility, multimedia integration, Internet protocol, and, most critical, shift to more learner-centered control of information.

The new software architecture is rules-based and built with objects. Ease of changes, purchasing new features through the objects, and integration to other software provide the needed ability to keep the software changing with changing needs in Maricopa. In the atmosphere of ten autonomous colleges, Maricopa will be well served by this flexibility. In the future era of rapid change and integration with other organizations, Maricopa will need software with those same attributes. The Internet architecture is another cornerstone for new systems. The Internet has merged video and audio with the computer media, JAVA software language is the great integrator of multimedia which makes it the vehicle for the new learningware developments.

JAVA is more than a programming language; it's a whole new computing platform. JAVA computing involves decision shift from a desk-top centric model to a network-centric one. JAVA has the potential to fundamentally change the way information systems are constructed, managed and used. As everyone connects to the Internet, whether they be faculty or students, and begins to exchange information, JAVA will be the software that puts education online. (Forester Research estimates that $3 million of JAVA applets were sold in 1996, a number that will increase to almost $700 million by the end of 1999.) At the present timeline, Maricopa will be among the first colleges to have a JAVA/WWW programmed student information system. The reengineered design specifications for creating a learner-centered system are a perfect fit for the power of JAVA. In addition, our JAVA-based administrative software architecture creates the foundation for the next generation of instructional software. (Bleed, 1997, p.9)

Distributed Learning Systems

The second innovation advantage that Maricopa currently holds in a strategic deck of cards is its commitment to distributed learning systems. A Center for Distributive Learning (CDL) is planned for more than one of our colleges, with Mesa Community College as the first college out of the chute. The online description of the Center for Distributed Learning offers this definition:

> [Distributed learning uses] a wide range of information technology to provide learning opportunities beyond the bounds of the traditional classroom. Some examples of distributed learning technologies include the World Wide Web, e-mail, video conferencing, groupware, simulations, news groups, distribution lists, chat rooms, MOOs, and instructional software. A distributed learning environment facilitates a learner-centered educational paradigm and promotes active learning.

As Maricopa evolves into an elaborate system of helpdesks, call centers, and course facilitation, the possibility exists that three to four thousand courses could end up on the Internet within the next two years. We are currently doubling Internet courses every semester. As Linda Thor, president of Rio Salado Community College, frames it, "Maricopa does not have courses up on the Internet; it has, in Rio's case, the whole college." This new educational delivery system, however, does not preclude the omnipresent need for student support for learning. Studies of online learning at Maricopa reveal that the best predictor of student success in Internet-based courses is a faculty phone call to the student during the first week of classes. Our experiences validate what we have always suspected–that technology very seldom stands alone. Elaborate support systems are needed to undergird technology, almost analogous to an iceberg in that technology is only the tip; underneath good technology are massive student support and increasingly intricate, self-organizing networks of learning communities.

Epilogue and Genesis

This chapter does not offer many solutions. Instead, it begs for higher education to develop a more coherent, visionary view of technology and asks that we not simply ride out its crests, waves, rivulets, and surges of progress. It calls not only for being impressed with technology's dazzling momentum, and its tumultuous nature, but also for constantly positioning and, at times, offering counterpoint to the technology solutions with which we seem so enamored. I like Kevin Kelly's article in *Wired*, in which he calls for the "devolution" as well as the "evolution" of our organizations:

> You've got to clear out the top of your organizations and you have to be ready to push back down into the valleys when you have reached the top of your peak. We have not learned to devolve our organizations very well and most organizations only have a short life at their highest point. They have to learn to devolve to the lower valleys and build the uphill path to even greater and different achievements. (Kelly, 1997, p. 192)

We are learning to undo and recreate ourselves at Maricopa, but ever so slowly. To be great at technology, we must also be critics of technology. We must look beyond simply the artifact stage of technology. Computers, in a sense, are passé. The massive amount of commerce growing off the Internet is making technology ever more pervasive, ever more self-organizing, ever more creative. We hope that Maricopa is more in the mode of critiquing, envisioning, and creating than in the mode of simply buying technology. We also hope that major users of technology, like community colleges, will learn to band together and create purchasing cartels to stop the blind commercial exploitation of users. Too often as users, community colleges buy inferior products rather than take on their own destinies and find their own solutions, which are almost always better than what is offered commercially.

It is ironic, indeed, that we are passing through a period in these millennial years at a point in time when Netscape is only a few years old. We are in a position in the development of our civilization where we have discoveries that make the invention of the printing press seem small. Is it not a wonder, knowing what the printing press did to change all of progress and civilization, that we do not have an engaging view of the future for technology that really projects what its true and hopeful potential can be? We need that vision and we need that coherent view.

As community colleges ride the tsunami of technological change and enter a new millennium, it is incumbent upon us to see the absurdities of our old Cartesian views of the universe, to look for larger patterns, and to lift up our technology agendas to fulfill the egalitarian mission we symbolize. Our new utopian future for technology application rests in a learning-centered ideal. The agendas prescribed by all the alternate futures call for technologies that allow the learner to rule. Whether responding to a future defined by cyberfreedoms, special interest collectives, or a media-defined youth culture, we must use educational technology to liberate the learner, or we will find ourselves prisoners of the past. At the same time, we must engage the human and organizational possibilities of technology to uphold our values of community and social responsibility. The vision for such a future must reside among our leaders.

References

Bleed, Ron. (1997, July 24). *Innovation Advantages for New Realities*. Report prepared for the Maricopa Community Colleges, Tempe, AZ.

Electronic Mail Description of the Center for Distributed Learning planned for Mesa Community College, 1998.

Kelly, K. (1997, September). "The New Rules of the New Economy." *Wired*, 5.09, 140-197.

Howe, N., Strauss, B., and Williams, I. (1993). *13th Gen: Abort, Retry, Ignore, Fail?* New York: Vintage Books.

CHAPTER 3

ADMINISTRATORS' ROLES IN THE ADOPTION OF TECHNOLOGY BY FACULTY: INSIDE THE TRADITIONAL CLASSROOM AND BEYOND

Alice Wildes Villadsen, Mary Kay Kickels, and Sunil Chand

Administrators in community colleges have been grappling with the issue of technology infusion into instruction for the past two decades. Prior to that time, technology in the classroom was found primarily in laboratory intensive curricula. Technology used as an aid to instruction in traditional classroom settings usually included overhead projectors, audio tapes, slides, films, videos, or, most awkwardly, the dreaded opaque projector.

Since the mid-1980s, certain faculty have been highly interested in using multimedia enhancements to enliven their teaching. Others have focused on the emerging technologies of distance education as an extension of traditional classrooms. While these faculty have embraced technological advancements as teaching aids, many other faculty have been reluctant to use technology. At times, administrators have felt like they were straddling two ice floes moving in opposite directions: the group of early adopters among the faculty demanding more and more sophisticated and costly technology, and the recalcitrant and reluctant faculty finding technology disturbing and threatening and wanting nothing to do with computers, television studios, or technology advocates.

The actual impact of technology-enhanced teaching on student learning is not fully known, although much classroom research is under way to discover just that. However, the need for community colleges to engage faculty in providing distance education is increasingly obvious. First, many students and their employers are asking us to provide distance learning options. In a 1997 survey by the Social and Economic Sciences Research Center at Washington State University, nearly 6 in 10 respondents reported that "cost or busy schedules are important barriers for them in taking more college courses" (*Workforce Economics Trends*, 1997, p. 7). Over 4 in 10 respondents reported that traditional college courses were not available when convenient. Only 15 percent reported ever having taken a course involving distance learning, but more than 70 percent thought that more courses using distance learning should be developed (*Workforce*, 1997). This study indicates the need for increased distance options, especially for community college students who are older, employed (often full time), and encouraged by their employers or by welfare reform initiatives to improve their skills.

A national survey suggests similar results. The Preliminary Report on Adult Learning Programs Survey Project for a Nation of Lifelong Learners (NLL) indicates that 83 percent of the 1,271 colleges and universities that responded reported that "flexibility in program" has been adopted as a means to deal with the needs of adult learners at their institutions. Among the respondents, 34 percent were offering courses delivered by at least one medium, and 33 percent were offering distance learning options for students (Maehl, 1997, pp. 2, 4). The report also indicated that business and industry sponsors of adult students expressed concern that "programs are not designed to contribute to the education and training needs of the sponsor," and that higher education is still too "rigid and traditional" to serve the current needs of adult learners (Maehl, 1997, p. 4).

A second reason for administrators to encourage faculty use of technology, both through distance education options and in traditional classroom settings, is the need for colleges to provide the right educational strategy for a group of increasingly diverse student learners. In his 1997 publication, *Creating More Learning-Centered Community Colleges*, Terry O'Banion includes as Principle III this descriptor: "The learning college creates and offers as many options for learning as possible. . . . If one option does not work, the learner should be able to navigate a new path to an alternative learning option" (p. 17).

Instructional options themselves continue to increase along with the pace of technology. Sherron and Boettcher (1997) report a prediction from a 1988 National University Continuing Education Association compendium that still seems to hold true:

- The evolution of new technologies appears to be continuing at a rapid pace.
- Each institution uses a unique mix or blend of technologies.

- No one technology dominates.
- A recurring theme is the three-pronged thrust that blends audio, video, and computer applications.

These themes, merged with the current categories of computing and communication products like the Internet, the World Wide Web, and video conferencing environments, provide numerous possibilities for learning options for community college students if faculty will pursue them and administrators will support their pursuits.

The Study

This chapter is a report on the first phase of a longitudinal study of the use of technology to improve learning in community colleges. Although the study began as an informal survey to determine what community college administrators are doing to encourage and to fund various technology applications within instruction, the researchers soon realized the value of long-term research into the evolving technology initiatives in community colleges. The identification of patterns, processes, models, and best practices can assist colleges as they go through the various stages of technology development.

To begin, an informal survey of the 20 League for Innovation in the Community College board member institutions (see appendix) was conducted during the 1997-1998 academic year. The designated League representatives at the 20 colleges responded or asked instructional colleagues to respond, or both, to seven basic questions. In addition, the researchers asked the 20 representatives to offer their best advice regarding approaches to the myriad of challenges resulting from technology infusion within the instructional units of their colleges. The 20 sets of narrative responses were then compiled by the authors and are presented below. In addition, the three researchers have included case studies of the history of technology in and beyond the classroom at their institutions: Central Piedmont Community College in Charlotte, North Carolina; Moraine Valley Community College in Palos Hills, Illinois; and Cuyahoga Community College in Cleveland, Ohio. The experiences of the 20 colleges participating in the study may aid other colleges as they deal with the complexities of providing technology resources for faculty to improve student learning.

Technology Within the Classroom

The first question asked of the surveyed institutions involved methods that have been used to support faculty in the use of various technologies, including multimedia presentations and other computer-assisted instruction, within a traditional classroom or laboratory setting: *How has your college encouraged faculty to adopt technology usage in the classroom?*

Made technology available to faculty. Such a simplistic response–that if faculty are to use technology in the classroom, it must be available–belies the complexity in community colleges' attempts to do just that: provide computers and software for faculty. With the life expectancy of computers and software becoming shorter and shorter, administrators are struggling to keep their interested faculty both initially equipped and regularly upgraded. However, all 20 colleges indicated that simply providing computing technology to individual faculty members is critical. Humber College also reported success with a computer purchase plan for college employees.

Provided or encouraged technology training. The provision of the computer and the software, of course, is not sufficient. Faculty must be trained to make the technology applicable and useful to them, and colleges reported a variety of training options. Technology training is sometimes accomplished on campus with college trainers; sometimes faculty are sent away to training institutes, such as the North Carolina Institute for Academic Technology; sometimes local computer information technology faculty are used to train their fellow faculty members; and sometimes external, contracted trainers come to the campus to train newly equipped faculty. However, in all cases, training is key.

Provided released time or financial incentives, or both, for technology training and course development. Often, training cannot be accomplished with a few hours or even weeks of intensive workshops. The responding colleges pointed out that faculty need time to devote to training and, even more importantly, to the development stage of technology infusion into instruction. Faculty often become frustrated when they gain expertise in computer-assisted instructional techniques and then find that, because of heavy teaching, advising, and committee schedules, they do not have time to incorporate technology into their courses. Incentives, therefore, are often necessary. Administrators need to find ways to provide incentives that encourage faculty to use technology to enhance classroom presentations.

Provided technical assistance and support for faculty adopters. Equally frustrating to faculty who are attempting to infuse technology into their teaching is an inability on the part of the institution encouraging such activity to provide technical assistance to faculty. Faculty are hired for their subject expertise and their ability to teach. Colleges should not expect faculty also to become computer technicians or sophisticated media specialists. Colleges must, therefore, think through the technical support issue before equipping faculty with sophisticated computer technology for classroom application. Many colleges in the survey have solved the technical support issue by opening technical assistance centers that can be used by faculty for both initial training and continuing support in course development. Others, such as Kirkwood with its Learning Technology Project, have set up and maintained websites to showcase instructional technology use, to provide links to resources on the Web, to provide a Web accessible database of instructional technology in use at the college, and to provide a listserv technology discussion group for faculty.

Set up "smart classrooms" for multimedia delivery. For faculty who are trained to deliver nontraditional, media-enhanced courses, classrooms appropriate for the use of instructional technology must be available. From classrooms equipped with networked interactive computer equipment to simpler ones with video-data projectors for multimedia teaching, the responding colleges have invested in creating technologically advanced classrooms for faculty use. These classrooms are often scheduled for maximum use by faculty representing many disciplines, and the colleges reported increasingly heavy use of these "smart" environments. These facilities are essential for the college wanting to encourage faculty use of technology to enhance teaching. How can institutions expect faculty to devote the time and energy to developing new instructional materials if spaces are not designated and equipped for the use of those materials?

Engaged faculty in campus technology teams and decisions. Administrators cannot expect to make all decisions regarding the infusion of technology into the classroom. Colleges reported that faculty themselves must be key players in the design of the campus technology plan; in decisions regarding the purchase and adoption of both hardware and software; in issues of hardware and software compatibility; and in decisions about financial investment in computing technology, its infrastructure, and the personnel needed to support such activity.

Showed that the college is serious about long-term investment in technology in the classroom. Instructional leaders and other college administrators must focus on the reality of technology as a support for learning. The use of technology in the classroom is not simply another passing educational fad. Administrator commitment can be demonstrated through such actions as emphasizing the educational value of technology in college goals, objectives, and routine internal communications; connecting the entire campus community electronically and using e-mail as a major means of campus linkages; and designating a portion of the budget for the purchase of classroom technology and training. Colleges have invested in technology by designing and building smart classrooms for faculty to use in teaching their courses. Such classrooms are designed for greater use of technology than are routine teaching space, and faculty often vie for the opportunity to teach in the smart classrooms.

Showcased faculty who are technology adopters. Several colleges have named progressive faculty technology users as mentors or coaches to other, less technically progressive faculty members. Others have encouraged faculty to develop idea exchanges among themselves about classroom applications for technology, including participation in the League for Innovation's virtual Technology and Learning Community (TLC). Some have supported faculty creativity by encouraging faculty participation in local "show and tell" programs, by sending faculty as college spokespersons to area clubs and organizations, and by encouraging faculty to become presenters at state, regional, and national professional association meetings.

Encouraged faculty to participate in external technology projects. Several colleges indicated that this encouragement is beneficial and that the external projects are at times grant related. Some faculty take the opportunity to return to industry for maintaining currency in technical applications in various disciplines, and they pay careful attention to the advice of local business and industry partners to ensure that classroom uses of technology mirror as much as possible the applications being used by industry trainers and proprietary organizations.

Technology Beyond the Traditional Classroom

As important as using current technology within classroom settings is, perhaps the more challenging and potentially more powerful issue that community college administrators must address is the growing need for distance applications in teaching. With more and more students requiring education "anyway, anyplace, anytime" (O'Banion, 1995-96, p. 22), the potential for distance education initiatives is limited only by our own imaginations. Administrators must find ways to encourage faculty to use their creativity and expertise to develop and then to teach courses delivered through video, interactive television, Web-based, and other computer-based instructional formats. The second question asked of the respondents addressed this challenge: *How does your college encourage faculty to develop other nontraditional instructional delivery options beyond the classroom?*

Asked for volunteers from among the faculty. The respondents acknowledged that not all faculty should be expected to develop and provide distance instruction, whether video, television, computer assisted, or computer based. However, all 20 of the surveyed institutions reported having found faculty with special interests and abilities to provide nontraditional, technology-based instruction. Several colleges also indicated that not all volunteers are suitable, and that guidelines for selection of appropriate faculty are important. Additionally, administrators need to focus on the development of technology-based distance options in disciplines that make sense educationally. For example, certain visual disciplines work well with video or CD-ROM options, and writing courses work well in interactive formats. The recruitment of volunteers must be accompanied by careful decisions that connect the faculty with the media and with the discipline.

Gave selected faculty time and, sometimes, money to do the development and pilot teaching. The development of distance classes takes time. Several colleges indicated that they had released faculty full time for development and teaching of distance options. In these cases, the simple load reduction, a time-tested method of giving faculty appropriate project time, had to be replaced with a complete freeing of the faculty for distance development. Colleges also reported variations in load reduction. Some explained that the teaching load was eliminated for a semester or quarter, others noted load reductions for the summer, and a few colleges reported indefinitely reassigning faculty to the virtual college initiative. Some colleges also offered pay incentives for distance course development and teaching. Others included plans for sharing possible royalty income from the products between the faculty developer and the supporting college. Finally, colleges with sabbatical options for faculty reported having used involvement in distance initiatives as a consideration in making positive sabbatical decisions.

Ensured appropriate technology, training, and technical support for faculty. To be productive innovators for distance education initiatives, faculty must be provided with appropriate technology, training, and technical support. The equipment, software, training, and technical support available for distance deliverers are, in and of themselves, incentives for energetic faculty who may be tired of traditional instructional modalities. Their colleagues can see the results of the innovative spirit of the distance faculty, and peer pressure has an impact on spreading the initiatives among the larger faculty group. Some of the colleges have provided faculty developers with laptops for use both on campus and at home in developing and in teaching online courses. Several of the 20 colleges reported that they are implementing online conferencing systems and that pilot projects are available for faculty application.

Provided high visibility to the faculty innovators and their technology applications. Some of the colleges reported that they encourage faculty developers by giving them special titles or access to travel and professional development funds. These faculty are often selected for both internal and external awards, and some colleges have adopted nontraditional development and delivery as a merit marker for faculty in performance appraisal, promotion, and tenure processes. Faculty are invited to present their products to colleagues both on the home campus and at professional meetings, and they are sometimes featured at board meetings or are invited to represent the college at community clubs and organizations. Internal publications are used to compliment their work, and news releases highlighting accomplishments of the faculty developers are provided to media. The League's Innovation of the Year award, a designation that often honors the technology adoption innovators, is available for internal recognition at each of the 20 institutions.

Used faculty on campus technology initiatives and teams. Unless faculty are involved in the campus decisions concerning the development of technology plans, the establishment of computing standards, the determination of guidelines for Internet course development, the selection of technology products, the development of policies for financial rewards, and other instructional issues, faculty are less likely to embrace the distance initiatives. Faculty make excellent members of technology teams and often thrive in an environment of joint decision making with instructional administrators. Several colleges indicated that they had used faculty to chair their technology initiatives.

Raised faculty awareness of appropriate distance technology options. Simple exposure to new advances in distance instruction creates in many faculty a desire to experiment. Respondents reported that they have organized vendor fairs on campus, hosted visiting professors who are skilled distance instructors, sent faculty to model institutions, and provided faculty travel to distance education workshops and seminars, all with good results.

Funding for Instructional Technology

Among the 20 colleges, the financial commitment to support instructional technology varied, but they all indicated that such a financial commitment must be long term. Although several colleges indicated that they had used grants and other short-term arrangements to finance technology initiatives, several of those questioned indicated that a "project" mentality is not sufficient to infuse technology throughout the teaching enterprise. The third question asked as part of the survey relates to funding sources used at the 20 institutions to support instructional technology: *How have you funded instructional technology initiatives at your college?*

Regular college budgets. Most colleges indicated that a base percentage of the institutional budget is devoted to technology purchases each year. Some states and counties provide special equipment allocations, usually based on college enrollment or types of programs offered.

Designated staff and program development allocations. Some respondents said that their colleges had made decisions to designate state or local staff and program development allocations for the training of faculty and technology support staff in the use of instructional technology. Some colleges had typically designated a portion of the college budget to training needs, a majority of which often was spent for faculty and staff training in technology.

College foundations and campaign funds. The college foundation was another frequently named source of technology support funds. Foundation monies have been used to equip specific labs and subject areas, to provide faculty with the equipment they need, and to ensure a general upgrade of campus computing services. Central Piedmont Community College reported a recent successful capital campaign that raised almost seven million dollars, with the funds devoted entirely to improving teaching technology.

Auxiliary enterprises. A few of the 20 colleges reported having used income from auxiliary services, such as bookstore profits, vending proceeds, and rental and lease revenue, as a means of supplementing state, county, and tuition dollars for upgrading faculty computers and developing smart classrooms, television studios, and technology assistance centers.

Profit from corporate and continuing education enterprises. Colleges within the survey group who have large corporate and continuing education (CCE) operations indicated that some income from CCE contracts had been used to upgrade teaching technology, usually specifically within the corporate and continuing education faculty, but sometimes also within the larger faculty population. Some colleges reported internal matching arrangements between CCE and traditional credit instructional units as well.

Grants. Almost all of the 20 institutions had at one time or another used federal, state, or local governmental grants or private foundation grants to supplement technology purchases in support of the instructional program. Several colleges reported successful grant initiatives that provided technology, training, faculty released time, renovation of existing facilities or construction of new ones, and technical support personnel.

Other sources. Some colleges used student laboratory or technology fees to aid in the general upgrade of technology on campuses, although none reported the use of these fees to support individual faculty initiatives. Others indicated that partnerships with local businesses and industries sometimes resulted in contributions of technology, software, materials, and training. Brookhaven College in the Dallas County Community College District, Texas, has received both hardware and software representing more than two million dollars from local industry to support a new geotechnology program. Finally, carefully constructed technology plans resulted in reallocation of technical resources between administrative and instructional needs, thus freeing funds for the purchase of current equipment for the most innovative faculty members.

Cost Efficiency

As community colleges have become more sophisticated in the application of technology to improve student learning and access, they have become increasingly conscious of the true costs of such initiatives. Not only is the technology itself expensive, but most colleges also admit that the technology is just the beginning of the costs. The full cost of technology ownership sees colleges invest in campus infrastructure, software upgrades, facilities construction and renovation, training, broadcasting and cable and television resources, faculty and staff time, and support staff. The researchers asked respondents to address cost issues associated with technology-enriched education: *Have you developed or used a cost/benefit analysis for technology-enhanced or technology-based instruction?*

Almost one-third of the 20 respondents indicated that they have developed or are developing cost models to help them make decisions about investing college resources in technology-enhanced instruction, particularly distance options like video and Internet courses. However, the colleges also acknowledged that projects to develop technology-based instruction are not likely to be cost effective, at least in the early stages. Most colleges expressed an understanding that technology-based or technology-enhanced instruction is an investment the colleges cannot afford to ignore.

Technical Expertise Requirements for Faculty

In the Information Age, community college faculty are expected to have computing skills. As distance education grows, the skills required of faculty increasingly include video and interactive television expertise and abilities to produce and teach interactive computer-based courses. To address this issue, researchers asked about expectations for faculty: *Have you developed a new or revised job description for faculty emerging from teaching technology initiatives?*

Colleges reported that they are beginning to respond to the new faculty skill sets by including technological expertise in faculty job descriptions. According to the survey, three-fourths of the colleges have rewritten job descriptions for all faculty to include computing or distance education expertise, or both; have revised job descriptions in certain disciplines to include technical skills; or have included technology skills as "desired" or "encouraged" characteristics. Colleges with faculty unions reported less movement than nonunion colleges in the revision of job descriptions, but some union colleges had made significant job description revisions.

Organizing for Instructional Technology Integration

With computing services having emerged from the financial, human resources, and student services areas of the college and with teaching applications having emerged from the instructional area, many colleges have a bifurcated organizational structure for technology. In the recent past, many colleges have combined administrative and instructional computing within one organizational structure to provide coordination, support, and financial resources more effectively. To elicit information about technology's place in the colleges, the researchers asked respondents to describe technology's integration into organizational structure: *How are classroom technology integration and distance teaching initiatives organized within your college?*

When asked about the organizational structure used at their colleges, one-fourth indicated that classroom technology and distance initiatives reported to the chief instructional officer. Four institutions said that all teaching technology was supervised by the chief administrative officer.

The other institutions were organized in a variety of ways: one model featured joint reporting between the chief instructional and the chief administrative offices, three colleges reported team management of technology, and two institutions combined the title and organization in "instruction and technology." All colleges reported concern and discussion on their campuses about the organization of technology in general, and several colleges indicated that they had recently completed new technology plans that would have significant organizational ramifications when implemented.

Words of Advice from the 20 Colleges

As a final component of the survey, respondents were asked to offer advice based on their experiences in encouraging faculty adoption of technology both in traditional classrooms and in distance applications. Many of the lessons are obvious; others are not. Penny Patz at DeAnza provided a reminder of a significant reality. Administrators, she said, cannot "jam technology down the throats of faculty. Instead, make it available. Peer pressure is still a mighty motivator for faculty adoption of technology to improve teaching/learning."

Have patience. Respondents indicated that no simple answers exist for technology infusion. Technology changes occur with overwhelming speed, but a similar quick pace simply is not possible in the encouragement of faculty and the development of technical applications. Persevere, and do not postpone dealing with campus technology. All colleges agreed that although they will never be "caught up" with technology needs, neither can they be "taken in by every new bell and whistle." A good technology plan will help the administrator deal with changes in technology expectations.

Do not leave faculty on the cutting edge without appropriate support services. Again and again, respondents indicated that moving too quickly into classroom and distance applications by giving faculty incentives to develop and teach with technology could very quickly turn into a disaster if the college is unable to provide sufficient technical support. Personnel with the expertise to aid faculty developers are not easy for colleges to hire, pay, and keep, yet their presence in the development process is critical to the success of the activity. Some respondents recounted problems of communication that can exist between the faculty developer and the technician, resulting in frustration and failure. It is imperative that the college provide faculty-friendly technicians as constant supporters of technically-enhanced teaching projects. One respondent said, "Providing the technology is the easy part. Having the resources to remain current and provide training and support for technology is the hard part."

Do not expect all faculty to adopt technology to improve their teaching. Finding the early adopters of technology and allowing their enthusiasm to spread is often the best way to see growth and creativity among faculty. Certainly, many faculty members are excellent at providing learning opportunities for their students without the infusion of technology into the process, and many students learn best in traditional settings. The administrator's role includes matching faculty members with suitable modalities and keeping reluctant faculty from discouraging enthusiastic colleagues.

Use faculty as advocates for technology; let faculty leaders take the lead. Respondents recommended that college administrators open technology committees and teams to faculty representation, ask faculty to chair or facilitate campus technology groups, and involve as many faculty as possible in all decisions the college makes about technology. Ownership in major and minor decisions at the college regarding technology turns faculty into advocates for that technology. Most responding institutions reported that faculty leadership in technology teams is a significant way to ensure enthusiastic faculty support for allocating campus resources to technology. Colleges also reported that faculty were involved in other aspects of technology integration, such as infusion, training, mentoring, evaluating, and implementing.

Do not expect faculty to be experts, necessarily, about the best technology for their particular needs or interests. Several colleges indicated that it is important to provide faculty with parameters to guide them through what is sometimes a maze of vendors, hardware, software, and assorted texts. Respondents suggested that vendor fairs, consultant recommendations, visits to colleges using the product, and encouragement of listserv participation are good ways to provide faculty with the resources they need to make sound decisions. College computer standards are necessary, and most colleges reported having a centralized check on technology and software purchases, a critical step in order for campus technicians and infrastructures to service faculty needs.

Do not expect bad teaching to become good teaching because of technology infusion. One instructional officer reminded administrators that technology is not a panacea. Bad overheads become bad PowerPoint presentations, bad videos, or bad Web classes. Teaching and learning are more complex than applying technology to a subject and expecting a miracle. For this reason, quality control is an important early step before decisions are made to invest resources in technology-based or technology-enhanced teaching projects. Keep the focus on student learning and make sure technology is a tool for supporting that learning. Standards for development of nontraditional, technology-based instructional units, courses, and modules should include a review process to ensure that good learning is occurring as a result of the new options.

Try to deal with faculty load and pay issues early. Because faculty time is required to create technology-based enhancements to existing traditional classes and to create distance courses, the college administrator should think through the issue of faculty load and come to some equitable solution before faculty become involved. Colleges should provide incentives for faculty who are interested in technology-based instructional development projects; however, the incentives do not necessarily have to be monetary. One colleague said, "Don't act like every new development requires extra pay. Acknowledge that these are additional ways of doing the job better." Most colleges reported that they provide faculty released time to work on technology projects; others use overload pay. A few colleges are moving to entirely new job descriptions and load expectations for faculty developers. Danger exists for the early faculty adopters whose enthusiasm for the technology-enhanced teaching options can turn sour if they begin to believe they are not being acknowledged for their hard work. As always, agreements need to be reached before rather than after a special project occurs.

Do not rely on ad hoc projects for advancing technology integration. Almost all twenty colleges reported that over the past ten years, they have used various ad hoc projects to encourage faculty adoption of technology in instruction. They noted that such projects were often very successful in developing small islands of creative energy and teaching excellence. However, the college representatives indicated that an "ad hoc approach" to technology integration simply was not the solution. Long range planning is essential for technology integration, with most colleges reporting the recent completion and implementation of technology plans for the future.

Keep tight reins on the hardware and hardware configurations. Some respondents advised that, with careful planning, colleges should be in a position to make wise decisions about hardware purchases and to ensure that all campus instructional projects requiring technology can be accommodated within the standard configurations. Faculty should have the lead role in technology use within instruction but cannot be allowed to make decisions that will not fit within the campus technology plan for purchase, installation, maintenance, and training.

Use every opportunity to provide professional development for faculty users. Respondents suggested that colleges host as many technology-based groups on campus as possible, and use their seminars and conferences for professional development opportunities for faculty. Santa Fe Community College in Gainesville, Florida, has developed an annual educational technology fair where vendors show their equipment and faculty demonstrate their uses of technology. This popular event, as well as the use of invited speakers providing workshops in retreat-style settings, has increased faculty use of technology at Santa Fe. Kirkwood Community College in Iowa has held technology fairs where faculty and staff demonstrate specific uses of technology in teaching and vendors display the latest technology, and at Delta College in Michigan, internal Internet conferences have been held and the college has sponsored a multimedia contest for high school students.

Find and use technology advocates among the college's board of trustees, advisory committees, and elected officials. Since the likelihood exists that technology will continue to be a major resource need, college advocates must understand the imperative for the college to remain current in technology applications within instruction. Respondents recommended that administrators keep the board involved and informed about technology-based instructional projects. They also advised that showcasing faculty developers at board, advisory committee, and community meetings can help develop a broad base of support for technology needs and possibilities.

Case Studies

In addition to reporting the results of the survey, the researchers produced three case studies to illustrate various practical approaches to encouraging faculty adoption of technology applications. These three cases do not reflect perfect solutions to the challenges administrators face; however, all three recount many of the findings in this study and support the veracity of the suggestions made by the twenty colleges included in the survey.

Cuyahoga Community College

Distance learning at Cuyahoga Community College began formally in 1975. In that year, one course was offered through television and drew 123 enrollees. Gradually, other delivery systems were added and today the college offers courses thorough broadcast television, interactive real time video, PC networks including both the Web and a college network, live cable, and independent learning through video and print materials. In the spring 2000 term, 69 courses enrolled over 2,300 students, taught mainly by full-time faculty.

The quality of these courses is assured by treating them in the same manner as all credit courses. Faculty propose and develop courses with dean review and approval, curriculum committee review, and approval of content, standards, and outcomes. Various strategies are used for student evaluation. Faculty who teach these courses undergo necessary training to assist in the transition from site-based to distance learning and are provided technical and logistical support by the Distance Learning Center staff.

Early in this decade, the college recognized the potential of live, interactive cable as a viable distance option. The college operated public access cable for the City of Cleveland, and one channel was reserved for college programming. Initially, packaged courses were broadcast over this channel, but distance education staff and faculty soon recognized the potential of offering live courses. Achieving this goal required adjustments to the TV studio and broadcast facilities, the identification and development of courses particularly suited to live cable, and special faculty and staff development. The college committed to each of these, and live cable was launched in 1992. The first class was College Survival

Skills, taught to 26 students by a counselor. In the spring 2000 term, nine courses enrolled 403 students. Most Cable College faculty are full time; however, one part time faculty member has taught via cable.

Live cable offers students a combination of site-based and distance options in a synchronous learning mode. Classes are offered at regularly scheduled times and meet in the TV studio under broadcast conditions. The class is carried live over cable, with students participating either in the studio or at remote sites. From remote sites, students call the studio on touch tone telephones to participate directly in class activities. All students have the same text and study guide, and all are required to submit completed assignments to the instructor as scheduled. Some cable classes may require in-person attendance from time to time or completion of assignments that require activity outside the remote site. Instructors are available for independent consultation on the phone, in person, or through e-mail. On average, one-third to one-half of the students in a cable college class attend from remote sites.

Holding a maximum of 40 students, the studio itself is equipped for instruction, broadcast, and interaction. Instruction is facilitated by three broadcast standard video cameras, a networked PC, an ELMO camera stand, a large screen monitor, and audio and video players. Each instructor is assigned a cable producer for technical support, and the instructor works closely with the producer to plan the course and to use the equipment in each session.

The video cameras transmit class images to remote sites. Zoom, focus, pan, and tilt functions are performed by the producer and control room director, as are audio and video functions. Before a class begins, the instructor and technical staff work together to create appropriate video and audio material, although purchased material is integrated whenever possible. The PC allows the instructor to include and transmit software such as Power Point or live Internet images, and the ELMO facilitates the use of hard copy materials; both the PC and the ELMO are under the instructor's direct control. The large screen monitor allows in-studio students to see all visuals being used; remote students view visuals directly on the their screens.

Broadcasts are controlled by the technical staff who manipulate the cameras and audio and video equipment. Technical staff operations free the instructor from these responsibilities and ensure seamless transitions between the media being used. In the control room, technical staff also monitor and regulate the quality of the broadcast image.

Interaction is supported by the addition of microphones and telephone lines for students. Each in-studio student has a microphone with audio controlled by the technical staff to assure broadcast quality. Microphone messages are carried within the studio and are broadcast immediately to remote sites. Incoming calls are received through a multiline phone bank controlled by technical staff who route messages to the studio and to the broadcast channel for everyone in the class to hear.

Since the fall 1997 term, Cable College has offered courses in dietetic technology, English, humanities, mathematics, speech, and college survival skills. Each instructor has been carefully selected and each course carefully developed. Courses are selected with a view to their effective delivery in video format since content must be compatible with and use the strengths of television. History is a good example, for it is amply supported and enhanced by video and audio materials that bring the subject to life. Interestingly, mathematics has proved successful because adapting to the medium allows the instructor to appeal directly to varied learning styles. Finally, courses should have broad appeal and the potential for generating an audience and enrollment.

Each course selected for Cable College must receive approval from the dean. The assigned faculty member, an instructional designer, and the assigned producer then jointly develop the course for cable. This team meets to review existing course content and delivery style and to adapt the course to television delivery for a distant audience. Adjustments may include altering and practicing presentation techniques that promote interaction and maintain the attention of the cable student; designing and developing television graphic material and video modules to support and supplement lectures; and preparing ancillary course materials such as syllabi, study guides, and handouts that must be available in advance for the remote student. The team also determines and arranges for the student support and communication options to be used, such as direct mail, voice mail, e-mail, or fax, and decides on the assessment and testing methods for the course, including on- and off-site options. Finally, the team goes through technical rehearsals to familiarize the instructor with the available equipment and technology. The result of this process is the development of courses with consistently high quality content, pedagogy, and technical standard.

Faculty are assigned to Cable College by academic deans on the basis of faculty interest and potential for success. Criteria include an openness to new approaches and suggestions for changes to pedagogy, a willingness to use technology and to be innovative, an ability to be engaging in presentation and to promote interaction, and a commitment to a long term engagement with Cable College. The first three of these criteria are important for success; the last is necessary because the investment in course and faculty development is substantial and needs to be recovered over time. Further, Cable College wishes to build on that investment through the accumulated experience of its faculty and staff, and that, too, needs adequate time. Faculty assignments are made at least a term before the course is first offered, and that term is used for development and training. Faculty are compensated for this work, usually receiving the equivalent of a course load in reassigned time.

Cable College now boasts a strong core of faculty and technical staff and a growing student body. The next steps will include enhancements to interaction that will follow technical improvements to cable delivery systems, especially as they begin to integrate audio, video, and PC response. Cable College is also studying the academic effectiveness of its effort in outcomes and is preparing cost/benefit analyses. Effectively, the enthusiasm of its staff, students, and faculty has already demonstrated Cable College's acceptance as a viable delivery option.

Moraine Valley Community College

Since the early eighties, Moraine Valley Community College in Chicago's southwest suburb of Palos Hills, Illinois has provided its community of learners with a number of instructional delivery modes that differ from traditional, campus-based, semester length course offerings. Like other postsecondary institutions at that time, Moraine Valley began experiencing increased enrollment among returning adults. Many of these new, nontraditional students were interested in taking their courses at locations close to their homes and at times convenient to their employment schedules and parenting responsibilities. This demographic shift, coupled with the introduction of the Alternative Learning unit at the college and the emergence of technology-based educational alternatives such as the telecourse, helped to fast forward the infusion of technology at the Moraine Valley. The college currently enrolls approximately 13,300 credit students and 14,000 noncredit students annually and provides educational services to 26 communities in suburban Cook County.

The telecourse at Moraine Valley greatly helped to modularize course content and provided students with greater flexibility in meeting course challenges. Interest in video-based courses grew steadily, as did the importance of computer technology. Soon, the need for fiber-optics on campus became evident. In 1991, the fiber-optic wires were installed, providing the technological infrastructure for "wiring the ivory tower" and laying the pathways for the electronic highway to pervade teaching and learning at Moraine Valley Community College.

During the past five years, the college has supported a number of initiatives focusing on the use of technology to promote faculty student interaction in the teaching and learning process. In 1994, Moraine Valley's administrators clearly acknowledged that technology was important to the institution's future when they decided to upgrade and expand the fiber-optic cabling that would serve over 90 campus instructional areas. The introduction of Project Vision and the installation of the Dynacom information system provided full multimedia delivery from a central distribution area to the campus classrooms. Using the fiber-optic cable network system, the faculty are able to receive full access to any media, including videotapes, compact discs, computer still video, television broadcasts, laser discs, slides, satellite transmission, and data links, in all rooms connected to the system. With the introduction of Dynacom, the college had the hardware and mixed media software necessary to provide faculty with new ways to express and expand course content. The effect is a teaching environment enriched by technology that enables instructors to bring more expressions and experiences of the world to classrooms. These learning opportunities are delivered easily and effectively through a fiber-optic network.

A compressed video distance learning network system was also introduced in 1994. At that time, the college became a member of a consortium of universities and colleges in the south metropolitan region of Chicago. With the support of a $119 million capital grant from the Illinois Community College Board, public and private two- and four-year institutions became operationally connected through dedicated T-1 lines. The introduction of a distance learning and telecommunications network prompted the college to provide training and development opportunities to support the faculty in developing new ways of teaching via the interactive network. As a result, instructors in mathematics, Latin history, radiologic technology, fashion merchandising, French, and other disciplines found themselves sharing information in new and different ways as they translated words, ideas, and expressions into interactive video via telephone lines, faxes, and video equipment. The college now has a distance learning unit at a local high school and sends general and specialized courses to students and faculty located in a remote part of the college's service area.

In 1995, while the college's administrators encouraged the use of the Dynacom multimedia system and assisted faculty in the use of interactive video learning, several faculty members in the communications and mathematics departments were actively involved in putting together a COM/MTH laboratory, a classroom in the learning resource center dedicated to teaching and learning with the use of computer technology. The following year, the Moraine Valley Community College Foundation provided a generous gift to the college, funding the purchase of computers to update the COM/MTH laboratory and to create a new open computer lab. This gift greatly expanded the use of technology in instruction.

At the same time, and consistent with the heightened interest in technology in the teaching and learning process at the college, the Vice President of Academic Affairs and the Dean of Learning Technologies reviewed the open positions in the division of academic affairs and redesigned several of these positions to reflect the need for competencies in interactive learning and computer technology. As a result, a Director of Interactive Learning was recruited and hired. The director was instrumental in introducing and developing a Center for Interactive Learning (LinC), a technology skunkworks, or dedicated area for faculty to develop multimedia approaches for classes.

In 1996, the college's Center for Faculty and Program Excellence (CFPE) and the Academic Affairs Council introduced Learning

Challenges, inviting faculty to present proposals that expanded student learning through innovative instructional approaches and the incorporation of technology. The Learning Challenge grants were extended to faculty members who presented creative and compelling approaches to the use of multimedia technology.

Also in 1996, all CFPE workshops focused on instructional technology, and the Center introduced personal and professional development opportunities for faculty to support the infusion of technology in instruction. To enhance the use of technology in the classroom, the Center also supports faculty attendance at conferences; this support is funded in part by revenues generated by the business and industry technology unit at the college.

In addition to the training and development efforts provided by the Center for Faculty and Program Excellence, the Educational Services and Innovations subdivision also provides technology training support. The librarians in the learning resource center present training sessions on the use of the Internet as well as assist faculty in the use of multimedia technology.

The Moraine college community is actively involved in technology planning and application. In December 1997, the division of Academic Affairs introduced the Learning Challenges for 1998, the Virtual College Project. The Virtual College Project is focused on the development of technology-based courses and the development of Web pages. Faculty were invited to serve on the project teams and to participate in innovating and developing asynchronous courses and Web pages for the college.

In early spring 1997, recognizing the growing impact of information technology on the institution, the president determined that Moraine Valley Community College needed a comprehensive technology plan. An outside consultant was hired to discuss technology planning with members of the college faculty and staff. By late summer 1997, it was determined that during the next 12 to 15 months, a technology plan would be written at the college.

The concept of a comprehensive plan was introduced after noting that less than half of American colleges and universities had a strategic plan for technology. As at most colleges, various departments at Moraine Valley had parts of a plan, often developed in isolation from other departments. Again, as with most colleges, a bifurcation existed among the academic and administrative leadership of information technology units at the college. The overarching goal in proceeding with this technology plan was to begin to develop a process for bridging those various areas of the college, as well as the infrastructure to support them.

The entire college community was invited to volunteer for any of ten groups that comprised the technology planning group. More than 70 individuals were assigned to topic-focused work teams, with co-chairs appointed to each team. The chairs of the ten teams, along with a vice president and the consultant, formed the Technology Leadership Team (TLT).

For more than a year, the TLT met biweekly, with work team meetings held as needed between these sessions. The external environmental analysis process provided an excellent training period during which time members became much more astute about their respective areas of responsibility. In January 1998, the findings of the external analysis were presented as part of a staff development day. This provided a bridge from the external world to the next planning phase, the internal environmental analysis.

During the internal phase, teams studied the history of each topic and interviewed college community members about needs and concerns for the future. The combination of knowing what is going on in the world, in higher education, and historically at Moraine Valley was very empowering. This input, combined with the external context, led the TLT to formulate detailed projects for recommendation. Projects were developed by the team and then reviewed collaboratively by both academic and administrative technology leaders. Sources of funding and the importance of the Total Cost of Ownership model were also addressed. Throughout the process, the TLT referenced policies and procedures needed to move the institution forward in the information technology arena. A complete set of recommendations was included in the final technology plan, providing a scenario for the future–if the recommendations were implemented. As of the fall 1999 semester, 18 of the 45 proposed technology projects have been funded and implemented by the college.

The heart of the planning process was the TLT, comprised of the co-chairs of the ten work teams: Alternative Delivery Systems, Classrooms, Computing, Instructional Design and Support, Learning Centers and Labs, Library and Information Resources, Networking, Policies and Procedures, Professional Development, and User Support. In addition, the members of the President's Executive Leadership Team served as advisors to the TLT. This dedicated group of individuals climbed a very rugged mountain on behalf of the faculty, staff, and students at Moraine Valley. Their stamina was remarkable; the results of their efforts will be seen for many years at the college.

The technology plan for the college, 1998-2001, Toward the Next Millennium, is a 300-plus page document that provides the vision for information technology and will guide the college's technology decisions in meeting changing informational needs and improving the process of teaching and learning at Moraine Valley Community College.

Central Piedmont Community College

Keeping abreast of the rising interest in and costs of instructional technology at Central Piedmont Community College in Charlotte, North Carolina, has been a challenge. Through Title III funding in 1987, CPCC entered the world of interactive television instruction. With money for its first studio, an interactive classroom on the central campus, and two receiving classrooms at area centers, the college proceeded to train its first cadre of interactive television instructors and provide its first distance education courses. That initial investment of federal funds has been supplemented through the intervening years with local dollars, other grants, college foundation funds, and two successful capital campaigns.

The addition of a local cable television channel with 24 hours of broadcast time expanded CPCC's opportunities to offer distance education as an option to its 30,000 credit and 30,000 noncredit students in the Charlotte-Mecklenburg region. However, with the growth of these options, shrinking state dollars, increasingly sophisticated technology, the advent of the North Carolina Information Highway, and a recently completed technology plan, the college has had to make some difficult decisions concerning the future direction of distance education.

Several issues were obvious. Although we had a staff of highly successful interactive television instructors, their numbers had not grown appreciably since the first Title III supported years, and, therefore, the course offerings were repetitive. Some of our faculty were retiring; others were looking for different challenges, such as online course development.

The cost of interactive television instruction was high. Our own cost analysis indicated that video instruction was more cost effective and seemed to be as successful with students, with the exception of developmental students who thrived on the interactive format and constant conversations with faculty members. Also, the cost of keeping the television studio appropriately equipped for interactive instruction and for video production continued to rise.

With the opening of new campuses on the perimeter of Charlotte, every penny for technology had to be maximized. What was the best investment of the college's dollars? Could we continue to offer the 20 or so interactive classes per term along with the video course offerings that were more economical, or should we look for a different mix of video and interactive courses? Should we continue to put technology dollars into interactive television instruction and not give full attention to other technologies for instruction such as computer-assisted courses, CD-ROM options, or Internet courses with e-mail communication as the primary teaching device?

All of these questions, and many others about the larger technology issues faced by the college, were at the base of a new direction that was launched at CPCC during the summer of 1997. With the completion of the college's technology plan, designed by a broadly representative technology team and with help from consultants, CPCC implemented recommendations from that report. The major actions included hiring an Associate Vice President for Technology charged with the centralization and unification of all administrative and instructional technology decisions and operations, opening the College Without Walls (CWW), and naming a director charged with coordinating all distance education options and marketing of CWW as a separate entity.

The new Associate Vice President for Technology's early actions included a complete inventory of all computing technology resources, the development of an integrated purchasing and redistribution plan, the upgrading of technical support services, and the coordination of infrastructures at all campuses. Early efforts have already resulted in stretching institutional technology dollars and hastening responses through the technology help desk.

The College Without Walls has taken several initiatives and has forged a new energetic team made up of the director, two faculty fully dedicated to CWW projects, several other faculty who serve on a released-load basis in the CWW, an instructional developer, a staff assistant, and several cooperative education students who aid in Web-related activities. The CWW is also supported by the CPCC television studio, including all video-based and interactive television offerings, and by the Technology Learning Center (TLC), a professional development lab that supports faculty who are developing technology-based or technology-enhanced instruction.

Since 1993, CPCC has been examining ways to encourage more faculty to engage in technology-enhanced instruction. In 1994 the Director of Library Services and the Assistant to the Vice President for Instruction designed a project called Tech Associates. Funded for the first year through college book store profits, the project allowed five faculty to apply for designation as Tech Associates and to be outfitted with laptops, training, and generous released time to design technology-enhanced teaching modules for use in their traditional courses. From that initial experience, which proved to be very successful and popular with faculty, the college decided to pursue outside funding and expand the concept of Tech Associates.

The need to infuse new faculty blood into the distance education initiative has now been addressed through a second major Title III grant, first funded in 1995. Focusing on upgrading the television studio to include computer technology within interactive and locally developed video productions, the grant also directs significant dollars into faculty development. Each year approximately 15 new Tech Associates are named to be a part of the Title III project. Faculty apply, are screened and selected by a local peer review committee, and are given laptop computers, training, access to technology conferences, released time, and projects. A director and support technician are available to aid them in training and project completion.

During the first two years, all Tech Associates were assigned the development of one module of instruction to be a part of a course called Workplace Readiness Skills. Such a course was badly needed in the college's curriculum, and the first year's experiment with locally funded Tech Associates proved that a common task for the associates would build a team approach to training. The Tech Associates first developed video modules with appropriate written materials for student use. The course, with thirty-minute modules on such subjects as workplace ethics, communications, teamsmanship, and total quality concepts, has now been piloted and is available for inclusion as a stand-alone course or as segments within existing courses. Secondly, the video modules were to be converted to an additional format besides video, one that was computer assisted, self-paced, and portable. The current group of Tech Associates is progressing well in the development project.

Tech Associates are being trained in skills that will serve well the College Without Walls initiative. Through the life of the five-year grant, approximately 60 faculty, along with the original five, will have been trained and equipped to provide appropriate instruction to distance students. The skills they develop for distance instruction will also serve them well in traditional settings and improve the overall quality of instruction for students at CPCC.

Final Remarks

The case studies and the survey of the twenty League for Innovation colleges indicate that these schools are involved in the struggle for effective use of technology to improve teaching and learning. As more and more community colleges face the challenges of infusing technology into instruction, they are likely to deal with issues similar to those identified by the colleges in this study, and this first phase of an ongoing study may assist colleges in meeting these challenges. Clearly, individual colleges will consider local needs and resources when making technology decisions; however, the technology effort can be aided through the sharing of experiences among colleges that are using technology to expand and improve learning opportunities for students. The findings of this study indicate that cost and currency of equipment and training, technology planning, professional development and incentives for faculty, adequate technical support services for faculty developers, and college infrastructure are common issues surrounding the inclusion of technology in community college instruction. Instructional administrators are now, and in the next century will continue to be, involved in making significant decisions concerning appropriate venues for learning, including interactive television classes, Web-based courses, video conferencing, fax and voice mail assignments, and the use of Internet and video disk resources in traditional and nontraditional settings. To secure faculty support of technology-based and technology-enhanced instruction, administrators need to address technology issues thoughtfully and with input from faculty and technical support staff. By taking this approach, community college leaders will be better able to ensure that technology is used effectively and appropriately not only to promote student learning, but to enhance administrator, faculty, and staff learning as well.

References

Maehl, W. H. (1997, August). Preliminary Report on Adult Learning Programs Survey Project for a Nation of Lifelong Learners (NLL). Santa Fe, NM.

National Alliance of Business. (1997, October). *Workforce Economics Trends*. Washington, DC: Author.

O'Banion, T. (1997). *Creating More Learning-Centered Community Colleges*. Mission Viejo, CA: League for Innovation in the Community College.

O'Banion, T. (1995-96). "A Learning College for the 21st Century." *Community College Journal*, 66(3), 18-23.

Sherron, G. T. & Boettcher, J. V. (1997). "Distance Learning: The Shift to Interactivity" (CAUSE Professional Paper Series, No. 17). Tallahassee: Florida State University, College of Education.

Appendix
College Participants in the Study

Central Piedmont Community College
Cuyahoga Community College
Dallas County Community College District
Delta College
Foothill-DeAnza Community College District
University of Hawaii Community College System
Humber College of Applied Arts and Technology
Johnson County Community College
Kern Community College District
Kirkwood Community College
Lane Community College
Maricopa Community College District
Miami-Dade Community College District
Monroe Community College
Moraine Valley Community College
San Diego Community College District
St. Louis Community College at Forest Park
Santa Fe Community College
Seattle Community College District
Sinclair Community College

CHAPTER 4

TECHNOLOGY, LEARNING, AND COMMUNITY (TLC): PERSPECTIVES FROM TEACHING EXCELLENCE AWARD RECIPIENTS

Mark David Milliron and Cindy L. Miles

The cold winds of criticism and the icy demands for accountability have dominated the closing decades of this century. But the new century holds promise of a fresh new spring for educators, and I see creativity and innovation blooming everywhere, but especially in the nation's community colleges.

Cross, 1998, p. 5

Creativity and innovation are hallmarks of the best community college faculty. Studies on community college education demonstrate that our faculty consider teaching to be their primary mission (Baker, Roueche, & Gillett-Karam, 1990; Roueche & Baker, 1987) and that they approach this mission as champions of a range of innovations, such as service learning, writing across the curriculum, cooperative learning, and learning communities (Cross, 1998; Exley, 1995; O'Banion, 1997a). As the current Learning Revolution amplifies our focus on educational outcomes (Barr & Tagg, 1995; Cross, 1998; O'Banion, 1997a, 1997b, 1998; Oblinger & Rush, 1997, 1998), however, community college faculty are newly challenged to find creative and meaningful methods to inspire student learning.

The forceful presence of technology in our lives adds further challenges and opportunities for faculty. Information technology has infused the educational enterprise, offering community college faculty a dazzling array of instructional tools and techniques (Anandam, 1998; Gilbert, 1997; Green, 1997). Technology to support instruction is hardly a new development, however. What were once revolutionary technologies are now a common part of almost every classroom experience, so much so that we hardly notice most of them. Consider one everyday technical resource in a standard classroom–electric lights. Each time we switch on the lights in a classroom, untold hours of research, development, trial, and refinement are reflected. The design used in most of today's light bulbs is based on technology that is 120-years old (half that, if fluorescent). Despite its earlier development, this technology has been in standard use in schools nationwide only in the last half of this century. In fact, comprehensive use was not in place until the last thirty years, after a focused national effort was administered by the Rural Electrification Administration (REA) to create an elaborate network to provide power to all parts of the country. In the history of higher education, universal access to this fundamental technology is somewhat recent, but it is hard for us to imagine a classroom today without electric lights.

We can draw several parallels between the electrification of classrooms and the current "wiring" of schools for the Internet. Just as electricity was a conduit for progress earlier this century, the Internet is heralded as the vehicle to bring education into the Information Age. Just as electrification spread rapidly in highly populated areas but was slow to reach smaller, poorer, or more rural schools, the "Information Superhighway" was quick to connect larger communities, but it is slow to arrive at institutions with fewer resources. And, like the REA campaign to bring light to all American communities, we are in the midst of a national movement to provide Internet access to all schools–the Net Day campaign, which enlists community volunteers to donate time, money, and other resources to wire schools and connect them with the Internet. It is interesting to note that both the electric light and the Internet offer instructors more flexibility and extend student access to learning tools and content. In this current connectivity venture, we can only hope that the Internet soon becomes so stable, useful, and common that we give it as little thought as we give to turning on the lights.

Indeed, in many ways the new millennium seems to promise a "new spring for educators." We will have more tools at our disposal, enhanced access to learning for students, and improved information on which to base key instructional decisions. At the same time that information technology offers more options, independence, and creativity for teachers and learners, it also stresses our educational communities with internal demands and external competition. To attain the true benefits of technology in coming years, we must grapple with these ambiguities and consider the full implications of technology use, both contributive and disruptive, on teaching and learning in two-year institutions.

This chapter is intended to fuel conversations about educational complexities and opportunities related to information technology by drawing on the expertise of community college teaching excellence award winners. It offers a basic framework for approaching the use of information technology in the community college based on research capturing the voices of award-winning faculty who shared their views on how to explore and embrace the **technology** available, and target it toward improving and expanding **learning**, while holding fast to a focus on **community**.

Studying Information Technology Use Among Community College Faculty

This chapter weaves findings from community college research and practice with data from a national study that began in 1997 at the National Institute for Staff and Organizational Development's (NISOD) annual International Conference on Teaching and Leadership Excellence, sponsored by The University of Texas at Austin. Each year, NISOD asks the CEOs of more than 600 member institutions to name their exemplary faculty to be recognized for teaching excellence. Colleges select faculty worthy of national recognition based on individual institutional criteria. More than 300 of the instructors selected each year attend the annual NISOD conference, where they are recognized as Teaching Excellence Award recipients. At the time of this study, NISOD and The University of Texas had recognized almost 7,000 faculty over the seven years of the program.

As part of a broader study on teaching excellence in the community college, these nationally recognized instructors were identified as a useful population from which to draw data on the use of information technology in community college instruction. This purposeful sampling (Patton, 1990) of faculty was chosen for their demonstrated ability in the classroom rather than for any savvy they might demonstrate with technology. Award-winning teachers were purposefully selected over technology advocates or "true believers." The research goal was to solicit perspectives from a collection of successful community college teachers who offered a high-quality instructional perspective regarding the application of technology to teaching and learning.

An Innovative and Interactive Study Design

This chapter focuses most attention on the rich findings drawn from the faculty in our study; however, for those interested in the study design and procedures, we provide the following brief overview of our methods. The study was conducted in a two-stage format, blending interactive qualitative techniques and standard quantitative survey methodologies. The "hybrid vigor" (Miles & Huberman, 1994, p. 310) of such mixed-method research techniques has been widely noted (Miller & Crabtree, 1994, Rossman & Wilson, 1991, Salomon, 1991). In this study, we called on the strengths of each methodological approach. First, we used an interactive qualitative method to explore the range of instructional technology applications and to solicit faculty perspectives about the positive and negative effects they associate with technology applications. Then, we turned to quantitative survey methods to test the agreement with these findings within a broader population of award-winning faculty and to construct a priority ranking of faculty views on the issues identified in the first study stage. The resulting triangulation of methods and sources contributed to the quality and rigor of the analysis. Following are details of the two study stages and a summary of key findings.

Stage One: Interactive Qualitative Focus Groups. The initial qualitative research stage of the study began with a series of two-hour focus group sessions held with teaching excellence award winners at the 1997 NISOD conference. Five focus group sessions were held, each with 45 to 50 faculty participants, for a total of 230 participants. The average age of focus group participants was 50; approximately 53 percent of the participants were male, and 47 percent were female. In each focus group, faculty participated in a process of collaborative brainstorming and idea clustering known in Total Quality Management circles as affinity diagramming. Affinity diagramming is a group process for organizing large amounts of language or textual information. Originally designed for strategic organizational management and planning (Brassard, 1989), affinity diagramming was used in this study as an interactive group data collection and analysis process. Faculty generated responses to research questions but also participated in group analysis of these responses, grounding the study findings in their collective experiences while giving voice to their individual perspectives.

For each focus group, seven questions were posted on the walls of a large conference room, two of which related specifically to technology use in instruction. The technology-focused questions were simple:

In what ways do you use information technology in instruction?

What do you see as the key issues (positives or problems) in the use of technology in instruction?

We reviewed the questions briefly with each group and asked faculty to write their responses on self-adhesive notecards and to post their responses next to the relevant questions on the wall, listing only one answer per card. We turned on low-level music and encouraged faculty to move around the room as desired. The brainstorming and posting process took approximately 45 minutes and generated high-energy movement and discussion.

After the brainstorming process, we divided the faculty into seven small groups–one for each question–to arrange the responses to each question into thematic clusters (affinity groups) that made sense together. This clustering process took another 30 to 45 minutes, after which the small groups reported on their findings. Finally, we facilitated discussion during which faculty members explained their responses and provided more depth to their written comments. The discussions were videotaped for secondary analysis.

After all the focus group sessions were complete, a research team led by the authors reviewed the affinity groups for each question from each session and created a master set of thematic clusters. The complete interactive qualitative methodology yielded 907 comments coded into 19 categories for the two questions on technology.

Stage Two: Quantitative Survey Method. In the second study stage, a questionnaire was produced and distributed that listed the research questions and thematic clusters (expressed as statements) generated by faculty in stage one, with an example comment for each thematic statement. The questionnaire asked respondents to record their level of agreement with each statement by choosing one item from a variation of a standard seven-point Likert scale:

YES! Yes yes ? no No NO!

In addition, respondents were asked to priority rank their responses by identifying the top three statements with which they most agreed.

The survey was sent to the entire population of 6,958 NISOD Teaching Excellence Award recipients. Several follow-up efforts were made to find addresses of faculty who had moved since receiving their awards and to locate those who had retired. A total of 1,670 faculty responded to the survey (a response rate of 24 percent). The demographics of survey respondents were similar to those of the focus groups–the average age of survey respondents was 50, 56 percent were male, and 44 percent were female. Their community college teaching experience averaged 17 years, and almost one in four planned to retire within five years.

Findings Focused on Teaching, Learning, and Community

In general, findings from the survey validated the work of the focus groups and provided additional insights into patterns of faculty perspectives on information technology applications in community college teaching and learning. Tables 1 and 2 (Appendix A) present a summary of the qualitative and quantitative responses to the two questions posed to study participants regarding the use of information technology in community college instruction.

Analysis of study findings from qualitative and quantitative data, derived from the responses of almost 2,000 award-winning community college faculty from around the world, revealed that faculty perceptions regarding information technology and instruction could be divided into three conceptual categories relating to *technology, learning,* and *community*. Study results pertaining to each of these concepts are explored in the following sections and placed in the broader context of discussions emerging from research and practice on the national higher education scene.

Technology Issues Identified by Award-Winning Faculty

One of the more intriguing findings of our study is that the most commonly cited uses of technology in instruction by teaching excellence award recipients are not instructor-based at all, but rather focused on student use. **Technology for student application and production** was the number one use of technology in instruction identified by this broad cohort of teaching excellence award recipients. Several faculty noted that students can now use technology tools to engage in meaningful inquiry and to produce professional quality print publications, multimedia presentations, interactive CD-ROMs, and custom websites, providing learning experience for themselves and others. Faculty comments related to the use of technology for student application and production include:

- *I get students on computers to file sample incident reports in Criminal Justice class and produce formal documents.*
- *Groups work together to produce PowerPoint presentations and websites on course topics.*
- *Students use computer-based writing software to collaborate on composition and editing.*
- *I assign research projects that require students to give/gather information using technology.*
- *I expect all work to look professional; I have students use word processors, spreadsheets, and PowerPoint to prepare their assignments to make sure it does.*
- *I require technology use in their oral presentations.*

The second most common technology application reported by faculty was **technology for student-driven learning**. Whether constructed by faculty using authoring programs like ToolBook or LearningSpace or prepared by software or publishing houses, whether these tools were available in-class, on the Web, or in a stand-alone lab, faculty in this study identified student-driven learning as one of the primary uses of technology in instruction. Faculty consistently mentioned computer-based tutorials, websites, and multimedia programs to foster improved student-driven learning:

- *Students are encouraged to use "tutoring" computer programs available in our math center.*
- *Students use software that accompanies ready texts for supplementary drills.*
- *I construct puzzles on class content using a puzzle maker program.*
- *Students are encouraged to take a computerized "student behavior inventory" which asks questions about study skills, time management, test taking, etc. and gives students a printout of results and ways to improve.*

- *There are some self-paced computer programs on some of our syllabi content. Students can do these programs in the computer lab and come to class prepared to move beyond the program in a higher level of discussion on that topic.*
- *I encourage individual computer practice for licensing exams to increase comfort level with exam construction, time limits, and computer use.*

The third most common cluster of technology applications for instruction mentioned by faculty was **technology for presentation**. According to focus group faculty, technology applications for presentation–PowerPoint, ToolBook, World Wide Web, CD-ROMs, and multimedia carts–are becoming standard teaching tools necessary to reach the "MTV generation" with more stimulating visuals that bring curriculum to life:

- *PowerPoint is a God-send.*
- *I use Power Point and ToolBook presentations for all formal lectures–give students copies of outline prior to class.*
- *We put lectures and overheads on WWW.*
- *I use the Internet to present interactive material in class to spark discussion.*
- *I've found that graphing calculators in higher levels of math classes can really give the student a concrete picture of what's happening. Not a replacement of analytical skills, but a reinforcement, a "visual confirmation" of the analysis done.*
- *I use interactive CD-ROM programs in the classroom and have them available for students to use/review in the computer learning lab.*

The subsequent cluster of technology applications encompasses **technology tools to improve communication** between students and faculty and among students using e-mail, bulletin boards, listservs, electronic forums, and real-time chats. Such interactive tools give instructors new and interesting options to reach our increasingly transitory and busy students. Moreover, faculty reported using these tools to reach other educators in their discipline areas around the country, an application which helps faculty in small programs or rural areas overcome the challenge of discipline isolation. Study responses indicate that communicative uses of technology are an increasingly important aspect of instruction:

- *I use e-mail to send and receive comments and papers from students.*
- *We encourage students to use e-mail to communicate with each other and with the instructor. We hope that will foster a sense of personal responsibility for learning. It also recognizes the need for communication outside the classroom in a contemporary way.*
- *Distance learning is a marvelous tool for doing role-plays, sharing information that is real-world oriented.*
- *I use "groupware" to hold and facilitate electronic meetings.*
- *I use e-mail and subscriptions to listservs to communicate with other teachers around the world with similar teaching issues to solve.*

Focus group faculty also identified a number of **applications of technology for research and reference**. Faculty explained that they often direct students to a variety of new research and reference technologies, which they said students must master to succeed in the workplace or in other institutions of higher education. Respondents described how library databases, virtual textbooks, and the World Wide Web leave the Dewey decimal system behind and enable students to search for and manipulate information in ways only dreamed of by their predecessors. Faculty also reported how they use these research tools to keep up with current trends in their discipline area. Most responses in this cluster focus on research applications of the Internet:

- *I suggest the students use the Internet to do research for both oral and written reports.*
- *Internet sites can inform pre-law students of school programs, admission standards, law school admission test preparation course, and access to particular info from law school libraries on agency decisions and case law.*
- *Information via technology–the Internet is great to use for research purposes, especially if you teach at a branch campus that has a limited amount of library and other research materials.*
- *My students and I use Internet sites to access specific, up-to-date information on state/local government agencies, progress of legislation, and access legislator's e-mail addresses.*
- *Internet research is valuable for the students and me.*

According to our study findings, **course management and assessment technologies** are changing the way faculty organize their instructional materials and evaluate student progress. Some faculty are creating dynamic syllabi that are available on the internal college network or over the Internet. Computer-adaptive testing, virtual teaching assistants, spreadsheets, databases, and online course staging technologies are assisting instructors in managing information in new ways for themselves and for students. Some faculty suggested that grade books are giving way to on-demand performance indicators available on a website 24 hours a day. Given the complexities of teaching in the community college and the challenges of becoming more learning-centered, faculty suggest that these tools could not have come at a better time:

- *All class notes are available on our class website.*
- *Distance learning students videotape their speeches for evaluation.*
- *Students use e-mail to send in papers and receive comments.*
- *I hold virtual office hours, using e-mail and chat.*
- *I have a website for my syllabus, I use a PowerPoint to organize my lecture material, and I use e-mail to give and receive assignments.*
- *I use QuestionMark software to design and deliver testing on line.*
- *Through computer-based testing, I can provide real-time feedback to my distance learning students.*

This study underscores the impressive range of technology tools available to educators. Nevertheless, findings suggest that even these award-winning instructors are slow to embrace and implement new technology developments, despite the growing array and significance of technology applications in community college instruction. For example, the clusters of technology for course management and technology for assessment were identified as key categories of instructional technology application by focus group faculty, but few survey respondents reported using these tools (only 31 percent and 14 percent, respectively). Moreover, several of the instructional presentation technologies mentioned by faculty involve more dated tools such as overhead projectors, VCRs, and 35-millimeter slide projectors.

Nonetheless, it appears that teaching excellence award winners are integrating technology into their instruction in growing numbers. One participant explained that faculty were slow to adopt new technology because it is seen as unreliable, a sentiment with which many in the group expressed agreement: "Only recently have many of these tools become stable enough for a teacher to trust that it wouldn't break down in the middle of class. Now I'm ready to use this stuff!" Most interesting, however, was the finding that the two most prevalent uses of technology for instruction involved the student as the primary user of the technology tool–student application and production, and student-driven learning. This observation suggests that successful community college faculty are demonstrating the finding of years of research on good teaching, which asserts that excellent faculty are those who actively engage the student in the learning process (Cross, 1998).

Learning Issues Identified by Award-Winning Faculty

Findings from our study of faculty perceptions of information technology echo the possibilities and challenges for learning associated with technology noted in other higher education discussions. A set of learning-related issues–learning for both students and faculty–emerged from responses to the question exploring what teaching excellence award recipients perceive to be the key issues (positives and problems) in the use of technology in instruction. The highest-ranking response reiterates Hooker's (1997) observation: **learning about technology itself is becoming essential, it is a "basic skill" our students need**. Faculty in this study indicate that the debate is no longer about whether or not technology will improve instructional productivity, reduce costs, or pay for itself. Information technology skills have become a core learning component that a community college student must master for successful transfer to a four-year school or into the workplace. More than 95 percent of our national sample of teaching excellence award-winners agreed:

- *The future is upon us. Every house will be connected by fiber optics in the next 5 to 10 years. Students, for employment in the future, will need to be technologically competent.*
- *With technology becoming an integral part of the industry, the students need to be introduced to these concepts before entering the work force.*
- *Students will be exposed to high tech on their first job. They must use current technology to succeed.*
- *Technology prepares students for the present and what will be dominant for the rest of their lives.*
- *We must insure that students have basic skills in technology and are comfortable before expecting more.*

- *Students, by using computers (word processing, Internet access, etc.) for my classes, learn or strengthen skills they will, in all likelihood, need in their work.*

The next core learning issue identified by these award-winning faculty members had to do with their own learning. Faculty contend that technology has become so complex and it changes so quickly that they have a difficult time staying up to speed. In terms of applying technology to instruction, most respondents agreed that **it takes a lot of time and training to use it well**:

- *Technology changes so fast that staying current is difficult.*
- *We lack of time to train to use technology. We have classes, but at times it's difficult for me to attend.*
- *I learn new software every semester, at times my head is spinning!*
- *Problem: When in hell do we have the time to produce the damn slide show?*
- *Faculty loads make it difficult to give technology the time necessary to create or use this resource to our best advantage.*
- *Unless you really understand the mechanics, you and students can get really frustrated.*

Training difficulties notwithstanding, more than 84 percent of the survey respondents agreed that **technology helps make teaching and learning more engaging**. In addition, respondents concur with Johnson's (1997) observation that, "community college students are becoming more accustomed to information technology, and they expect the associated innovations to be a part of their educational experiences" (p. 2). Focus group faculty noted that multimedia presentation technologies, interactive communication tools, student-driven learning options, and a host of other technological capabilities help students connect to learning in new ways:

- *It can capture students' interests and make otherwise dull information come alive for them.*
- *Using technology adds dimension to subject matter. Away with using only the written page for instruction!*
- *I can show invasive or private activities that students may avoid (peri care) or not have an opportunity to experience (surgery).*
- *It gives me the ability to make the classroom or the course work experience more exciting.*

- *It gives students the ability to "see" the material to be learned.*
- *I can show how the normal curve superimposes the histogram for some distribution. Demonstrate the probability of an event by showing the integration of the curve. Show the regression line that passes through the scatter plot.*
- *Technology opens up opportunities to bring real-time examples into classroom–e.g. in nursing, technology allows the student to "see and hear" the patient.*
- *It helps add clarity–makes visual what is abstract on the page.*

Moreover, study faculty noted that, **when used well, technology use in instruction can help facilitate different kinds of learning**. They pointed out that the connection capabilities made possible by information technology could enhance interactive and collaborative learning. Sophisticated presentation technologies and skillful management of information by instructors were reported to stimulate different learning styles and illuminate intricate or perplexing concepts. Respondents noted that students' use of the technology tools to access and analyze information helped foster critical thinking and the construction of knowledge. More than 92 percent of surveyed faculty agreed that differentiated learning was enhanced by the use of technology:

- *Technology gives students more avenues of learning–some are readers and some are watchers, and some are listeners.*
- *It is another way to teach students with different learning styles.*
- *It reinforces and stimulates all "senses" for learning.*
- *It provides different methods of instruction to students with varied learning styles.*
- *Technology allows students another avenue to learn.*
- *It allows learners to show their skills and become a peer teacher in a community of teachers/learners.*
- *It enhances learning by appealing to different types of learners.*
- *A picture is worth a thousand words–multiple methods of learning.*

Faculty asserted that effective technology use not only appeals to students with a range of learning styles, but it also **gives students more control of their learning**, particularly through asynchronous options like computer-based tutorials and Web-supported materials. Faculty stressed that such technologies are giving new meaning to old concepts of self-paced learning:

- *Technology offers cutting-edge ways to allow students to follow and expand their own ideas.*
- *Video material can be stopped, started, segmented, or whole to make a point.*
- *Students take responsibility for their own learning.*
- *Students can take a greater part in their learning.*
- *The information age is realized in instruction—rather than being told this is the information age, students actively participate in developing the age.*
- *Students can learn at their own pace when they can access technology in and out of the traditional classroom.*
- *It allows for individual adjustment—e.g., slower students can spend time as needed in hands-on learning*
- *It allows the faster ones to move on, keep interested, get more value for the education.*

One major learning challenge associated with the powerful learning options offered by information technology that was repeatedly emphasized by study faculty is that **some instructors are tempted to use technology for its novelty rather than utility**. Respondents stressed that without a sharp focus on its intended purpose of enhancing learning, technology use can easily deteriorate into what one faculty member called, "the gee whiz factor," with little or no learning to show for the hours of effort:

- *Too much "entertainment" and "fun" may actually slow down or minimize serious learning or just "miss the point."*
- *There may be more focus on gadgets than on students and learning.*
- *Overuse of technology becomes a crutch to teaching rather than a supplement to or addition to taught information.*
- *Too many instructors try to use technology for the sake of using technology. If it will not enhance the learning, don't use it.*
- *Support is more concerned with technological efficiency than effectiveness for teaching. It's simply technology for the sake of technology.*
- *Students can be dazzled by the method and ignore the content.*

It is encouraging to hear the voices of faculty ring with the language of learning. As the Learning Revolution spreads throughout higher education, we can be confident that our best faculty care deeply about how to use technology to improve learning. Their comments reassure us that, when used well, technology is a formidable learning tool. However, their comments also remind us that the important phrase to remember is, *when used well.* Information technology use in education–even when highlighted by elaborate websites, chat rooms, and interactive video–neither equates to nor automatically creates good teaching. In fact, as Terry O'Banion articulates this challenge, "Technology has the powerful potential for extending and expanding really bad teaching, poor instructional design, and outdated content." Our challenge in applying technology to instruction, then, is to keep a strong focus on learning processes and outcomes. When we can document improved and expanded learning for our students, we will know technology use in education is working.

Community Issues Related to Technology

Faculty in this study unearthed a number of issues that point directly to community, a notion that has been at the heart of the community college enterprise since its inception. Faculty identified a series of topics they felt must be considered for a college community to effectively embrace, and for students to be well served by, technology. The first of these is the acknowledgment that **technology for instruction can get very expensive.** There are serious budgetary implications for technology that can test the most cooperative and closely knit college communities. Faculty recounted tales of technology "money pits" and disputes over allocations of limited technology resources among college areas that stressed institutional relationships as well as budgets:

- *Training needs to be a budgeted item just like equipment and software.*
- *There are not enough computers! My office mate and I share one, and we both use PowerPoint!*
- *There is serious frustration in not having the resources to create what I know can be done.*
- *Our classrooms are built for the 60s, not the 90s or the 21st century.*
- *Computer labs are expensive to set up and become outdated the day of the grand opening (they're also expensive to maintain).*

- *There is unequal access to technology—some faculty have the latest computer and printer in their private office, others are in a broom closet with three other faculty and antiquated technology where they have to beg and borrow computer time here and there, stopping and starting their work and going from one word processor such as WordPerfect to another such as Word on a different computer.*

In addition, faculty in this study remind us not to leave anyone behind in our zeal to move forward with technology. Study participants point out that community colleges can be the gateway to information technology inclusion for all citizens, much like public libraries were for the printed book, but we must face the challenge that **our students do not have equal access to technology**. Faculty contend that not only must we give students access to e-mail and the Internet, we also must offer basic skills necessary to bring the economically and technically disadvantaged into the Information Age. Respondents challenge us to work to ensure that all community college students can benefit equitably from the information technology infrastructures we develop:

- *Not all students have access to computers/Internet either on or off campus.*
- *Using e-mail with students allows them to communicate with me outside their classroom both locally and globally, but they have to have e-mail to participate.*
- *We can't leave anyone out. What about those students who don't have computers?*
- *The Internet is great, if you can get to it.*
- *We need technology accessibility for anyone in the world.*

Faculty also point to **ubiquitous hardware and software problems** that frustrate educators trying to adapt to new technologies. Respondents underscore the human implications of technical instabilities and failures and describe how these add stress to the college community. If challenges of technology unreliability are not addressed, focus group faculty explained, selling instructors on the value of using technology in the classroom will be difficult at best.

- *Hardware/software problems are very time consuming and distracting.*

- *Classroom use of technology demands a back-up plan, as it is prone to crashing.*
- *You must plan ahead and be prepared for the unexpected–you **will** have technology problems.*
- *A lot of the "bugs" have not been worked out–valuable class time can be lost because equipment, computers, etc., do not function properly.*
- *Damned stuff does not always work.*

The constantly changing and spontaneously crashing hardware and software does little to help confront another key issue raised by faculty, **fear and resistance about the use of technology**. Resistance to change is a formidable challenge for an organization undertaking any major new initiative, and often such resistance finds its basis in fear. As study participants related, technology conjures a number of fears for faculty: basic technophobia, fear of appearing ignorant in front of peers and students, fear of failure when relinquishing proven traditional teaching approaches, fear of loss of classroom control. And, students share many of these fears. Further exacerbating the anxiety surrounding technology use are divisions in the college community along lines of technology advocates and resistors. Study respondents note that **"true believers" can cause problems** by "promising the moon in a minute," when most faculty are struggling just to get the technology to their class on time. Moreover, the technologically savvy sometimes are condescending toward technical neophytes or contemptuous of those who are thoughtfully critical of technology. Challenges related to fear and resistance of technology were reflected in a number of faculty comments:

- *Instructors refuse to change with the times.*
- *Students excited about technology may have frustrations because instructors are behind the times.*
- *There is resistance to learning new techniques–both students and faculty, but more faculty.*
- *Some teachers are still scared.*
- *Too many colleagues fear technology.*
- *Technology frightens students with little or no exposure.*
- *Technology can be intimidating to the nontraditional student. This intimidation could hurt the learning. It has been my experience that older women are terribly afraid of computers.*

- *One problem is techno-able folks patronizing the techno-novice. No one wants to learn something they have been made to feel inadequate about.*

The final and most substantive community-related technology issue revolves around **maintaining the human touch while using technology in instruction**. Focus group faculty noted that in our complex community college context–characterized by at-risk, part-time, older, or single-parent students interacting with our multidimensional mission to prepare college transfer students, produce technical workers, and provide training for the local workforce–our struggles with technology and its effectiveness in instruction are unique in higher education. This context makes it imperative that we carefully craft our technology-based communications. One unintended critical inflection read into an e-mail sent to an unsure community college "virtual student" can quickly turn him into a nonexistent student. Moreover, the exemplary faculty in our study were quick to explain that they have come to rely on nonverbal communication–the confused look, the nodding head, or the unfocused stare–as their gauge of student learning and teaching effectiveness. They expressed concern about losing these human touches and wondered, for example, "What are the telltale communication signs of confusion or effectiveness in an online course?"

Focus group participants discussed the importance of breaking through the impersonality of technology to cultivate a sense of caring and community. Concern for the "human" issues related to the use of instructional technology was a key category identified by focus group faculty, a priority identified by more than 80 percent of survey respondents:

- *On Wednesday of this week, I shall be teaching my first e-mail class. I worry about the lack of face-to-face (i.e., fully human) interaction.*
- *Technology can never replace the human need for warmth and compassion given by a caring teacher.*
- *Technology can actually get in the way of teaching and learning. You can rely on it so much you forget how your students are responding or reacting.*
- *Students (and some instructors) are fearful that the environment will become too depersonalized. Used inappropriately technology can be cold, isolating.*

- *Technology should enhance the ability of faculty to draw students into the circle of learning. The most important factor in instruction is, I believe, the acting/exhibitionist piece of good teachers which catches the students and makes them yearn to hear/learn more. Technology shouldn't be in the way.*
- *In an ITV classroom, discussion is hard. It is stilted and shortened and people don't "connect" to you or to each other in the same way.*
- *You lose the human element in some cases. I like the personal interaction with students, seeing their bright faces when something is clear and their blank stares when something isn't.*
- *Teaching emanates from love, which cannot be excluded from the process. Technology per se cannot build that special bridge between teacher and student that results from learning.*

Putting a Little TLC into Community College Instruction

This study has several apparent limitations. First, the faculty chosen as "teaching excellence award recipients" are members of a purposeful sample, but the criteria for selecting these exemplars of "teaching excellence" are unique to each of the NISOD member schools. Nevertheless, this variance in selection criteria for award recipients may, in fact, lead to a better reflection of the diversity of community college teaching excellence in our findings.

In addition, personal priorities or interests may have biased the affinity diagramming process that engaged faculty participants and the research team. While every attempt was made to include all participants equally in this process, strong personalities always exist in groups, which can influence such activities. Finally, the response rate on the quantitative survey is small (24 percent). However, since the survey did not include comparative statistics and attempted to capture as much of the population as possible (rather than using a representative sampling technique), this response rate is admissible and is further offset by the high number of respondents (1,670).

These and other limitations notwithstanding, the study reported here is a broad-based and comprehensive attempt to capture the perspectives of community college teaching excellence award winners regarding how they use technology and the key issues they perceive to surround the use of these increasingly significant tools. Bringing these **technology** tools to bear to improve and expand **learning**, while maintaining a strong sense of **community**, is the challenge we hear in these faculty voices.

As noted, this study cohort was not composed of technology "true believers." Nonetheless, these faculty members used information **technology** in numerous creative ways. Their most prominent applications engaged students as active participants in information technology usage–an approach reported by successful faculty across discipline areas. Encouraging students to use technology to produce coursework and to apply concepts was first on the teaching excellence award recipients' lists of technology uses, followed closely by promoting technology for student-driven learning. Faculty also described widespread use of technology products to enhance and expand their instructional presentation capabilities, helping "bring [instructional] material to life" and stimulate different types of learners (e.g., visual or auditory learners). Next, faculty reported using technology to improve their communication with students and to facilitate interactions among students through e-mail, online chats, and threaded discussions. Faculty also described how new technology applications for research and reference have enabled them and their students to obtain the most current information easily and rapidly. Finally, faculty reported that technology tools for course management and assessment are leading them to experiment with new organizational and testing strategies.

A striking characteristic of the faculty participants in this study was their thoughtfulness surrounding sensitive issues regarding technology uses in instruction. Mirroring the focus on **learning** spreading throughout higher education, this cohort provided several notable insights into core learning issues. First, they agreed that learning with and about technology is becoming an essential "basic skill" for community college students. They pointed out that when students leave our institutions, they are entering a world of work or university transfer that uses technology at almost every turn. We do our students a serious disservice if we do not incorporate technology into their educational experiences.

Although dedicated to using these new tools to enhance student learning and to prepare students for successful transition into work or the university, faculty in this study identified a number of challenges hampering the meaningful integration of technology into instruction. A prevalent response among this cohort was that, despite claims of user-friendliness and ease of use, effective use of technology in the classroom requires a significant commitment of time and training. Faculty felt that, if used clumsily with too little preparation or training, or if combined with already poorly conceived instruction, technology might in fact inhibit learning. But when used well, they agreed that information technology could make teaching more engaging and facilitate different kinds of learning. Moreover, faculty emphasized that effective use of instructional technology can give students more control of their learning by offering them flexibility to learn in new and powerful ways outside of the classroom, on their own schedules.

These faculty clearly assessed the use of information technology to facilitate learning as vital, but suggested that technology use must be undertaken with consideration of several key issues that affect the college **community**. They reminded us that information technology remains an expensive educational investment that can lead to conflict over expenditures, resource allocations among divisions, and cost-to-benefit assessments. In addition, faculty stressed that not all students (or faculty) have equal access to technology, a situation with the potential to create a technology-based caste system within our institutions. In addition, findings suggest that technology hardware and software continue to malfunction frequently enough to raise the tempers and frustrations of faculty and students, which does little to reduce the fear and resistance that surround technology use in education. All these challenges are exacerbated by a core of true believers who advocate for the hegemony of technology, sometimes without regard for the insightful technology critic or sensitive technology novice.

Still, these award-winning faculty acknowledge the inescapable significance of technology to society and education, and they challenge us to overcome the shortcomings of technology applications and to strive to maintain the caring connection to the students we seek to empower through education. The men and women who so candidly shared their experiences and perspectives in this exploration of the intersection of technology and community college instruction remind us that while using the great new technology tools, we must not lose sight of the "human" things that faculty do to touch students each day, in and out of the classroom.

Suggestions for Putting TLC into Instruction

In closing, we offer a collection of suggestions for community and technical college educators to consider as they grapple with the issues related to technology, learning, and community that derive from the findings of this study. No single institution likely will find all of these proposals to be feasible or even appropriate. Nonetheless, judging from the responses and experience of this spectrum of community college teaching excellence award winners, any institution would be well served to bring together key personnel to give these suggestions serious consideration.

Technology Suggestions

1. Ensure that students have access to the technology necessary to produce their work and learn how to learn. Word processing, presentation software, spreadsheets, e-mail accounts, and Internet access are a minimum for all students to engage their educational opportunities on equal footing. Optimally, use of these technologies should be encouraged in most classes (i.e., "technology across the curriculum").

2. Expand access to asynchronous, technology-enabled learning options, such as Web tutorials and computer-based training, to allow students to drive their own learning. Allowing students to interact with learning materials at their own pace provides flexibility for individual learning styles while developing useful technology skills.

3. Provide access for faculty to the software, hardware, and training necessary to make effective use of presentation technologies in their classroom. Faculty in this study contend that visual, multimedia presentation technologies can "bring instruction to life."

4. Encourage technology applications that increase and improve communication between faculty and students and among college personnel at-large. In the community college context of increasingly busy and transitory students, flexible communication media are essential for bringing working students into contact with instructors. Effective communication technologies are particularly valuable tools for part-time faculty and their students. Few part-time faculty have offices

or voice mail on campus, and giving them college e-mail accounts greatly enhances their connectivity with students and colleagues.

5. Foster the use of the Internet and other technology-based research tools in instruction. Build curricula that encourage students to access research materials using technology. In addition, set a goal of providing all faculty members desktop access to the Internet to facilitate research in their discipline areas. Teaching five to six classes per term leaves little time for disciplinary upgrade; bringing the needed information to faculty desktops seems the least we can do.

6. Explore the many uses of technology to facilitate course management and assessment. The better tools faculty have to manage the increasing number and diversity of students coming their way, the better their instruction will be.

Learning Suggestions

1. Develop an information technology literacy component in your programs. Faculty in this study suggest that we do our students serious disservice by failing to recognize that the use of technology is a new "basic skill." Moreover, consider developing a basic information technology literacy component in your hiring and evaluation procedures for faculty. Perhaps we do our faculty an even greater disservice by not setting this standard for them.

2. Implement strategies to provide the necessary time and training to enable faculty to use technology effectively. This is by no means a simple suggestion in terms of logistics or budgeting. However, we can no more expect our faculty to make good use of technology without appropriate learning opportunities than we can expect our students to pass the final exam on the first day of instruction.

3. Catalog and showcase the different ways that instructors are using technology to improve instruction. Develop an institutional website that features model instructional uses each month. Develop teams for sharing experiences in applying technology in instruction, along the lines of the Great Teacher Seminar framework.

4. Enlist faculty who are further along on their technology journey to serve as mentors. Develop or expand teaching and learning centers to facilitate quality use of technology. Remember the maxim from faculty in this study, that technology can make instruction more engaging *when used well*. Encourage technology uses that appeal to different learning styles, uses that can be documented to improve learning.

5. Foster technology applications that encourage students to take control of their learning. The most important contribution of instructional technology in the Information Age may be to empower and motivate students to take responsibility for their own learning.

Community Suggestions

1. Deal with the expense of information technology openly and honestly–avoid "it will save us money in the long run" rhetoric. Make decisions about technology purchases based on learning and community goals. Develop as many alternative and stable funding strategies as possible to bring technology to the college without sacrificing other mission-critical services.

2. Strive to provide increased technology access and technical support, in particular, to students and staff who do not have technology available at home.

3. Avoid major system upgrades or equipment changes during pressing times in the academic calendar. Just before fall registration may not be the best time to implement a new administrative software package or instructional scheduling program.

4. Develop surefire strategies to respond promptly to hardware and software breakdowns in instruction. At the same time, encourage faculty to develop contingency plans for those times when *nothing* will make the system work.

5. Listen respectfully to those expressing resistance to technology. Do not dismiss the intelligent critics, as they sometimes can save thousands, even millions, of dollars in inappropriate

hardware and software purchases. Nevertheless, understand that some individuals will never accept technology and will fight for its demise at every turn. Search for balance, and always attempt to approach technology decisions thoughtfully, allowing for balanced contributions to the discussion. Beware of placing vocal "true believers" on the vanguard of your technology implementation efforts, as they can be perceived as patronizing or overzealous by those accepting technology at a slower pace.

6. Never lose sight of the essential human touch in instruction. People reach other people and change lives through teaching and learning. Remember that technology is merely the medium, a tool of our trade. As we move deeper into the Information Age, we cannot lose sight of this reality nor emphasize enough the need for caring and connected instruction. Community colleges traditionally have taken a holistic approach to learning and human development. To help balance detrimental effects of the ubiquitous technology in our lives, community colleges may be challenged with reinvigorating their emphasis on wellness and community.

In a caring educational community, learning and student success are at the center of all institutional processes, and technology is put in its place as a creative servant to these ends. Indeed, as Pat Cross (1998) points out, creativity and innovation are flourishing throughout today's community college. And, according to the faculty whose perspectives enliven this study, a focus on integrating TLC–**technology, learning, and community**–into instruction, can help us realize the promise of a "new spring" of educational opportunities for community colleges. These faculty voices encourage us to bring similar thoughtfulness and energy to all of the challenges that face us in the new millennium.

An earlier version of this report was published by the League for Innovation in the Community College (1998) as Technology, Learning and Community (TLC): Perspectives from Teaching Excellence Award Recipients.

References

Anandam, K. (1998). *Integrating Technology on Campus: Human Sensibilities and Technical Possibilities.* New Directions for Community Colleges, 101. San Francisco: Jossey-Bass.

Baker, G. A, Roueche, J. E., & Gillett-Karam, R. (1987). *Teaching as Leading: Profiles of Excellence in the Open-Door College.* Washington, DC: Community College Press.

Barr, R. B., & Tagg, J. (1995, November/December). "From Teaching to Learning: A New Paradigm for Undergraduate Education." *Change,* 27 (6), 13-25.

Brassard, M. (1989). *The Memory Jogger Plus+: Seven Management and Planning Tools.* Methuen, MA: Goal/QPC.

Cross, K. P. (1998). *Opening Windows on Learning.* The Cross Papers Number 2. Mission Viejo, CA: League for Innovation in the Community College.

Davis, B., & Wessel, D. (1998). *Prosperity: The Coming 20-Year Boom and What It Means to You.* New York: Random House.

Exley, B. (1995). *Partners in Action and Learning: 1994-1995 Annual Report.* Miami, FL: Miami-Dade Community College.

Gilbert, S. W. (1997). *Levers for Change: TLTR Workbook (Teaching, Learning, & Technology Roundtable Program: Regional TLTR).* Washington, DC: American Association of Higher Education.

Graves, W. H. (1998) A Strategy for IT Investments. In D. G. Oblinger & S. C. Rush (Eds.), *The Future Compatible Campus: Planning, Designing, and Implementing Information Technology in the Academy.* Bolton, MA: Anker.

Green, K. C. (1997). *Campus Computing Survey: The Seventh National Survey of Desktop Computing and Information Technology in Higher Education.* Encino, CA: Campus Computing.

Healy, J. M. (1994). *Your Child's Growing Mind: A Practical Guide to Brain Development and Learning from Birth to Adolescence*. New York: Doubleday.

Hooker, M. (1997). The Transformation of Higher Education. In D. G. Oblinger & S. C. Rush (Eds.), *The Learning Revolution: The Challenge of Information Technology in the Academy* (pp. 20-34). Bolton, MA: Anker.

Johnson, S. (1997). "Leadership in the Information Age." *Leadership Abstracts*, 10(5). Mission Viejo, CA: League for Innovation in the Community College.

Mander, J. (1992). *In Absence of the Sacred: The Failure of Technology and the Survival of the Indian Nations*. San Francisco: Sierra Club.

McClenney, K. (1998). "Perched at the Millennium: Perspectives on Innovation, Transformation, and Tomorrow." *Leadership Abstracts*, 11(8). Mission Viejo, CA: League for Innovation in the Community College.

Miles, M. B. & Huberman, A. M. (1994). *Qualitative Data Analysis: An Expanded Sourcebook* (2nd ed.). Thousand Oaks, CA: Sage.

Miller, W. L., & Crabtree, B. F. (1994). Clinical Research. In N. K. Denzin & Y. S. Lincoln (Eds.), *Handbook of Qualitative Research* (pp. 340-352). Thousand Oaks, CA: Sage.

Milliron, M.D., & Miles, C.M. (1998). *Technology, Learning, & Community (TLC): Perspectives from Teaching Excellence Award Recipients*. Mission Viejo, CA: League for Innovation in the Community College.

O'Banion, T. (1997a). *A Learning College for the 21st Century*. Published jointly by the American Association of Community Colleges and the American Council on Education. Phoenix, AZ: Oryx Press.

O'Banion, T. (1997b). "The Purpose, Process, and Product of the Learning Revolution in the Community College." *Leadership Abstracts*, 11(7). Mission Viejo, CA: League for Innovation in the Community College.

O'Banion, T. (1997c). "The Learning Revolution: A Guide for Community College Trustees." *Trustee Quarterly*, 1, 1-19.

O'Banion T. (1998, May). The Learning College of the Twenty-First Century. Keynote address. National Institute for Staff and Organizational Development (NISOD) International Conference on Teaching and Leadership Excellence, Austin, TX.

Oblinger, D. G. & Rush, S. C. (Eds.) (1997). *The Learning Revolution: The Challenge of Information Technology in the Academy.* Bolton, MA: Anker.

Oblinger, D.G. & Rush, S.C. (Eds.) (1998). *The Future Compatible Campus: Planning, Designing, and Implementing Information Technology in the Academy.* Bolton, MA: Anker.

Patton, M. Q. (1990). *Qualitative Evaluation and Research Methods* (2nd ed.). Newbury Park, CA: Sage.

Rossman, G. B., & Wilson, B. L. (1991). "Numbers and Words Revisited: Being 'Shamelessly Eclectic.'" *Evaluation Review*, 9 (5), 627-64.

Roueche, J.E. & Baker, G.A. III. (1987). *Access and Excellence: The Open Door College.* Washington, DC: Community College Press.

Salomon, G. (1991). "Transcending the Qualitative-Quantitative Debate: The Analytic and Systematic Approaches to Educational Research." *Educational Researcher*, 20(6), 10-18.

APPENDIX A

Tables 1 and 2 present a summary of the qualitative and quantitative responses to the two questions posed to study participants regarding the use of information technology in community college instruction. Each table highlights one technology-focused question and the thematic clusters of responses derived from the focus groups, with an example comment from that cluster. To the left of each category and comment are the Likert scale responses from the national survey and the mean response for each comment. To the right is the weighted ranking of survey responses. Focus group responses are listed in order of overall priority ranking of survey responses.

TABLE 1. **Summary of Findings for Question One**

1: In what ways do you use information technology in instruction?									
YES! 1	Yes 2	Yes 3	Neutral 4	No 5	No 6	NO! 7	Mean Score	Focus Group Responses *(categories and sample responses)*	Rank
19%	19%	21%	14%	15%	6%	6%	3.3	**Technology for student application/ production–**"*I expect all work to look professional and have students use word processors, spreadsheets, and PowerPoint to prepare their assignments to make sure it does.*"	1
18%	18%	21%	15%	15%	6%	7%	3.4	**Technology for student-driven learning–**"*There are some self-paced computer programs on some of our syllabi content–students can do these programs in the computer lab and come to class prepared to move beyond the program in a higher level of discussion on that topic.*"	2
17%	13%	18%	15%	18%	9%	10%	3.7	**Technology for presentation–** "*I Use PowerPoint to create classroom presentations and student handouts–it's been a God-send.*"	3
20%	13%	17%	11%	16%	9%	14%	3.7	**Technology for communication/ interactions–**"*My students can reach me 24 hours a day for chats via e-mail or fax.*"	4
13%	16%	24%	14%	17%	8%	8%	3.6	**Technology for research and reference–** "*I assign Internet research.*"	5
8%	9%	14%	12%	29%	12%	16%	4.5	**Technology for course management–** "*I put my syllabus online, collect papers via e-mail, and produce grade sheets on spreadsheets.*"	6
3%	4%	7%	17%	33%	16%	20%	5.0	**Technology for assessment–** "*I use QuestionMark software to design and deliver testing online.*"	7

TABLE 2. Summary of Findings for Question Two

2: What do you see as the key issues (positives or problems) in the use of technology in instruction?									
YES! 1	Yes 2	Yes 3	Neutral 4	No 5	No 6	NO! 7	Mean Score	Focus Group Responses (categories and sample responses)	Rank
50%	29%	16%	4%	1%	0%	0%	1.8	It's becoming a 'basic skill' our students need–"Students will be exposed to high tech on their first job. They must use current technology to succeed."	1
35%	30%	23%	5%	4%	2%	1%	2.2	It takes a lot of time and training to use well–"[Technology] changes so fast that staying current is difficult."	2
33%	23%	25%	12%	4%	2%	1%	2.4	Need to keep the human touch– "With Internet courses and interactive TV, students can sometimes feel alienated."	3
26%	33%	25%	12%	3%	1%	0%	2.4	It can make your teaching more engaging– "The ability to make the classroom or the course work experience more exciting."	4
31%	37%	24%	6%	1%	0%	0%	2.1	Can help facilitate different kinds of learning–" It gives students more avenues of learning–some are readers, some are watchers, and some are listeners."	5
37%	27%	22%	9%	3%	1%	1%	2.2	It can get very expensive–"Computer labs are expensive to set-up and become outdated the day of the grand opening (also expensive to maintain)."	6
30%	24%	22%	8%	8%	4%	4%	2.7	Students don't have equal access to technology–"Not all students have access to computers/Internet either on or off campus."	7
21%	25%	30%	14%	7%	2%	1%	2.7	The hardware and software can be problematic–"Hardware and software problems are very time consuming and distracting."	8
22%	33%	26%	15%	3%	1%	0%	2.5	Gives students more control of learning (e.g., asynchronous learning)–"Students can can work in self-directed fashion–it bridges time and space gaps."	9
16%	22%	28%	18%	10%	4%	2%	3.1	Some are tempted to use technology for the novelty, not the utility–"More focus on gadgets than on students and learning."	10
15%	25%	29%	13%	11%	4%	3%	3.0	There's a great deal of fear/resistance around the use of technology–"Resistance to learning new techniques–students and faculty–but more faculty."	11
10%	17%	27%	29%	11%	4%	2%	3.4	True believers can cause problems– Techno-able folks patronizing the techno-novice. No one wants to learn something they've been made to feel inadequate about."	12

CHAPTER 5

CYBER-COUNSELING, VIRTUAL REGISTRATION, AND STUDENT SELF-SERVICE: STUDENT SERVICES IN THE INFORMATION AGE

Carol Cross

If Rip Van Winkle were a community college registrar from the 1960s before he took his nap, what a jolt he would get if he woke up today and toured a technologically advanced community college. He would learn about students across the country taking a virtual tour of the campus via the Internet before submitting high school transcripts and admission applications online. He might wonder about the fiscal health of the college when he saw only a few students standing in line to register for classes. But, he soon would be pointed to electronic kiosks scattered across campus that students were using to access their records and sign up for new classes, and to students registering from home via telephone, perhaps even monitoring the availability of the classes on the college's cable television station. And he would be astonished to learn that students could use their student ID "smart cards" to check out library books, debit tuition and book payments from their electronically transferred financial aid payments, and find out their grades at the end of the semester.

Similarly, if Snow White had been a community college counselor thirty years ago, she would be amazed to see what had happened to her job after a 1999 Prince Charming awakened her from her slumbers. She would now have at her fingertips a wealth of information on each student she advised: high school records, academic goals and performance at the college, test results in academic skills and vocational aptitudes, even an individual learning style diagnostic and study skills prescription. She might automatically receive notices of students exhibiting early warning signals for failure–excessive absences, low midterm grades, missing homework or term papers–so that she could intervene before students got into academic trouble. She would have multiple resources available to suggest for students with special needs: computers that read texts aloud, software that displays complex concepts visually, and courseware geared for students with Attention Deficit Disorder and other learning disabilities. Snow White and her students could perform instant degree audits to discover course requirements for graduation or transfer, allowing them to make routine decisions in seconds and have time to explore students' deeper interests and more complex needs.

Indeed, when looking at the ways information technology is now used for student services at community colleges from the vantage point of the 1960s, the current technology offerings seem almost like a fairy tale. The ways community colleges have used technology to expand access, increase productivity, enhance existing services, and explore new possibilities in student services over the past 40 years sometimes seem as if they could have been created only by a very powerful wizard.

However, this would not be a fairy tale unless it had a wicked witch, an evil giant, a dreaded curse, or a bloodthirsty monster, and the tale of technology applications in student services has its demons as well as heroes. Beneath the surface of the magic kingdom of technology-facilitated student services lie slumbering dragons that conjure dark questions: Will technology depersonalize the community college experience, particularly for those with weaker skills and fewer support structures? Will it ultimately reduce access or make information and services harder to get for the most disadvantaged students? Will it drain college coffers in elusive searches for increased productivity? Will staff end up spending most of their time dealing with technology rather than with students? Educators grappling with these demons may wonder if the technology fairy tale will have a happy ending after all.

Of course, few people in higher education today base their educational decisions on fairy tales; we prefer facts and data to anecdotes and conjecture. To that end, this chapter offers the results of a study of the ways information technology is being used in student services and the effects these technology applications are having on student development. These questions are examined in the context of discussions about current revolutions in technology and learning, as well as prospects of what the future might hold for student services.

Setting the Stage

When examining the application of information technology to student services in the community college, tales of good and bad magic abound.

Moving rhetoric about the positive transformational effect of technology and ominous warnings about how it dehumanizes educational services are easy to find. Publications and conferences offer extensive theorizing about future directions of the student services profession and sincere calls for strategic development of a vision for technology-facilitated student services. Indeed, excellent overviews (such as Baier & Strong, 1994) address current concerns, review best practices, and describe outstanding examples of the many ways technology is being infused into the student services arena.

Such profiles are good resources for a broad perspective on this subject. However, what these profiles often lack are hard data that strip away the hyperbole and demonstrate how extensively technology has actually infiltrated community colleges as a whole. Furthermore, little information is available that quantifies the impact of information technology on student services. Describing an institution's implementation of certain technologies is one thing; specifying the difference those technologies are making in the overall student services process is quite another. Many of the technological benefits of such programs may be lauded by higher-level administrators at conferences or in publications; however, that enthusiasm may not be shared by lower-level, front-line personnel who are the ones most actively involved in using the technology. Finally, amid the swirl of claims and counterclaims, it is difficult to get a sense of which benefits or concerns are shared by a majority of student services professionals working in community colleges and which ones are promulgated by narrow constituencies with a particular axe to grind.

Information about the infiltration of information technology into student services differs significantly from similar information about instructional services. Far less national data are compiled on the student services use of technology than on the instructional use of technology. Nothing equivalent to K. C. Green's annual *Campus Computing Survey* (www.campuscomputing.net) exists to indicate how much money community colleges spend to support student services through technology, nor to detail the trends in applying that technology in specific areas. In most studies, student service applications are lumped into the infrastructure category, a valid categorization of such things as integrated student databases, but not very helpful for providing a national picture of technology trends in student services.

This leads to a situation in which certain technological innovations in student services appear to be accepted by practitioners. Few lament the passing of the "good old days" of card-based registration, in which the seemingly endless lines and redundant bureaucracies were an ordeal for students and staff alike. But, it is difficult to determine how broadly student services technologies are actually being implemented or to validate claims of rosy promises and dire consequences of using technology in this arena.

To get a snapshot of the use of technology in student services, the author used the Internet to conduct a national online survey of 50 community college educators representing the full range of student service functions. The survey, which targeted student service personnel who were employed at two-year institutions with a commitment to using information technology, gathered three categories of data:

1) the leading ways respondents' institutions use technology in student services,
2) the respondents' subjective assessments of the impact of that technology, and
3) the respondents' opinions regarding some of the major claims, positive and negative, of using technology in student services, based on their own experience.

In some cases, information from survey responses was supplemented by college documents or other resources on the application of technology at participants' institutions. In a few instances, the author conducted follow-up telephone or e-mail interviews with student services representatives to clarify how information technology was being implemented, and whether and how the infusion of technology had changed student service operations at their institutions.

The study was aimed at getting the opinions of student service personnel whose colleges professed a commitment to information technology, evidenced primarily by their membership in the League for Innovation. However, the study, which was designed by the author in consultation with a number of community college student service professionals, did not assume that each respondent would necessarily share his or her employer's views about the benefits of technology.

Indeed, a recurrent theme among at least some faculty and staff has been that such technology was being imposed upon them; therefore, the study was designed so the views of such critics could be heard in an anonymous context. On the other hand, the study was intended for people with at least minimal hands-on experience with technology. Thus, all solicitation and respondent participation was conducted through e-mail and Internet to ensure that respondents had at least some computer experience.

Obviously, this study sample is not statistically representative of community colleges at large. However, the intent of the survey was to determine how a sample of technologically active institutions are specifically using information technology in student services, and how the experiences of practitioners compare to some of the theories and concerns surrounding IT use as described in the literature. Furthermore, although the survey sample was small, study findings support qualitative descriptions of case studies and best practices contained in most national literature. Therefore, the survey tends to quantify and validate current writings about such trends that have not been substantiated by much quantitative data.

A Framework for Analyzing the Use of Technology

O'Banion (1997b) points out that one of the key barriers to productive dialogue and real change in education is the lack of a common and precise vocabulary. Today, when everyone is consumed with the need for change, vague descriptors like "new paradigm," "learning revolution," and "institutional transformation" are bandied about, leaving people to argue about the terms themselves rather than to engage in productive debate about the underlying concepts. To avoid such semantic debate or descriptive ambiguity when assessing the impact of technology in the student services area, the author suggests a framework with which to characterize the progressive effects of technology application. This framework defines a three-stage process–**Duplication**, **Application**, and **Transformation** (DAT)–of innovative technological adoption.

Phase I: Duplication. Most initial uses of an innovative technology merely replicate what is already being done with the old technology, whether human, animal, mechanical, or digital. At first, people view the innovative technique through the paradigm of what they already know, and they conceive of the new as an extension or variation of the old. Thus, for example, the first cars were horseless carriages, and early film was termed moving pictures. Given this tendency to see the new technology through the eyes of the old, it is no surprise that new technology is generally operated in parallel with the traditional methodology, becoming a secondary or duplicate technique for producing goods or performing services. New uses are usually not revolutionary or even evolutionary, but modified replications of current practice.

The use of the term *duplication* is not intended to denigrate. In fact, two major contributions of new technology occur during this phase. First, such duplication extends access, for it makes the traditional goods or services more widely available or available in a new form that reaches new populations. For access conscious institutions like community colleges, this is a major benefit. Second, the duplication phase gives first-time adopters experience with the new technology that may deepen their understanding of its operation and potential. For many, if they did not initially use a new technology to replicate something with which they were familiar, they would probably never use it at all and might never discover its latent possibilities. Therefore, a new technology rarely takes away from or replaces an existing technique from the start. Instead, the new is layered on top of the old, and they operate in tandem.

The printing press, the last great technological invention to truly transform education, was first used to produce more copies of the same handwritten academic, classical, and liturgical texts which teachers always had used. Indeed, the first printers, known as scriptors, took great pains to make their manuscripts look like traditional ones, with each printing house reproducing the idiosyncratic script styles, punctuation, and abbreviations popular among the hand scribes in that community who continued to toil on their labor-intensive documents. The initial adoption phase of this new innovation had no impact upon the process of education which relied primarily on an oral tradition requiring great oration and memory skills, but it did relieve the tremendous problem of access to texts for teachers and students.

Phase II: Application. After some hands-on experience with the technology, however, most people begin to see new ways to use it. This begins a rich period of experimentation, or the *application* phase. During application, adopters rethink their use of a technology in light of its new possibilities, and attempt to use the technology in ways that will allow them to perform old tasks better or to undertake untried activities. The benefits of this stage are increased efficiency or effectiveness, along with expanded access.

Application is probably the messiest, most difficult, and most contentious phase of the technological adoption process. It is a time of breakthrough achievements and glorious failures as people determine what the technology and their organizational structure can accommodate. Although nonadherents may have been passively suspicious or wary of the new technology in the first phase, by the application phase the new technology poses a direct challenge to their established way of doing things and usually provokes some active opposition. It is a time when the new technology does battle with the old methodology as both compete for resources, advocates, personnel, and market share.

In the printing press example, the application phase was marked by the development of many features of books we now take for granted, such as standardized fonts, punctuation, spelling, indexing, and cataloging. These features made written documents universal and transportable, providing the basis for an objective body of knowledge that is the foundation of modern education. Printers also began expanding into new markets and reproducing information that had not been transcribed before, such as maps, guidebooks, currency conversion tables, and how-to manuals. As printers gained a better understanding of innovative ways to apply the capabilities of this new technology, hand scribes condemned these new products as works of the devil and argued that paper was transitory compared with the reliable and proven medium of parchment. Meanwhile, with the advent of affordable books produced by the presses, students were no longer dependent on the text monopoly of the universities and began reading and acquiring knowledge on their own. Many professors of the time predicted the downfall of Western civilization, led by radical young students who were seduced by popular but intellectually inferior books, who challenged the authority of their professors and the traditions of the university, and who exhibited deplorable basic skills in memorizing and reciting texts.

Phase III: Transformation. Ultimately, the full adoption of truly new technologies leads to the transformation of the organization into either an enterprise that does in a revolutionary way what it always did or becomes an entirely new enterprise. A particular technology achieves transformational status when the behaviors of individuals are reorganized in meaningful ways around the possibilities inherent in that technology. For example, the automobile did much more than replace the horse and buggy; it generated new patterns of mobility and community, connected a nation through a network of highways, fostered the urban and suburban lifestyle in which the majority of us now live, and created one of the major pillars of the American economy. The moving picture was first used merely a means of capturing stage performances on film, but movies have evolved into a completely different art form and industry than the theater from which they emanated.

Clearly, the printing press and its products generated an entirely new approach to higher education. This technology not only replaced historical approaches to instruction, making reading rather than memorization and recitation the predominant academic skill, but it also transformed the curriculum by facilitating a shared and verifiable set of facts and theories. Such common and objective understanding, in turn, formed the basis of modernism, the approach that has been the prevailing intellectual movement from the Enlightenment to current times.

How Is Technology Being Used in Student Services?

Using the DAT model, which offers a standardized approach to categorizing the uses of technology through the duplication, application, and transformation stages of adoption in an organization, the data from the survey group can be examined. The first part of the survey asked whether specific technological applications were being used in seven broad areas of student services: student recruitment, registration and records, financial aid and financial management, advising and counseling, testing and placement, student support services (including services for disabled and at-risk students), and student activities. Figure 5A lists those technologies that are being used by more than 50 percent of the respondents' institutions.

Figure 5A. Technology Uses in Student Services Reported by Majority of Respondents

Technology Uses	Percent Use
Use of Internet for student recruitment	92%
Telephone registration	78%
Computerized information on transfer institutions used for student counseling/advisement	58%
Use of technological assistive/adaptive devices for disabled students	58%
Use of computerized learning aids for physically disabled students	58%
Electronic submission of Federal Student Aid forms	54%

Other technologies that were said to be in use by a substantial percentage (between 20 and 49 percent) of respondents are noted in Figure 5B.

Figure 5B. Technology Uses in Student Services Reported by 20 Percent to 49 Percent of Respondents

Technology Uses	Percent Use
Use of Internet to provide counseling and advisement	48%
Computer-based testing for vocational interests and aptitudes	48%
Use of computerized learning aids for learning-disabled students	48%
Student records available on demand via kiosks, intranet, and/or Internet	46%
Use of Internet/intranet to advertise student activities and/or recruit participation	44%
Computerized and/or online Federal Student Aid information	44%
Interactive resources (computerized, interactive videodisc and/or Internet) on colleges and program requirements available in addition to personal advisor	42%

Figure 5B, continued

Technology Uses	Percent Use
Computerized or online nonfederal student scholarship information	40%
Computer-based testing for academic placement	36%
Use of computerized learning aids for at-risk students	34%
Use of Internet/intranet for internal operation of student government, clubs, or other student activities	32%
Internet/online registration	30%
Computer-based testing for personal learning style	28%
Advertisement of institution through computerized database or CD-ROM for student recruitment	26%
Ability to receive student transcript online	26%
Online database on university transfer credits that gives immediate feedback on required or transferable courses	24%
Use of computerized/online aids for learning communities	22%

The leading uses of technologies reported by the study respondents are not surprising when considered from the DAT theory of technological adoption. That is, most of the highest percentage uses could be considered to be in the *duplication stage*, in which technology is used to expand, but not replace, existing services. For example, most colleges have not eliminated their high school visitations and traditional promotional materials, but have supplemented these with recruitment via the Internet, which is often targeted toward new, nontraditional, or distant student populations not normally reached through traditional means. Adaptive devices and computer-based learning aids have not changed the way most classes are taught, but they do offer students with disabilities enhanced ways to participate and succeed in traditional courses.

Uses that seem to fit more within the *applications phase*–more innovative uses that further exploit the potential of the new technology–were reported for fewer colleges. A number of applications with midrange response rates could be considered to fall into the phase of applying information technology to student services. Two examples illustrate such uses: (1) student counseling via the Internet or computer often allows students to explore more options than their time-limited sessions with a live counselor, and (2) computerized adaptive testing bases the content and difficulty level of successive questions on a student's individual performance on prior questions. These applications differ substantially from the traditional alternatives of face-to-face advisement or standardized, paper-based placement exams, both in terms of the experience and the results for students and staff.

Finally, most of the uses that might be considered truly new or *transformative* in the educational process would be expected to have the lowest rates of use. Accordingly, the survey data indicate that technology to support such new educational concepts as assessing personal learning styles or creating learning communities were reported by only 28 and 22 percent of institutions, respectively. Other technology applications that suggest a definite departure from traditional student service processes failed to garner even a 20 percent usage rate among the focus group, as indicated in Figure 5C.

Figure 5C. Technology Uses in Student Services Reported by Less than 20 Percent of Respondents

Technology Uses	Percent Use
Student activities involving the creative, recreational, or nonacademic use of computers	18%
Use of interactive counseling resources (computerized, interactive videodisc, or online resources) required as prerequisite to seeing a counselor	8%
Computerized personal financial planning tools available in addition to scholarship/student financial aid materials	8%
Computerized midsemester monitoring/early intervention system for students showing indications of failure in courses	6%
Computerized "one-stop" center that provides information and assistance to both college and community services	6%
Use of "smart card" technology for student ID/library/payment/information access card	4%
Use of artificial intelligence/computerized expert system in student counseling	4%

Two applications with high rates of reported use are somewhat of a deviation from this general picture, however. The second most highly reported technology application, telephone registration, has not eliminated in-house registration; nevertheless, for most colleges the process of adding this option has caused them to revamp substantially their registration processes, both telephone-based and traditional. This application arguably falls into the *application* or *transformation* phase, even though both new and old systems are being maintained. Similarly, on-demand student record access to online or electronic kiosk information systems was reported by a large number of institutions (46 percent). A system by which students retrieve their personal academic and financial information at will via kiosks, Internet, or intranet signifies a much different information management philosophy from one in which the registrar's office is the sole repository of student records. Study respondents indicate that this approach affects the behavior of both students and staff; therefore, this application may also bridge the *application* and *transformation* phases of technology adoption.

What Impact Are These Technologies Having?

Attributing *transformational* status to any information technology used in student services is a highly subjective and uncertain form of analysis. Even though some of these technology applications may have the potential for dramatically altering the provision and use of student services, these applications may be designated as transformational only if the institution changes its fundamental structures or procedures as a result of adopting this technology. The degree to which such changes are occurring in various community colleges is perhaps best assessed by those experiencing these effects within the institution. To begin to understand the perceptions of student services personnel regarding such effects, survey respondents were asked to assess the impact information technology was having on their institutions for each of the seven student services areas and for student services overall. Respondents chose one of five options from the scale in Figure 5D to describe the impact of information technology (IT).

Figure 5D. Ranking the Impact of Information Technology (IT) on Student Services

Transformational Impact	Major Impact	Minor Impact	In Planning Stages for IT use	No Plans to use IT
4	3	2	1	0

Figure 5E displays the mean scores describing respondents' perceptions of the impact of information technology on student services in their institutions.

Figure 5E. Impact of Information Technology Uses on Student Services

Student Services Area	IT Impact Rating
Registration and Records	2.96
Student Recruitment	2.70
Financial Aid	2.45
Student Support Services	2.22
Counseling	2.19
Testing and Placement	1.98
Student Activities	1.76
Student Services Overall	2.70

These results suggest that, to date, no area of student services has been transformed by the inclusion of information technology at the majority of institutions. However, most colleges report that technology has had either a major or minor impact in most areas of student services and on the student services process overall. The two student services areas noted to be affected most dramatically by technology–registration and records and student recruitment–correlate with the top two leading uses of information technology reported earlier. In fact, 30 percent of respondents appraised the impact of technology in the registration and records divisions of their institutions as transformational.

Interestingly, the impact of technology use on student services overall was rated higher than its impact on most of the individual student services areas. This finding may simply demonstrate perceptions of the cumulative impact of a number of lesser effects, or it may point to efforts in many institutions to use technology to improve coordination among student services divisions that are not yet visible in individual areas. Still, we cannot draw conclusions about the quality, negative or positive, of effects reported without evaluating the final category of survey data: perceptions about the benefits and challenges associated with technology applications in student services.

What Benefits and Problems Are Technology Users Encountering?

Analysis of responses to the first part of the survey brought some focus to the many ways information technology is being used and the perceptions of student services personnel about the impact of these applications. The final portion of the survey explored respondents' subjective assessments of various claims and criticisms found in the literature and in public discussions about using technology in student affairs.

Study participants were asked to respond to each of twenty statements about the use of information technology in student services, indicating their responses by choosing one of five scale options: Strongly Agree, Agree, Neutral or Undecided, Disagree, or Strongly Disagree. The twenty items were randomly ordered statements of ten benefits of using technology in student services commonly posited by technological advocates (positive claims) and ten criticisms of such technology applications raised by student service professionals concerned about the impact of technology (negative claims). The statements were not identified as supportive or critical in the survey. Respondents were allowed anonymity (that is, originating e-mail addresses were not captured, although respondents could report their names and institutions if they wanted), and, regarding each statement, they were encouraged to report their honest opinions rather than official policies of their institutions.

The results were analyzed using a five-point scale like that used to assess the impact of technology (i.e., Strongly Agree = 4 points, Strongly Disagree = 0 points). Thus, the higher the score, the greater the agreement and the lower the score, the lesser the agreement with the statement. Figure 5F lists the statements according to their positive or negative orientation to technology applications in student services, ranked by their mean response scores from greatest to least agreement with the statements.

Figure 5F. Mean Responses to Positive and Negative Claims About Effects of Technology Use on Student Services

Positive Claims		Negative Claims		
Strongly Agree	*Agree*	*Neutral/Undecided*	*Disagree*	*Strongly Disagree*
4	*3*	*2*	*1*	*0*
Technology allows student service personnel easy access to more information on students, improving the advising process.	3.44	Computer games and recreational uses of the Internet are seductive time wasters that divert significant amounts of students' time and attention from more productive activities.		2.36
Overall, I believe technology allows us to serve students better.	3.42	Student service personnel do not receive sufficient training and/or other support in the use of technology to make the investment in equipment cost effective.		2.22
Use of technology increases access to student services.	3.42	The growing use of electronic mail and the Internet increases student isolation and "cocooning" among students with weak social skills.		2.08
Technology facilitates data collection and analysis that allows student service personnel to better plan and evaluate their programs, thus enhancing job performance.	3.22	Distance Learning and Computer-Based Instruction require different skills than traditional classes and thus increase the workload of student services personnel.		1.92
Technology provides routine information required in prescriptive advising, allowing counselors to devote more time to personalized and developmental advising.	3.21	The use of technology reduces student privacy because more people can get personal information, both legitimately and by breaking into files.		1.70

Figure 5F. continued

Positive Claims			Negative Claims	
Strongly Agree	*Agree*	*Neutral/Undecided*	*Disagree*	*Strongly Disagree*
4	*3*	*2*	*1*	*0*
Technology empowers students to be responsible for and to monitor their own academic progress and/or to make their own decisions.	3.08		Technology puts an additional burden on student services personnel and takes away time they would otherwise spend with students.	1.56
Electronic communication, such as the Internet, gives busy students increased opportunities to form relationships with their peers, instructors, and other people in the college.	3.04		The power and anonymity of the Internet/intranet encourage students to engage in racial and sexual harassment, hate crimes, hacking, or other inappropriate or illegal activities.	1.50
Technology gives student services personnel easy access to more information on internal and transfer college programs, improving the advising process.	3.04		Use of technology makes student services more impersonal.	1.42
Technology enables students with special needs, such as the disabled, to participate more fully in the complete college experience.	2.84		Technology gives students information they are not equipped to interpret and apply correctly, leading students to make mistakes.	1.31
Technology allows us to provide student services more efficiently, thus enabling us to serve large numbers of students with a stable or reduced budget.	2.70		Money is being invested in student service technology that would be better spent on acquiring additional student service personnel.	1.18

As the scores show, although the statements of promise and concern were intermingled on the survey, a clear delineation is found between their cumulative scores. The lowest ranked positive claim receives higher levels of agreement than the highest ranked negative claim. The mean response for eight of the ten positive statements is greater than 3.0, suggesting general agreement with these statements. None of the negative claims achieve this general agreement level. In addition, no statements, positive or negative, are rejected outright by respondents overall. Seven of the ten negative statements fall in the 1.0 to 2.0 category (undecided, with a tendency toward disagreement) and the other three have scores between 2.0 and 2.5 (undecided, with a tendency toward agreement).

Taken as a whole, these findings indicate that study participants are generally positive about the use of information technology in student services. Respondents agree most strongly with claims that information technology provides greater access to information and services for students and staff, that it facilitates more personalized or developmental advising, and that it improves student services processes overall. Claims that money would be better spent on additional personnel instead of on technology, that students will misuse the information or power that information technology provides, or that technology depersonalizes the student service process received the lowest levels of agreement.

The most troubling issues identified by respondents are the potential for recreational computer use to become a time waster or an isolating agent for students and the deficiency of training and support for student service personnel in using information technology. Respondents appear ambivalent about whether distance and technology-facilitated learning require more student services than do regular classes, whether student privacy is at risk due to information technology, and whether technology takes away from time spent with students. In terms of information technology benefits, respondents are most ambivalent about claims that technology assists special needs populations to participate more fully in the college and improves productivity in the student service arena.

What Is "The Big Picture" Suggested by the Survey?

In examining all three sets of data, as supported by other national literature and individual case studies, eight trends in integrating information technology into the student services area seem to emerge.

1. Student service personnel support investment in information technology. Respondents largely reject the idea that money spent on information technology in their areas would be better spent on additional staff, and generally assess technology as having a decided impact on their institutions. They express almost blanket acceptance of the claim that technology allows them to serve students better overall. Altogether, they appear to be fairly satisfied with the results to date of their institutions' investments in technology. A major, related concern seems to be a lack of user support and training resources for use of technology applications, a concern they share with instructional and administrative personnel, according to Green's 1999 *Campus Computing Project* report and Milliron and Leach's (1997) *Community Colleges Winning through Innovation* study. Student services personnel are also somewhat unsure about claims for improving their productivity through information technology, another view mirrored in instructional computing.

2. Overall, information technology has had a meaningful, positive impact on student services, but it has yet to truly transform most student affairs operations. Although respondents seem to support investments in information technology and report promising inroads, most feel that technology has not had a major impact on student services at their institutions. Few claim that the use of information technology has substantively transformed what they are doing, although the impact on registration and records operations seems to be heading in that direction.

3. Better, more complete, timely, and accessible information is increasingly available via technology to support both students and student service personnel. Respondents note the advantages of greater access to information for students and for themselves. They agree that increased information allows them to provide better counseling and other services and to plan and evaluate their operations better. They believe that more information allows students to take responsibility for their own decisions and monitor their own progress. Faster, easier access to routine information via technology allows more time for personalized and developmental advising, which studies indicate students almost universally prefer but rarely get (Herndon, Kaiser, & Creamer, 1996). Study respondents feel that the benefits of student empowerment and the improved quality and access to information provided by information technology outweigh problems of personal privacy issues or of students misapplying or even abusing information from technology-based sources.

4. Student service personnel appear to be using technology to enhance, not deter, the community college's traditional "high touch" approach. The suggestion that information technology makes student services more impersonal receives the lowest agreement rating of any statement on the survey. Conversely, the item ranked highest in terms of agreement is the proposal that by providing better access to information on the student, technology allows student service personnel to improve student advising. It appears that front-line personnel who actually use the technology share their institutions' perception of the benefits of IT in student services.

Benefits of enhanced and improved services to students are rated more highly than departmental benefits of enhanced productivity or processes. Respondents also agree that using information technology to perform routine student services tasks and provide answers to frequently asked student inquiries gives them more time to provide personalized service with individual students. User-friendly, integrated student information systems that are the goal appear to be having the greatest effect on student services, and that effect is largely to help student services personnel better meet individual student needs.

The differences between respondents' views about the effects of electronic communication on students provide another indication that many student services professionals recognize the high-touch benefits of IT. Respondents were asked their views on whether electronic communication increases students' opportunities to form relationships with their peers, instructors, and others in the college community or increases student isolation, particularly among students with weak social skills. Study participants rate their agreement with the relationship-building perspective well above their concurrence with the isolation view. These findings indicate that, although slightly concerned about potential negative effects, respondents currently find information technology to be more of a connective force than an isolating or dehumanizing force for students.

5. Some of the older, lower-tech, less cutting-edge or "sexy" technology applications are having the greatest impact on student services. Although current literature tends to emphasize the latest, trendiest technologies–for example, the new smart cards that students use to shop at the college bookstore or cafeteria, to check out library books, and to access their own course records–some of the older technology-based workhorses are having the greatest impact on student services at community colleges. Computerized student databases are certainly among the oldest information technologies used in student affairs, but this seems to be the application that comes closest to transforming student services operations. Even the student information kiosks that are popping up on campuses across the country have been around since at least 1989.

The impact of student information systems is likely a confluence of several factors: (a) the technology has evolved greatly in the decades since it was first introduced, particularly in terms of ease of use for individuals with little or no technology training; (b) student services staff have developed sufficient experience and expertise with this technology to create systems that truly meet their needs rather than just adopting what is available; and (c) this application has penetrated most areas of student services more deeply than other technology applications. Like student information systems, telephone registration systems have been around for more than 15 years, so they are another relatively longstanding technology innovation. This technology is not only widely used at community colleges, but also generally well-regarded by students and staff. Again, this is a technology that is familiar, easy to use, and considered to be an almost standard operation now, but it has had a considerable impact on improving services for students.

Nevertheless, while older, more pervasive, and easy to use applications would seem to have the greatest impact, these qualities alone do not guarantee widespread adoption among student service operations. For example, only a few respondents report using any form of television in student services, despite television's omnipresence in society, and its role, at least until very recently, as the major conduit of community college distance education courses.

6. The Internet is rapidly gaining popularity and usage in student services. The major exception to the previous point may be the Internet. Just as faculty appear to be embracing the use of the Internet in their classes, student services personnel are swiftly adopting the use of the Internet in their work. Given how recently community colleges established access to this global network, progress in the use of Internet technologies in student services is remarkable. In this study, student recruitment via the Internet is the single most reported use of information technology in student services overall, and other Internet-based services are among the most widely used in each student services division except for student support services. Particularly significant is the fact that almost a third of respondents report that they had implemented registration via the Internet, one of the more complicated and sophisticated uses of the Internet in student services. Again, since the majority of community colleges have gained access to the Internet within the past three years, this is a broad penetration of a relatively complicated technological application in a short time span.

Although study respondents are somewhat concerned about the potential for the Internet to drain students' time in unproductive pursuits, few appear to have experienced problems with students using the Internet to access other student's records, to hack into college information systems, or to distribute illegal, harassing, or inappropriate communications.

7. Some established and relatively pervasive technological applications seem to have a limited impact on student services. Two student services areas in which technology has a fairly high level of penetration and has been used for some time are academic testing and placement and student support services, particularly for students with disabilities. Computerized adaptive testing software for college-level placement has been commercially available since the early 1980s, and computer-based vocational testing has been available for more than a decade. With their commitment to accessibility, community colleges have embraced adaptive technologies for students with physical disabilities, many of which have been available for nearly twenty years, and have been pioneers in using hardware and software solutions for students with learning disabilities or limited English proficiencies.

Despite the relative longevity and high adoption levels of these technology applications, however, respondents seem to feel that technology has had only a minor impact on these service operations. When study participants assess the impact of technology on various student services areas, only student activities earn a lower impact rating than testing and placement. Agreement with the claim that technology enables special needs students to participate more fully in the college experience received the next to lowest agreement rating of the positive claims about technology. These findings suggest that although technology is widely used to serve students with academic and physical challenges, the problems in these areas may be resistant to technology-based solutions. These are areas in which the community college's longstanding concerns about maintaining access are surfacing, and, at least for the present, student services personnel seem to feel that these are areas in which the human touch may still be more critical than high-tech tools.

8. Student services departments are using information technology to integrate operations and resources not only within their institutions, but also between their colleges and other organizations. Information technology is not only making life easier for students as they move from office to office within a particular institution, but also making their movement between institutions easier. Student services operations are making great strides in coordinating their exchange of information with the K-12 systems from which their students come, the colleges and universities to which their students transfer, and the government and community agencies that provide funding and other support to their students. Nearly 60 percent of survey respondents indicated they now have computerized information on transfer institutions, and 54 percent submit federal financial aid forms electronically. Approximately one-quarter of all those surveyed have an online university-based degree audit program that provides them with immediate feedback on which courses will transfer to other university programs in their states, as with California's statewide ACCESS network. This is a promisingly high percentage, given the difficulty states have had in settling the complex and contentious articulation issue, let alone the challenge of keeping such information current and instantly accessible online. Although it was among items at the bottom of the list of technological benefits noted by study respondents, they clearly agreed that having such information available resulted in better service for the students, even if it has not been fully implemented at their institutions.

Summary of Findings

The trends suggested by this survey are not earth shattering, and most student services professionals would find few surprises in the analysis. Furthermore, the data support neither the technology-facilitated, student-centered nirvana depicted by some technological advocates nor the doom and gloom, Chicken Little predictions that information technology is turning student services at community colleges into dehumanizing processes. In most areas, at least when viewing the comprehensive data, information technology seems to have had only a minor-to-major, rather than transformational, impact on student services to date. Thus far, community colleges seem not to have tapped the full potential of their new technology-based tools in any student services arena.

However, the survey does suggest that community colleges are on the right track in implementing technology in student services. Respondents seem convinced that institutional investments in information technology are improving student services, and are doing so to a greater extent than would be possible if those resources were put into traditional expenditures such as additional staff. They are generally positive about the proposed benefits of using technology and do not report major concerns regarding implementing technology. Student service personnel who are applying the technology first-hand seem to share their institutions' enthusiasm for it. Few respondents seem to be experiencing the depersonalization, the privacy abuses, the misplaced focus on technology rather than on students, or other demons that skeptics are watching for as technology infiltrates the realm of student services.

Community colleges also appear to be focusing their resources in student services on more established, fundamental technologies, rather than on the trendy technology *du jour*. Nevertheless, the Internet is rapidly moving into student services, apparently with a significant role to play in most student services areas.

What Does the Future Hold for Student Services?

Among the institutions represented in this study, most student services departments seem to be in the *application* phase of the *duplication-application-transformation* cycle of technology implementation. The implementation trends also suggest that ultimately information technology will have as great an impact on education as the printing press had on early universities. More than any of the Industrial Age technological developments, which transformed national economies as well as social structures but left traditional higher educational processes relatively intact, television and computers parallel the printing press in the impact of technological advancement on education. All three innovations (a) undermine the information or knowledge monopoly previously held by the academic professorate; (b) foster a geometric proliferation of information that traditional educational organizations are not equipped to handle; (c) challenge the very nature of data, knowledge, and education; and (d) require and facilitate the development of new cognitive skills that alter the most fundamental processes of education.

It follows that if the very nature of education–the curriculum, the instructional processes, and the organizational structures–changes, student services cannot remain untouched. The underlying purpose of student services is to recruit, enroll, place, advise, support, and develop students as they pursue their instructional programs, and if those instructional programs change dramatically, the service units must adjust correspondingly.

Therefore, student services personnel anticipating the stories that will unfold for them in the new millennium should look to the new directions that instructional programs are taking and prepare themselves to support the new educational structures that are emerging. Several characteristics of the new model for higher education emerging from the Learning Revolution are clear:

1. Education is centered on the individual learner and is freed from the traditional confines of time and space; students can access what they want, when they want it, where they want it, and how they want it.

2. Institutional quality is assessed on the basis of demonstrable learning outcomes rather than on educational holdings (numbers of books, libraries, or buildings) or inputs (numbers of students, class size, or hours spent in class).

3. Education is continual and integrated rather than discrete in time and subject matter. Instruction is focused on preparing students to be lifelong learners who will return to educational experiences periodically throughout their lives and who can connect new information with knowledge from prior learning or another subject area.

4. Multiple educational options are available within institutions and among institutions and other organizations offering instruction, introducing a new competitiveness never before seen in higher education.

5. The cognitive processes of education are shifting their focus from content to information acquisition, manipulation, interpretation, evaluation, and communication skills, and the hegemony of the written or spoken word is being challenged by multisensory information sources.

Such educational trends are signposts to the future of student services in the community college. Student services must simultaneously diversify–as with registration, which can be conducted in person, by mail, by on-campus kiosk, by off-campus Internet, or by telephone–and integrate, creating a seamless flow of information with many different entry points and options. The needs of the student, not those of the staff or the institutional structures, will be the focal point around which all else revolves. Student services personnel must find ways to accommodate student needs, often through thoughtful use of information technology to develop structures that are unbound by time and space and that integrate multiple informational sources, including video, graphics, audio, and perhaps even virtual reality.

A New Heyday for Student Development

Undergoing real transformation is seldom an easy or comfortable experience, and student services personnel may go through tremendous levels of anxiety as they look toward this future. However, as the curtain rises on the 21st Century fairy tale of higher education, it may be that this transformational break with the past will bring student services to new levels of importance and effectiveness within the community college.

First, student services personnel, who tend to be less steeped in academic tradition and who have the experience in marketing the college to students, may make the transition to a more competitive environment more easily than will their faculty peers. Second, if education is merely becoming another commodity to students, as Sacks (1996) suggests, student services may give community colleges the customer service edge to compete with the onslaught of private and public educational providers. In fact, Doucette (1997) and Bleed (as cited in Rooney, 1996) predict that the student services unit may gain new roles in brokering support services at the community college for educational content provided by other organizations. Furthermore, research indicates that distance education and other alternative instructional systems are best suited for strong, highly skilled, and motivated students. Student support services will likely become even more critical as the primary community college clientele–returning students, first-generation college students, and students with weaker academic skills–attempt to take advantage of these new educational methodologies.

Finally, the rallying cry among community colleges for using technology and process reengineering to support an institutional focus on student learning (O'Banion, 1997a) is in alignment with the most deeply held beliefs of most student services personnel. Indeed, this may be an opportunity for a reconciliation of the academic and student development missions that have diverged from the earliest days of most community colleges. As noted by Bloland, Stamatakos, and Rogers (1996), many institutions developed a fracture between faculty and student affairs in the 1960s and 1970s, when student development programs often were seen as promoting radical, unproven, or "flaky" extracurricular experiences for students or providing only trivial administrative services. With recent movements such as the American College Personnel Association's Student Learning Initiative and the Learning Revolution, professors, administrators, and student services personnel are embracing student learning as their preeminent professional responsibility.

As faculty debate the requirements for becoming a learning-centered college with a focus on student outcomes rather than institutional processes, the time for moving from *student services* to *student development* may be at hand. As the Learning Revolution progresses, student services personnel will be called on to demonstrate not only an accounting of the services they have provided, but also a demonstration of the learning experiences they have produced for their students.

To function as essential components of a student-centered institution, student affairs departments will need to organize and orient themselves around the needs of students, not the needs of the institution. This may require rethinking, reengineering, and regrouping the traditional components of student affairs to improve the way the student interacts with the organization. Such a technology-facilitated, learning-centered reorganization of college functions might include a number of divisions organized by student outcomes rather than by institutional structures:

Informing Learners. Complete information about the college–its programs, its calendar, its fees, its personnel, its services–would be available via many modes, including CD-ROM, the Internet, interactive television, and kiosks at public buildings throughout the community. Such information would be searchable and would respond to information requests, enabling potential students to determine quickly whether the college has the courses, programs, or support services they need, as well as the steps they must take to enroll and successfully meet their goals. Once students have enrolled, the information would expand to include all their personal academic information–assessment tests, advising recommendations, course grades, degree audits–all private but accessible through use of the student smart card, again via computer, the Internet, kiosks, or the telephone.

Enrolling Learners. Students would have multiple options for registering for classes, including using the Internet and the telephone, with the registration process integrated with previous educational information, such as electronically submitted transcripts from other institutions, and financial aid programs. Registration payment options would include cash, checks, credit cards, and emerging forms of cyber-payments. Registration, in most cases, would be an ongoing process, with the ability to start classes continually throughout the year.

Assessing Learner Capabilities and Challenges. Computer-based testing typically used for placement purposes in math and English classes would be expanded to include other developmental measures, such as learning styles, vocational aptitude, and personality profiling. Such testing would be accompanied by counseling on ways to maximize individual strengths and overcome personal weaknesses. For example, oral learners would be taught ways to study most effectively using their voices, while introverts might be introduced to more intimate ways to communicate, such as using the Internet.

Advising Learners. With more factual and background information available prior to counseling sessions and greater information available to learners and staff, student services professionals would concentrate more on individualized developmental advising and less on communicating repetitive information about degree and program requirements. Counseling and advising sessions would be conducted via multiple delivery modes including personal visits, telephone, Internet, and interactive television.

Supporting Learners. The diverse support mechanisms from student and academic affairs would be integrated through searchable online student support centers which students, faculty, and student services personnel could use to access myriad resources for student tracking, tutoring, technology-assisted learning, risk intervention, and student development activities. These highly sophisticated systems would link currently separate divisions, but would appear to users as a transparent integrated support system and would include such services as student orientation delivered over CD-ROM or the Internet, adaptive devices for disabled students, computerized early warning alert systems, and online tutoring.

Connecting Learners. Linked closely to the role of supporting learners, this functional area would include programs, processes, activities, and technologies that help connect students to one another and to the institution. A variety of powerful networking technologies as well as traditional college systems would be used to build communities of learners, which extensive research has shown can increase academic performance and persistence. This burgeoning area would include learning communities, interactive and online class discussions and activities, mentoring programs, and technology-facilitated student activities.

Forwarding Learners. This area would facilitate the next step for the student making the transition from the community college to work, community service, or further education. Technology-enhanced transition mechanisms would include computerized university degree audits, electronic transfer agreements, and résumé or portfolio maintenance as part of the student smart card; searchable databases of job openings, and occupational recruitment available via satellite or the Internet.

The above framework paints a portrait of student services that is ongoing rather than bound to a semester-driven, "feast or famine" schedule; that is holistically focused on the comprehensive needs of students rather than on departmental or organizational boundaries; and that uses technology to link students and support learning anytime and anyplace. We may seem to have returned to the realm of fantasy and fairy tales; however, all the technology applications described here are already developed, in place, and being tested, at least in rudimentary form, in some community colleges today. The only magic involved is the power that arises when dedicated professionals equipped with the latest technological tools become committed to reinventing their student affairs operations not simply to provide student services, but to facilitate fully the development and learning of community college students in the 21st Century.

References

Baier, J. L., & Strong, T. S. (Eds). (1994). *Technology in Student Affairs: Issues, Applications, and Trends*. Lanham: University Press of America.

Bloland, P. A., Stamatakos, L. C., & Rogers, R. R. (1996, March/April). "Redirecting the Role of Student Affairs to Focus on Student Learning." *Journal of College Student Development*, 217-226.

Doucette, D. (1997, February). "The Community College Niche in a Competitive Higher Education Market." *Leadership Abstracts*, 10(2). Mission Viejo, CA: League for Innovation in the Community College.

Green, K. C. (1997). *The 1997 National Survey of Information Technology in Higher Education*. Encino, CA: The Campus Computing Project.

Green, K. C. (1999). *The 1999 National Survey of Information Technology in Higher Education*. Encino, CA: The Campus Computing Project.

Herndon, J. B., Kaiser, J., & Creamer, D. S. (1996, November/December). "Student Preferences for Advising Style in Community College Environments." *Journal of College Student Development*, 637-648.

Milliron, M. D, & Leach, E. R. (1997, October). "Community Colleges Winning Through Innovation: Taking on the Changes and Choices of Leadership in the Twenty-First Century." *Leadership Abstracts*, Special Edition. Mission Viejo, CA: League for Innovation in the Community College.

O'Banion, T. (1997a). *A Learning College for the 21st Century*. Published jointly by the American Association of Community Colleges and the American Council on Education. Phoenix, AZ: Onyx Press.

O'Banion, T. (1997b). *Creating More Learning-Centered Community Colleges*. Mission Viejo, CA: League for Innovation in the Community College.

Rooney, M. (1996, Winter/Spring). "Ron Bleed, Maricopa Info-Tech Vice Chancellor, Sees Critical Role for Student Service Professionals." *Eleven Update: The A.C.P.A. Commission XI Newsletter* (World Wide Web edition). [Online]. Available: www.acpa.nche.edu/comm/comm11/upindex.htm.

Sacks, P. (1996). *Generation X Goes to College: An Eye-Opening Account of Teaching in Postmodern America*. Chicago: Open Court.

CHAPTER 6

KEEPING UP TO SPEED WHEN YOU'RE MOVING TOO FAST ALREADY: INSTRUCTIONAL TECHNOLOGY STAFF DEVELOPMENT PROGRAMS AND USER SUPPORT

Lynn Sullivan Taber

"Will you walk a little faster?" said a whiting to a snail,
"There's a porpoise close behind us, and he's treading on my tail."
-Lewis Carroll, *Alice's Adventures in Wonderland*

Many people in developed countries feel as though a "porpoise is treading on their tail." Given the ubiquity of telecommunication advances, we must learn to move with the world, but often we find keeping up the pace somewhat difficult. Examples abound. Many banks transfer funds electronically, so we can no longer float checks, gaining a few free days before the check will clear. Many grocery stores have transferred their inventories to databases and require computer transactions in order to sell goods. In many industries, when the computer is down, we wait. We wait until the computer is up again. Smaller companies or stores changing computer operating systems or major software risk losing sales or being unable to generate a payroll until the bugs are worked out. The preponderance of information available through e-mail communications, the media, and the Internet bombard and overwhelm us. In fact, many of us sense in our everyday lives that we are not only failing to keep up, but also falling behind. We feel the push to "walk a little faster."

People throughout the world are in the process of adapting to this heightened pace, and those involved in the teaching and learning processes are no exception. Two-year colleges pride themselves on their ability to be responsive and innovative. To live up to this reputation, these institutions must light the way by assisting faculty, students, and communities to access and effectively use the variety of technological advances erupting worldwide.

When confronting challenges such as those presented by our increasingly digital society, it is useful for administrators and faculty to have data about the current situation and options to explore. There is no one way to approach the challenges presented by instructional technology advances; we can learn from the experiences of others, including community colleges that are on the cutting edge.

To gather baseline data and discover options for working efficiently and effectively with instructional technology, the researcher conducted a study with the following objectives:

1. To identify the type and estimate the extent of instructional technology and faculty development presently in community colleges
2. To identify the type and estimate the extent of instructional technology user support presently available in community colleges
3. To summarize the findings, to identify trends and institutional examples that will inform, and to suggest applications for practice

The findings of this study are presented in this chapter.

Integrating Instructional Technology into the Classroom

> "The time has come," the Walrus said,
> "To talk of many things:
> Of shoes–and ships–and sealing wax–
> Of cabbages–and kings–
> And why the sea is boiling hot–
> And whether pigs have wings."
> -Lewis Carroll, *Alice's Adventures in Wonderland*

Colleges throughout the world realize the importance of incorporating technological advancements into their institutions. Wide-ranging discussions are ongoing as college personnel consider what to do about incorporating technology into the classroom, when to do it, how to do it, and (especially) how to finance it. Educational professionals' versions of "shoes–and ships–and sealing wax," and "whether pigs have wings," with regard to instructional technology, may be heard at conference tables, at professional meetings and seminars, on listservs, and through practically any other discussion medium involving educators. In a 1995 study conducted by the Community College League of California, for example, nearly 600 California community college trustees, faculty, administrators, staff, and students participated in forums held on ten campuses and at an annual convention. At each meeting, participants were asked to address the same question: "What skills and needs will students bring to our community colleges in the next five to fifteen years and how can our colleges respond in the best interest of students?" A summary of the responses follows.

1. A major curriculum demand will be to prepare students to hunt, gather, learn, and manufacture information.
2. Students are continually bombarded with technological stimulation. The curriculum will need to address the use of technology as an aide to learning. Students will expect educational stimulation beyond the traditional lecture format.
3. Colleges must develop technologies and strategies to deliver learning on demand, particularly for independent and distant learners (including those at work-based sites).
4. Some community college leaders believe the curriculum will need to be adapted to distance learning technology and to the technical advances of both students and the institution.
5. Faculty will need ongoing training in advanced technology.
6. Colleges should encourage instructor retraining to meet shifting curriculum demands.

(Community College League of California, 1996, pp. 8-9)

Although these responses emerged from the California system, it is likely that two-year colleges in most states would have provided similar observations.

This chapter does not argue the merits of instructional technology. The working assumptions are: (1) technology in support of instruction can be effective in enhancing student learning if used appropriately, and (2) technology can be efficient in making education available to a larger number of individuals than a campus classroom location can.

Issues about these changes in the learning and teaching processes have arisen as a result of discussions about the integration of technology into the classroom:

[Technology] has improved access to resources, brought about effective and efficient delivery of instruction, addressed various student learning styles, enabled distance learning, and increased the interest of students. The primary teaching methodology of faculty is being transformed from the traditional "lecture and listen" to a more dynamic interactive process. As a result of the training, a faculty member becomes a facilitator of learning rather than the "fount of knowledge." (Henderson, 1996, p. 4)

The future direction is clear: faculty are well advised to become technologically literate and innovative in the classroom.

Instructional Technology Faculty Development

Despite the advances of technology, some institutions have not integrated technology into their classrooms. In addition to inadequate financial resources, two other major factors contribute to this lack of technology use. One has to do with a lack of trained personnel capable of selecting and maintaining appropriate hardware and software. The other concerns the need for faculty who are trained to use discipline-specific technologies in the classroom or for distance education:

The critical role of teachers in effective learning means that all must have training, preparation, and institutional support to successfully teach with technology. . . . Few teachers have had either teacher education or field experiences that enable them to be effective distance education teachers or successfully use technology in their own classroom. (Office of Technology Assessment, 1989, p.17)

Faculty must also dedicate time to self-training because of the increasing gap between the preparation and expectation levels of students and faculty. Today's students are more likely to be computer literate and to expect to use technology to accomplish their academic and occupational goals. Alvarez (1996) describes these students thus:

Students who grow up in a technological age will not accept lectures that fail to draw upon the information resources on the Internet and elsewhere. Schools that do not provide their faculty with classrooms where dynamic audio and visual media are easily used will be unable to attract good students. (p. 2)

Because the effectiveness of student learning may be influenced by expertise in the use of instructionally-related technologies,[1] training and development must be available and accessible to two-year college faculty. Surveying two-year colleges to determine the type and level of faculty development in instructional technology currently under way, and identifying programs and activities that are transportable to other campuses, can provide ideas and insights for faculty and administrators. Therefore, the first question this study poses is, *"To what extent do community colleges presently offer faculty development in instructional technologies?"*

Providing User Support for Faculty

Unlike the instructional technology literature, which offers an abundance of articles, examples, product descriptions, and research studies, a comprehensive search of the user support literature reveals very little research and few observations about faculty user support services in two-year colleges. Sources researched include the ERIC data base from 1990 to the present; the *Journal of Educational Technology*; the 1996 and 1997 convention programs of the League for Innovation in Technology and the American Association of Community Colleges; and selected National Association of College and University Business Officers (NACUBO) journals published since 1995. A significant source of ideas and information is provided in the instructional technology listserv, www.aahe.org/general/partner_tlt.htm, managed by Steven W. Gilbert of the American Association of Higher Education. The organization is called the Teaching, Learning & Technology Affiliate of AAHE - The TLT Group - and membership is free. Several educators wrote that increased user support services would be required, but did not address the topic in depth. For example, one wrote: "Hardware is no longer the primary cost consideration in information technology. . . . The surprise for most of us was the need for continuing or even expanding support activity" (Barone, 1996, p. 11).

Experts who can provide prompt troubleshooting services for hardware and software problems are essential for faculty who rely on technological tools to deliver instruction. As faculty learn more about technology, or as new technologies become available, questions and

---

[1] As yet, there is no conclusive, widespread evidence in the research literature that the use of technology in the classroom improves student learning.

problems arise that require technical assistance. In this study, services designed to address these kinds of needs are referred to as user support activities.

In spite of the dearth of published information currently available, informal communication in the field indicates that some colleges are making excellent progress in providing user support services. To uncover and disseminate information about such programs and services, the second question in the survey asked, *"To what extent and in what ways do selected two-year colleges provide user support services for faculty who are integrating technology into their classrooms?"*

Methodology

In 1997, all colleges of the League for Innovation in the Community College and the League's Alliance for Community College Innovation–approximately 500 institutions at that time–were mailed a survey (Appendix A) addressed to the individual responsible for staff development or a similar function. The survey asked respondents to identify (1) faculty development programs and services available for instructional technology and (2) an individual at the institution with responsibility for faculty user support services. This survey was developed by the author and was reviewed for accuracy, completeness, and appropriateness by instructional technology faculty at The University of Alabama[2] and by staff members at the League for Innovation. Three secondary objectives of the survey were aimed at identifying differences or similarities in instructional development opportunities and user support services by (1) student FTE, (2) college type (rural, suburban, or urban), and (3) the annual budget of each institution. While we suspected and found great similarity between the annual budget and FTE of each institution, we wanted to confirm our suspicion. In addition, in preparation for a later study on rural institutions, the author wanted to determine differences or similarities among rural, suburban, and urban institutions. A list of technical definitions for words used in the survey was compiled and may be found in Appendix B. This list was not attached to the e-mail survey. In retrospect, it would have been advisable to have included the list, as different interpretations of the terminology used may have led to varying responses.

---

[2] Appreciation is extended to Professors George Marsh, Anna McFadden, Barrie Jo Price, and Margaret Rice for their professional assistance and support.

Colleges were given five weeks to respond. One hundred fourteen colleges returned usable surveys, a 23 percent return rate; see Figure 6A for sample characteristics. Using SPSS software, a database was constructed that contains all of the reported data and was used for the data analysis underlying the study findings.

Selecting Exemplary Programs and Services

To identify colleges with strong programs, respondents were asked to name one or two colleges they perceived as having a particularly strong instructional faculty development program for technology. From the results of this snowball sample question, four institutions were selected for further exploration. In addition, reviews of program presentations on this topic were conducted in several places: (1) at the 1995 and 1996 National Institute for Staff and Organization Development (NISOD) conferences; (2) at the 1995 and 1996 American Association of Community Colleges (AACC) conferences; (3) at the 1995 and 1996 League for Innovation technology conferences; (4) through the identification of the 1996 and 1997 AACC's National Council on Staff, Program, and Organizational Development (NCSPOD) award-winning staff development programs; (5) through a review of the score achieved by each institution when the number of instructional technology services offered were tallied, and (6) by considering word-of-mouth information. From this input, four additional college programs were selected to be featured in this chapter, for a total of eight institutions.

We contacted managers of these programs for more detailed information about their *instructional development for technology* programs and services. Space does not permit detailed descriptions of all identified college programs and services; however, several institutions' program components were selected to be profiled in this chapter.

In the fax survey, respondents were also asked to indicate if their institutions provided *user support services* for faculty involved with instructional technology. Employees responsible for these services, if identified, were subsequently contacted through a short e-mail survey (Appendix C). Of those who replied, the institutions with the strongest user support services were contacted for additional information. Several institutions' programs for user support were selected to be profiled in this chapter. In sum, the researcher used several methods to survey two-year colleges with regard to (a) *faculty instructional technology development opportunities* and (b) *faculty user support* services for instructional technology.

Survey data analysis consisted of calculating descriptive statistics, including sums, means, and percentages, and creating crosstab tables to assist in looking for trends. The Mantel-Haenszel test for linear association was used when appropriate. Results of the data analysis are outlined in the findings sections of the chapter.

Sample Characteristics. The sample of 114 two-year colleges consisted of member and associate colleges of the League for Innovation in the Community College who returned a completed survey. The characteristics of the responding colleges are summarized in Figure 6A.

Figure 6A. Sample Characteristics of Responding Institutions

College Type		Student FTE		Annual College Budget	
Rural	40	0 - 3,000	41	0 - $10M	24
Suburban	35	3,001 - 6,000	24	$10.01M - $20M	26
Urban	35	6,001 - 9,000	17	$20.01M - $30M	15
Total	110	9,001 - 12,000	9	$30.01M - $40M	13
Unknown	4	12,000+	13	$40.01M - $50M	4
TOTAL	114	Total	104	$50.01M - $60M	3
		Unknown	10	$60.01M - $70M	5
		TOTAL	114	$70M+	6
				Total	96
				Unknown	18
				TOTAL	114

A phone conversation with Kent Phillipe on September 19, 1997, researcher at AACC, indicated that the study sample breakdowns of student FTE and annual college budget were similar proportionally to the entire population of AACC member colleges along these two dimensions. This was not the case when reviewing the sample in terms of college type (rural, suburban, urban). Fewer urban and more rural colleges responded to the survey than those represented in the AACC membership. This factor should be kept in mind when the study findings are considered.

Findings

Faculty Development in Instructional Technology in Two-Year Colleges

The study's first research question asked, "To what extent do community colleges presently offer faculty development in instructional technologies?" The following list includes the *most* commonly reported training opportunities for faculty (85 percent or more of the colleges):

1. The Internet
2. E-mail
3. Presentation Software
4. Use of the Internet for Instructional Purposes
5. The Use of Home Pages
6. The Development of Home Pages on the World Wide Web (WWW)

The survey question asked respondents to indicate which *training opportunities* were available on their campuses but *not* what equipment was located on campus. Although it is probable that the equipment required for the technology is on campus, we cannot conclude that this is the case.

The *least* commonly reported technologies and training opportunities (25 percent or fewer of the colleges) are included in the following list:

1. Photography in Visual Media Production
2. The Use of Virtual Labs (in chemistry, biology, automotive technology, etc.)
3. Television Production in Visual Media Production
4. Audio Recording (in automedia)
5. Audiographics in Distance Education

Each of these technologies requires more complicated and expensive technology than access to e-mail or to the Internet. The use of these technologies may also be perceived as more complicated or difficult.

Further analysis of the data yielded information regarding trends in instructional technology faculty development available by college type, student FTE, and annual college budget.

Faculty Development Opportunities by College Type

Figure 6B shows the *most* commonly mentioned training opportunities by rural, suburban, and urban colleges. While 90 percent of each category of colleges report training in e-mail, the Internet, and presentation software, only the suburban and urban institutions reported additional technology training in 85 percent or more of the sites.

Figure 6B. Instructional Technology Faculty Development Opportunities Most Available (85 Percent) by College Type

Rank	Rural	Suburban	Urban
1	Internet (92%)	E-mail (100%)	Internet (100%)
2	E-mail (92%)	Internet (97%)	E-mail (100%)
3	Presentation software (90%)	Presentation software (97%)	Presentation software (97%)
4		Home page development (94%)	Internet for instructional purposes (94%)
5		Home page use (94%)	Home page use (94%)
6		Internet for instructional purposes (94%)	Home page development (84%)
7		Databases (87%)	Tool software graphics (85%)
8		Tutorials (86%)	

The suburban and urban colleges are more likely to offer more faculty development opportunities in instructional technology than are the rural colleges. Almost all rural colleges, however, offer training in the three most popular uses of computer technology: Internet, e-mail, and presentation packages. The rural colleges are *least likely* to offer some of the more sophisticated instructional technology. For example, fifteen percent or fewer of the rural colleges offered training in auto recording in automedia, online editing, television production, and the use of virtual laboratories (i.e., for chemistry and biology classes). At least fifteen percent of suburban and urban colleges offered training in all surveyed technologies except audiographics.

Faculty Development Opportunities by Student FTE

The data were reviewed to determine if there were discernible trends of instructional technology faculty development opportunities by student FTE differences. Using the Mantel-Haenszel test for linear association, the levels of availability of training in each instructional technology were assessed across the five levels of student FTE. We explored these associations to determine if there were differences in availability due to student FTE size. Figure 6C presents the fourteen technology skills that showed a significant linear relationship.

Eight of the fourteen instructional technology training opportunities showed a significant linear relationship that was negatively skewed. That is, the largest FTE institutions were more likely to offer faculty development in the following technologies than were the smaller institutions:

1. Tutorial
2. Simulation
3. WWW Synchronous
4. WWW Asynchronous
5. Use of Online Video
6. Audio Media: Audio Recording
7. Virtual Labs
8. Use of Listservs

Figure 6C. Significant Relationships Between Faculty Development in Instructional Technology and Student FTE[3]

Technology or Skill	0-3,000		3,001-6,000		6,001-9,000		9,001-12,000		12,000+		Significance
	n	%	n	%	n	%	n	%	n	%	
Hypermedia	10	28	12	52	16	94	7	78	8	73	.000***[4]
Develop. CD ROM Present.	4	11	15	65	14	82	5	56	6	55	.000***
Audio Media: Audio Record.	4	11	3	13	4	27	3	38	5	50	.002***
WWW Synchronous	17	45	14	64	11	69	8	89	10	83	.002***
Online Editing Tech.	6	17	7	30	10	59	4	44	6	50	.006***
Asynch. Environments	11	31	9	41	11	79	7	78	6	55	.006***
WWW Asynchronous	17	52	16	70	11	73	7	78	10	91	.01***
Video Editing	6	17	11	48	9	60	4	50	5	46	.015**
Use of Listservs	17	47	13	54	11	65	6	67	9	82	.03*
Use of Chat Rooms	11	31	9	39	11	69	4	44	7	58	.036*
Virtual Labs	6	17	8	35	5	31	4	44	5	46	.04*
Tutorial	22	61	18	82	14	83	8	89	10	83	.05*
Simulation	15	41	15	68	10	63	5	63	8	73	.05*
Use of Online Video	9	25	7	30	7	44	3	38	6	55	.05*
Total Possible Responses for Each Category	40		24		17		9		13		

[3] The shaded cell in each row contains the greatest percentage of schools offering professional development in that technology. The level of significance of the Mantel-Haenszel Test for Linear Association of each row is shown in the far right column.

[4] *** ≤ .010; ** ≤ .025; * ≤ .05

The following six instructional technology training opportunities showed a significant linear relationship in a shape approximating a normal curve, or more accurately, a hill:

1. Video Editing
2. Hypermedia
3. Develop CD Rom Presentations
4. Online Editing Techniques
5. Asynchronous Environments
6. Use of Chat Rooms

These findings suggest that mid-size institutions with a student FTE of between 6,001 and 9,000 are significantly more likely to offer training in the above technologies than are smaller or larger institutions.

Faculty Development Opportunities by Annual Budget

Training in the use of the Internet specifically for instruction is offered by all responding colleges with an annual budget of $20 million or larger, with the exception of the colleges in the $60 million to $70 million category. One hundred percent of the colleges with annual budgets over $60 million teach the use of databases. Internet, e-mail, and presentation software are taught in at least 87 percent of colleges, regardless of their annual budget. Faculty development in aspects of distance learning are least available in all two-year colleges.

As common sense would indicate, generally, training in the more expensive technologies is most available at the colleges with the largest annual budgets. The anomaly in the data regarding those schools with budgets in the mid-size range is addressed in the discussion section of this chapter.

Overall Assessment: Some Colleges Offer (Much) More Than Others

To compare the total numbers of training opportunities available in the responding institutions, we compiled the total number of *yes* or *no* responses each institution noted on its survey response form. A *yes* was assigned a value of two, and a *no* was assigned a value of one. If a college representative answered *yes* to every question on the survey, that perfect score would be 90. Forty-two of 114 colleges (37 percent) scored 71 or above (Figure 6D). The numbers associated with each variable category represent the number of colleges in that category. The percentages reflect the proportion of schools in each category that scored 71 or above.

This analysis suggests that urban colleges with student FTE of 3,001 to 9,000 and an annual budget of $20 million to $30 million or between $50 million and $70 million are most likely to offer a substantial proportion of the professional development opportunities in instructional technology listed in the study survey.

Figure 6D. Most Technology Development Available by College Type, Student FTE, and Annual Budget[5]

College Type			Student FTE			Annual Budget		
Type	**n**	**%**	**Student FTE**	**n**	**%**	**Budget**	**n**	**%**
Rural	9	23	0-3,000	10	25	$0-10M	5	21
Suburban	15	43	3,001-6,000	12	50	$10-20M	4	15
Urban	18	51	6,001-9,000	10	59	$20-30M	9	60
Total	**42**		9,001-12,000	3	34	$30-40M	6	46
			12,000+	5	38	$40-50M	1	25
			Subtotal	40		$50-60M	2	67
			Unknown FTE	2		$60-70M	3	60
			Total	**42**		$70M+	2	34
						Subtotal	32	
						Unknown	10	
						Total	**42**	

[5] The survey question asked about availability of training, not attendance at such training. As a result, we have no way to judge how many college faculty and staff are making use of these professional development opportunities.

Summary: Faculty Development Findings

At least 85 percent of all responding colleges reported faculty development opportunities in six areas:
1. Internet
2. E-mail
3. Presentation Software
4. Internet for Instructional Purposes
5. The Use of Home Pages
6. The Development of Home Pages on the WWW

When trying to establish the extent to which community colleges presently offer faculty development in instructional technologies, it is helpful to review the technologies with the least amount of training available. Across all institutions, five development opportunities are least (25 percent) available:

1. Photography in Visual Media Production
2. The Use of Virtual Labs
3. TV Production in Visual Media Production
4. Audio Recording in Automedia
5. Audiographics in Distance Education

Rural, suburban, and urban colleges rarely offer development opportunities in TV production, in visual media production, audio recording in automedia, or audiographics in distance education. Of the development opportunities listed on the survey, audiographics in distance education is offered least often. Training in the use of virtual laboratories is not common in rural or urban institutions or in colleges with less than 3,000 FTE.

One result suggests that mid-size institutions with a student FTE between 6,001 and 9,000 are more likely to offer training in certain technologies, such as chat rooms, online editing techniques, video editing, hypermedia, developing CD Rom presentations, and use of asynchronous environments, than are smaller or larger institutions. This is a perplexing finding, and a follow-up study to uncover the reasons behind these relationships would be helpful. Such a study could include determining if the particular mid-sized institutions that responded to this survey were recipients of federal or private foundation grants focused on expanding technology available to faculty and students. This might not explain the entire finding, however, because online editing techniques and the use of chat rooms are not expensive instructional technologies.

User Support Services

The second research question of this study was, *"To what extent and in what ways do selected two-year colleges provide user support services for faculty who are integrating technology into their classrooms?"*

Survey Results

The survey asked respondents to name the individual(s) responsible for user support in their institutions. The phrase "user support services" was not defined so answers may have been based on different assumptions. Of the respondents, 36 (22 percent) did not report a name, 63 (55 percent) wrote an individual's name with a title such as dean or director, and 15 (13 percent) mentioned an individual with a title specific to the user support function.

Two points must be made here. The first is that the reporting of titles that do not describe user support activities does not mean that no user support activities or services are provided by the people holding those titles. The second point is that titles specific to a function, service, or value tend to indicate an institutional commitment to a function, service, or value.

To determine if the institutions' annual budgets had an effect on user support staff titles, we analyzed the survey data and determined that no institutions with an annual budget of at least $40 million reported an employee with the user support function specifically in her or his position title.

Summary: User Support Findings

An interesting finding is that just 15 colleges (13 percent) reported having an employee with a title specific to the user support function. We found no distinguishable difference between the frequency of user support titles among rural, suburban, and urban colleges; 13 to 15 percent of each type reported specific titles. We have recently seen an increase in the number of technology or information services positions at the vice-presidential level in two-year colleges. As colleges become more aware of the importance of providing comprehensive user support, we expect an increase in positions focusing on the delivery of user support services.

When examining the data for student FTE differences, it was noted that colleges with 9,001-12,000 FTE had the largest percentage (22 percent) of positions with user support titles. However, this was not substantially different from the other FTE categories and the "n"s were small.

No institution with an annual budget of $40 million or more reported having an employee with a specific title including the words "user support." These institutions reported individuals with more general titles, including instructional technologist, computer technician, programmer/trainer, and network manager. In fact, the largest percentage of institutions, 52 percent, reported that user support was the responsibility of staff with more general titles including deans, directors, network managers, or programmer/trainers. Some of the positions reported to an administrative vice president; others could be found in the academic function. More than one-third of the institutions for which the researcher had annual budget data did not list a user support contact person at all. Descriptions of some institutions' user support programs and services appear in the following paragraphs.

Model Community College Programs

In addition to having an opportunity to report faculty development and user support services, each survey respondent was asked to indicate one or two of the "best professional development for technology programs" in the United States. This snowball sample technique yielded the names of four institutions: Maricopa Community Colleges (AZ), especially Glendale Community College; Miami-Dade Community College District (FL) and the Kendall Campus in particular; Johnson County Community College (KS); and Fayetteville Technical Community College (NC). In the following pages, we highlight selected aspects of the programs and services offered at these institutions, as well as programs at four additional colleges: Mott Community College (MI); Metropolitan

Community College (NE); Monroe Community College (NY); and Schoolcraft College (MI). These four additional institutions were selected using a method described earlier in this chapter.

Maricopa Community Colleges

Glendale Community College (GCC) of the Maricopa Community Colleges sponsors a Training and Employee Development Center (TED). The Center's mission is "to provide quality comprehensive learning opportunities that are courteous, timely, and responsive to employees' needs, thereby enhancing GCC's ability to provide quality education and service to its students and the community" (www.gc.maricopa.edu/~TED/ mission.htm). Glendale recently inaugurated a new approach, the Instructional Palette, for using technology to enhance learning:

> The Instructional Palette provides faculty members with an array of technical tools and electronic resources from which they can select when designing their courses. These tools and resources are simple to set up and use, readily available, easily integrated with each other, and accommodating of differences in subject matter and teaching style. The Instructional Palette provides for widespread access to information consistent with laws regarding copyright, enhanced use of a variety of educational strategies, and extensive means for communication, both publicly and privately, in formal and informal environments, to benefit a diverse group of learners. Some faculty members are already using the instructional strategies that the palette provides, so there is a wealth of expertise to share with others. However, as more faculty explore the design possibilities, we think that we will discover new uses and more effective combinations of elements, especially as students begin to use these tools themselves. (Page 1, Instructional Palette, URL: www.gc.maricopa.edu/~TED/mission.htm)

At the time of the survey, the suite of available tools consisted of productivity tools and a range of network resources to promote expanded learning, critical thinking, personal development, and civic responsibility. Tools included Windows95, Microsoft Office97 (Word, Excel, Access, and PowerPoint), a choice of Web browser (Netscape or Internet Explorer), enhanced utilities (including FTP and ZIP clients), and 10 Mb of personal storage space on the network. E-mail and computer conferencing are included. The institution's goal is to make the suite available to all students, faculty, and staff.

The staff believes that the following considerations are important when considering a palette approach to integrating technology into instruction:

- Is the network easily maintained?
- Is the palette expandable?
- Can the institution provide adequate support for the tools?
- Can faculty and students access the palette easily?
- Does the network storage accommodate the enrollment patterns of students and the pacing of their educational careers at minimum cost? (Page 2, Instructional Palette, www.gc.maricopa.edu/~TED/ mission.htm).

The Innovation Center at Glendale Community College

The Innovation Center helps faculty and other staff find, develop, and implement projects that involve multimedia, databases, or publishing. "Multimedia projects incorporate text, sound, graphics, and full-motion video into highly engaging and widely-accessible learning environments" (www.gc.maricopa.edu/~IC/ projects.html). The Center has the resources to develop and produce these projects, but it also can identify multimedia material available commercially. Some database projects involve collecting and organizing new data, and others involve making data already collected accessible. Projects that involve publishing, linking, or updating information for the classroom or for campus, community, or world audiences comprise the third category.

Many projects encompass more than one of the types described above. Examples of current or completed projects include a multimedia physical science project, a database of international students, and computerized testing for the departments of nursing, psychology, and mathematics.

User Support Services at Maricopa's Glendale Community College

A unit of the Training and Employee Development Center (TED), the Technology Help Desk's main function is to provide technical support for

Glendale Community College's employees. Users may request hardware, software, and communication services. The Technology Help Desk is staffed from 7:00 a.m. to 6:00 p.m. Monday through Thursday and on Fridays between 7:00 a.m. and 4:30 p.m.

Miami-Dade Community College District

Miami-Dade Community College District (MDCCD) has a long history of commitment to providing faculty development of all types. A well-known department at Miami-Dade, the Center for Faculty, Staff and Program Development, has recently been renamed College Training and Development (CT&D) and has reevaluated its vision, mission, scope, and objectives. According to Mardee Jenrette, District Director of Training, Development, and Project Implementation at MDCCD, the purpose of the CT&D is "to help employees develop skills needed for current jobs, assist them in responding to job changes, and prepare them for future job requirements." The unit will serve all faculty, staff, administrators, and full- and part-time students directly and indirectly. In addition to expanding from an effort previously focused on the Kendall campus to one with a collegewide focus, the CT&D has been conducting focus groups and using other vehicles to identify training priorities, share ideas, and listen to concerns as they move in new directions. Exemplary college programs are being identified so they can be shared more broadly. Priority programming areas include training to enhance student learning and student success and training in technology. Student success training will include classroom strategies for faculty, academic advisement skills and knowledge building for full-time and adjunct faculty and for student services personnel, teaching fundamentals for new full-time and adjunct faculty, and workforce development. Technology training will allow the college to implement the recommendations of the Florida Software Consortium and the College Technology Committee to assist departments as they come online or upgrade and to support expanded use of educational applications.

The first series of workshops offered through MDCCD's new CT&D included introductions to Windows and to a variety of software applications, including word processing, spreadsheet, database, presentation, electronic grade books, multimedia, authoring, Internet, e-mail, and Web basics software. Workshops on specialty software such as PhotoVista for Macintosh users and QuickTime VR construction were also offered. Ongoing employee assessment will determine needs and offer assistance in these computer skill areas: (1) basic skills; (2) productivity skills; (3) advanced computer maintenance skills; (4) online resource skills; (5) online instruction skills; (6) computer media skills (graphics, animation, sound, and video); (7) presentation skills; (8) authoring skills; (9) classroom assessment and evaluation skills; and (10) classroom instruction skills. Future training may be delivered via multimedia tutorials, videotapes, books, simulations, and learning and review sessions.

Faculty are involved in delivering development experiences at MDCCD. Using a faculty rotation strategy, some are hired to conduct or develop workshops. This rotation takes up 40 percent of the faculty member's time and an adjunct faculty member is hired to cover the participant's classes.

Marie Nock, Director, College Training and Development, outlined four challenges for continual instructional technology faculty development: (1) serving the entire college well since human resources were not increased as the service area expanded from one campus to collegewide, (2) finding ways to get time for faculty to develop courseware, (3) networking all departments, and (4) placing computers on the desks of the 600 remaining faculty. Nock noted that part of her vision is the importance of linking instructional technology faculty development to the organizational development of the institution. She believes that integration of technology into the curriculum requires planned change. Finally, she underscored the fact that most faculty did not come to the community college with technology skills, noting that "they need to be trained, given incentives, recognition, options, and time to make the desired state a reality."

User Support Services at MDCCD

This section of the chapter was contributed by Robert Calabrese, Associate Dean for Learning Resources at the Kendall Campus of the Miami-Dade Community College District via a personal e-mail communication on September 11, 1999. The blurring of lines between the types of technology-based services required by students, faculty, and staff for educational and administrative issues prompted MDCCD to develop a Division of Learning Resources at each of its campuses. Learning

Resources includes the Campus Network Services, Library, and Media Services departments. The logic for this amalgamation was purely based on the needs of students, faculty, and staff. Consider a faculty member developing an instructional tool or needing to use a computer in the classroom, a staff member seeking methods for improving the scheduling of classrooms, or an administrator attempting to design a new student computer laboratory. Some faculty and staff members have the time and skills to accomplish these tasks; others do not. The institution must determine the costs of staff training, design consulting, construction errors, maintenance problems, and the operation and evaluation of the product or facility. Training is an excellent solution, but many personnel need a place for ongoing support or someone to provide services for them. If an individual cannot master all the required skills, a project which could have very positive implications for the students and ultimately for the institution may be forgotten or delayed.

The learning resources structure was implemented in August 1998 on a collegewide basis after several years of campus trials to resolve these and other issues. The five associate deans for learning resources currently administer approximately 2,950 faculty and staff accounts and 8,500 total computers on the college's collective academic and administrative network, which spans six campuses, two outreach centers, and numerous ancillary sites. We are responsible for ensuring that departments are assisted in the design, construction, maintenance, operation, and evaluation of all technology projects; that staff adhere to the standards developed for the purchase of equipment and materials; and that campuses are not duplicating services or projects without consultation. The standardization, the sharing of ideas and best practice issues, and the individual talents of the associate deans have accelerated the implementation of major projects in departments, at individual campuses, and across the college. Finally, one of the most important outcomes of the implementation of the learning resource structure is its ability to champion the needs of the technology team and, ultimately, our students by understanding the consequences involved with the implementation of technology in the classrooms, laboratories, research spaces, and offices.

Johnson County Community College

Johnson County Community College (JCCC) in Kansas provides

faculty development for instructional technology in several ways. Services come primarily from the Educational Technology Center (ETC) and the staff development program. In its inaugural year (1996-1997), the ETC offered Web Wizard workshops designed to train faculty how to develop and maintain their own Web pages, advise faculty on possible components for technologically-enhanced classrooms, and provide assistance in the development of online courses and such projects as creating the *Online Grammar Handbook*. The ETC is responsible to the Dean of Instruction who reports to the Vice President for Academic Affairs. Several projects are planned for the future:

1. Developing training materials and offering faculty workshops on digitizing and distributing text, graphics, sound, animation, and video over the Web
2. Exploring and testing the use of Web-based forms, Web database access, Web testing, Web forums, and Web-based interactivity for instructional uses
3. Exploring the potential instructional applications of QuickTime VR, VRML, 3D modeling, digital animation, voice recognition systems, personal digital assistants, Internet Explorer, and desktop digital video conferencing
4. Continuing to upgrade and acquire appropriate hardware, software, and personnel for the ETC to facilitate the development of interactive media and other instructional computing projects, provide faculty access to a media development center of instructional technology tools, provide the opportunity for research and development on topics related to instructional technology and the curriculum, and provide appropriately equipped ETC training labs for staff development computer training and to support the development by faculty of interactive instructional materials.

Faculty are invited to submit formal proposals for instructional computing projects. A detailed application must be completed, including statements about the intended audience, objectives of the project, and resources and materials needed to implement the project. After approval to proceed is obtained from the faculty member's program director, the ETC conducts a technical evaluation of the project, establishing a timeline; detailing required equipment; outlining audio, video, and computer generated image requirements for the project; and establishing whether these multimedia assets exist (on laser disk, disk, or tape) or must be created. If the proposer's division administrator approves the plan, a development team is created to work with the faculty member. The faculty member's involvement in the project includes several activities:

- Provide the content and the initial script for the project
- Work with ETC staff to locate print media, existing graphics, and text for the project
- Work with the ETC to story board the project
- Secure copyright permissions
- Participate in ongoing team project meetings
- Participate in training sessions and forums related to the successful completion of the project

Jonathan Bacon, the ETC's coordinator, noted that it is "not a truism that faculty are not interested," citing the substantial response from faculty to these initiatives.

The ETC also collaborates with the college's Staff Development Center for Teaching and Learning, which reports directly to the Vice President for Academic Affairs. Collaborations between the two units include working together on the college's Distance Learning Team, and supporting faculty instructional technology projects. The Distance Learning Team was established to provide a network of support for faculty efforts in distance learning. The October 1996 newsletter of the Center for Teaching and Learning reported these team goals:

1. Serving as a resource for faculty and staff in the area of distance learning and technology
2. Developing distance learning instructional models that can be implemented and refined by faculty involved in distance learning
3. Developing recommendations for distance learning policies and procedures

At the time of the survey, over 60 JCCC faculty were offering either an entire course or part of an on-campus course with some form of distance learning.

According to Helen Burnstad, Director of Staff Development, the Center for Teaching and Learning is "by faculty and for faculty." One of the Center's collegewide technology projects, funded with assistance from major grants from IBM and Apple, has trained faculty to use technology in the classroom. Computer and Information Systems (CIS) faculty secured release time to work as administrative interns with the project. Staff development activities also include the efforts of a Technology Training Coordinator who organizes software training sessions for all college staff.

User Support Services at Johnson County Community College

The Executive Director of Information Services oversees the work of three categories of user support services: administrative computer, network, and academic computer. The college is implementing BANNER, a commercial product designed to manage its student, financial aid, human resources and payroll, admissions and records, and finance systems. A bundle of user support services are available to college staff who are involved in the implementation process. The administrative computer services function provides these support activities. The network services unit provides network users with support by staffing a Help Desk and by providing assistance with Internet-related needs, microcomputer hardware and software support, microcomputer maintenance, and voice communications assistance. Academic Computer Services gives support to the academic computer labs, including technical support, and provides instructional support services.

Fayetteville Technical Community College

Fayetteville Technical Community College (FTCC) is North Carolina's second largest community college, serving over 40,000 students each year. FTCC is the state's leader in online distance education courses. The number of online offerings has grown steadily since courses were first offered in 1995. The College offered 24 online courses in the fall 1997 semester, and in the spring 1998 semester, 33 online courses were offered, enrolling over 540 students in a range of courses, including expository writing, chemistry (lecture only), auditing, embalming theory, and introduction to video concepts. Current Virtual Campus "desktops" may be visited at www.faytech.cc.nc.us/infodesk/vcampus/vcnframe.html.

FTCC's Virtual Campus Project, initiated in the fall 1997 semester by President Larry B. Norris, represented the college's vision to expand online distance education offerings to include at least three complete degree programs by the fall semester 1999. Two of the three targeted programs are statewide programs: Funeral Service Education and Media Integration Technology. The other targeted program, Speech-Language Pathology Assistant, is a regional program offered by only three other North Carolina community colleges. To reach its distance education goals sooner than planned, the Virtual Campus Project complemented online offerings with the college's telecourse and course-by-cassette offerings; fourteen were offered in the spring 1998 semester, enrolling nearly 300 students. The Virtual College Project also offered courses through its North Carolina Information Highway (NCIH) networked interactive classroom; three courses were offered in the spring 1998 semester, broadcast to four sister community colleges.

Two instructors have been given half-time teaching loads so they can devote time to faculty development activities for the Virtual Campus Project. All faculty wishing to teach one of the Internet-based classes must complete the course entitled *Designing an Online Classroom*, developed by one of Fayetteville's faculty members, and faculty who teach Internet-based classes are provided the most advanced computers available at the college. Technology workshops are held throughout the year for all faculty wishing to improve their computer skills. These workshops normally concentrate on new hardware and software releases and their applicability to instructional delivery. Attending technology workshops and enrolling in *Designing an Online Classroom* are considered normal professional development activities and do not generate faculty release time.

Fayetteville is the home of Ft. Bragg, a major Army base, so many members of FTCC's student body are serving in the military or are international students. This can sometimes result in major fluxes in enrollment. During the Gulf War, for example, the college lost 30 percent of its students. With Internet courses, some transferred military personnel can continue their coursework from remote locations. In addition, a handicapped student recuperating from surgery wrote that she appreciated having the Internet course option, but students have other reasons for taking online courses. For example, some students use Internet classes as an option when two courses they need are offered at the same time; the program allows these students to enroll in one "in person" course and one Internet course.

User Support Services at Fayetteville

The Data Management Office at FTCC provides user support for more than 1,500 computers in the instructional labs and faculty offices. A combination of full-time lab technicians and part-time student lab assistants accounts for approximately ten FTE support positions. The college has a maintenance contract that covers all hardware. One full-time technician and one part-time student assistant provide installation, maintenance, and upgrades for hardware and software. The Fayetteville user support providers report to the Office of the Associate Vice-President for Curriculum Programs. At Fayetteville, all user training for hardware and software is referred to as "user support."

Selected Program Components from Other Colleges

Mott Community College

Mott Community College (Michigan) anticipated the increasing demand for distance learning and made a commitment to develop a "sound and highly-respected" degree-granting telecourse program. In 1992, Mott's administration made the decision to offer two associate degrees entirely by distance learning. Prior to this decision, the matter of choosing which courses would be offered via distance learning was determined primarily by faculty interest. Distance learning courses tended to be offered by faculty who enjoyed trying new methods and innovations. The decision to offer entire degrees via distance learning meant that course offerings would be determined by degree and program requirements. Rather than distance learning offerings being the province of the 15 percent of the faculty who were innovative teachers willing to try something new, the distance learning program would have to depend on a large number of mainstream faculty who were more averse to taking risks with their careers and their professional images.

A broad-based approach to meeting this challenge involved the development of a comprehensive program model consistent with Mott's specific needs. Professional development needs were identified using the DACUM process, and an adapted version of DACUM was used to develop a *Standards and Practices* document that outlined requirements for faculty teaching distance learning courses.

Mott staff concluded that "competence leads to confidence." Mainstream faculty are willing to engage in distance learning when they are confident that what they are doing is professionally credible in their own eyes and those of their colleagues. The DACUM process helped build confidence because it engaged a large number of faculty working in collaboration to define the skills and competencies expected of them by their peers. According to Bill Angus (personal communication, January 19, 1998), Dean of Educational Technology at Mott, the significance of the phrase "competence leads to confidence" rests on the distinction between the small community of innovators who are willing to try new approaches of all kinds and the much larger population of mainstream faculty who need to become engaged and committed when a college decides to offer entire degrees by distance learning. Continuing assessment plays a critical role in providing feedback to facilitate innovative professional development, standards, and practices and in meeting the needs of Mott Community College's students, faculty, and staff.

Metropolitan Community College

In Omaha, Nebraska, Metropolitan Community College's (MCC) Faculty Development program is committed to achieving its vision of effectively using available technologies to provide educational opportunities that enhance student learning. Because MCC recognizes the diversity of technology training needs among faculty, the college maintains a traditional, broad-based laboratory curriculum permitting learners to focus on developing technology skills or to receive a wide range of individualized and project-based support. The college is capitalizing on opportunities to develop mutually beneficial partnerships with both local and national technologically advanced businesses, maximizing the potential benefits of the college's investment in technology-enhanced learning while further assuring the relevance of these efforts to the workplace of the next century. In the following paragraphs, several types of programs and services that are available for faculty to learn about instructional technology are described.

Traditional classroom and laboratory instruction is provided throughout the year on regularly scheduled faculty development days, evenings, weekends, and other convenient times for faculty schedules. Technology courses are available at the basic, beginning, intermediate, and advanced levels in the areas of computer basics, networking, information access, Windows, e-mail, personal information management tools, word processing and keyboarding, telephony, and Internet. A *Technology Skills Self-Evaluation Grid* is available to assess individual skill levels to determine which courses would be most appropriate. Course offerings in the broad technology components are keyed to the skill levels identified in the *Technology Skills Self-Evaluation Grid*.

In addition to traditional classroom software training, faculty have the opportunity to participate in online technology modules and numerous seminars such as Tools to Evaluate Online Courses, Technology and Human Existence, Maximizing Student E-Mail in the Classroom, and Incorporating Active Learning to the Distance Learning Classroom.

During the summer, *Advanced Media Seminars* are offered to faculty. During the 20-hour workshops, Instructional Design Services staff supports faculty in the design, development, and production of materials for use in distance education, technology classrooms, and online learning.

Media Skills Workshops (MSW) and *Distance Skills Workshops* (DSW) are adaptations of the Instructional Skills Workshop (ISW) originally developed under the auspices of the Ministry of Advanced Education, Province of British Columbia. Both workshops are 24 hours in length and are experientially based to provide participants with opportunities to create and to deliver presentations using appropriate media or a variety of distance learning delivery systems.

The *Jumpstart Project* is a collaborative partnership between Educational Services, Student and Instructional Services, and Instructional Design Services to encourage and to support faculty exploration and innovation in a learner-centered environment. The Jumpstart Project focus is on the development of modules, courses, and media to support student learning in the classroom and on the Web. Faculty who are selected to participate in this program are provided funding for release time and materials acquisition.

Support and training of part-time faculty in the use of program-adopted presentation technology is provided through specialized orientations and updates. A peer-based faculty support system that includes content experts, mentoring, faculty orientation, faculty resource representatives, and a multitude of classroom sessions to assist part-time faculty is available. As they incorporate technology into the classroom, this support can focus on orientation, integration, and assistance.

Faculty may also participate in Individualized Professional Development and Customized Training opportunities to enhance technology skills. These two options allow faculty the flexibility to learn technologies specific to their disciplines.

In 1998, MCC opened a Teaching, Learning, and Technology Center (TLTC). The TLTC is designed to provide an environment in which collaborative relationships can develop and participants can discover new techniques to promote learning. Participants can also learn strategies for continually improving the quality of instruction and service to students. The facility houses a technology training lab with desktop units that have state-of-the-art video, audio, and document conferencing capabilities and an interactive telephone lab for training sessions on telephone and voice mail technologies.

The Design and Support Service team of Instructional Design Services (IDS) is also located in the TLTC. The second floor facility houses multimedia production computers, digitizing flatbed scanners, digital cameras, and a complement of multimedia, presentation, graphic and imaging, Web authoring, and media production software. IDS team members work with both full- and part-time faculty, individually or in groups, to enable them to select, design, and produce course materials and use delivery methods that are most appropriate to content and diverse learning styles.

The Faculty Development office is coordinated by a full-time faculty member on release time for a two-year rotation. Along with this coordination, a part-time Technology Training Coordinator plans and schedules technology training support for faculty. These offices report to the Director of Personnel Development in the Office of Planning and Instructional Effectiveness area.

Instructional Design Services is made up of two teams. The Design and Support Services team consists of six full-time professionals with expertise in visual and graphic design, video and audio production, instructional design, Web page development, online course development, photography, multimedia software, and networking and computer maintenance. The Operations team is made up of five members with experience in broadcast engineering, audiovisual equipment repair, and television systems maintenance. The IDS teams report to the Director of Technology Enhanced Learning in the Vice President of Student and Instructional Services office.

A distinctive aspect of the faculty development program at MCC is that it is embedded in a collegewide Faculty and Staff Development Plan and Catalog of Courses. In addition to two collegewide events, Fall Opening and Spring Celebration, each year all employees are required to participate in a minimum of 32 contact hours of in-house faculty or staff development activities. As part of the 32-hour minimum, a core curriculum is designed each year and required of all employees. During the 1999-2000 year, one part of the collegewide core curriculum requirement is the completion of a technology-related course. The college requires supervisors and managers to support employees in developing the technical, professional, and leadership behaviors required for ongoing quality performance and to model those behaviors as well (MCC's Faculty and Staff Development Plan and Catalog of Courses, 1999-2000).

User Support Programs and Services

Instructional Design Services maintains a standard hardware profile and software load throughout the college's forty-two technology rooms and four distance learning rooms. All technology rooms include a multimedia networked computer, a visual presenter and VCR (a video disk player is available upon request), and either television monitors or a ceiling mounted projector for display. The standard software load consists of Windows 95, MS Office 97, Internet Explorer and Navigator, QuickTime

4.0, Real Player G2 and Media Player, Shockwave, Authorware, and Flash plug-ins, Astound 6.0 player, McAfee, and Adobe Reader.

IDS maintains a spare inventory of all hardware in the technology rooms and the standard software load including the operating system is "ghosted" onto a CD-ROM. This ensures minimum downtime for all resources in the technology rooms.

A multimedia computer technician providing on-call support during the 8 a.m. to 5 p.m. college work week rounds out the Design and Support Service's team. Additional technical support during the evening and weekend is provided through the college's Help Desk.

Monroe Community College

At Monroe Community College (MCC) in New York, the Office of Educational Technology Services and Professional Development (ETS/Professional Development) provides professional services and facilities to MCC students, faculty, staff, and administration. The office designs, develops, and supports instructional development for instruction and asynchronous learning–including the SUNY Learning Network–for local and distance education. The Office offers workshops, share sessions, conferences, classes, and consultation to all MCC employees. During 1995-96, 340 faculty and staff took at least one of the 111 classes and 806 sessions that were taught. Thirty-nine niche training sessions were presented on specialized topics for selected academic and administrative departments.

MCC has organized three units to deliver particular services: Instructional Technologies Development, Faculty Innovation Center, and Electronic Learning Center. The Instructional Technologies Development unit assists faculty and staff in developing courses, modules, and materials for use in the smart classrooms, the learning centers, distance learning, presentations, and conferences. Assistance in development, programming, or both, is offered in World Wide Web, courseware, multimedia, presentations, classroom materials, and research into new technologies. Consultation on developing instructional modules and materials is also available.

The Faculty Innovation Center (FIC) is located in a laboratory staffed by experts who provide consultation on courseware, technology, and World Wide Web development. Training activities are sponsored by the FIC in several areas: (1) multimedia development computers (Windows and Macintosh), (2) World Wide Web and Internet connectivity, (3) 35 mm slide and document scanning, (4) computer to videotape transfer, (5) color and laser printing, and (6) scheduling of and orientation to the smart classrooms. The Electronic Learning Center (ELC) features knowledgeable staff that support students in writing papers, developing projects, using the World Wide Web and Internet for research, using word processing and spreadsheet software, using databases, using or creating videotapes and audiotapes for courses, and performing in discipline-specific simulations.

The training area provides technical skill building activities for faculty and staff and manages associated training facilities. Several options are available: (1) a catalog of topical proficiency tracks with a schedule of session dates and times, (2) niche training on a variety of subjects, (3) information sharing workshops, including Celebrating Learning and the Brown Bag series, (4) professional development seminars or workshops as requested, (5) the ETS's Newsletter, (6) technology documentation ("recipe cards"), and (7) coordination of the training facilities.

Schoolcraft College

Sharon Szabo of Schoolcraft College (Michigan) described the college's faculty user support services (personal e-mail communication, August 4, 1997) as having two components: a Computer Information Systems (CIS) professor who divides his time between teaching students and helping faculty from other disciplines integrate technology into their classrooms, and a learning technologies team of faculty who help with faculty training, support, and special projects.

The faculty training program includes an extensive training class in Windows and Microsoft Office. After successful completion of this course, the instructor is provided a new computer for his or her office desk, and about 85 percent of the faculty have completed the training. These faculty are networked to a printer and have access to campus e-mail and the Internet. Additional sessions are scheduled for further training as requested by faculty. Individual tutoring time is available in a Learning

Technologies Office equipped with three computers that are connected to the Internet and to a scanner; all three also have zip drives.

Classroom projection systems are supplied when the faculty indicate need and merit. Forty-five percent of main campus classrooms and labs have some type of computer projector system with several more requests being processed. When these systems are in place, about 55 percent of the classrooms will be equipped with computer projection capability. Preliminary findings indicate that lack of sufficient resources still is a major concern.

Resources

> *Shake, shake, hazel-tree,*
> *Gold and silver over me!*
> -K. Webb, *Ashputtel*

There is no question that "keeping up to speed" requires an incoming flow of resources. However, the Community College League of California (1996) concluded that community college districts in the state must be prepared to serve students in spite of inadequate state support. A majority of states are encountering the challenge of reduced or level state support. A need exists for practitioners and researchers to describe the user support they need and the steps that colleges have taken or plan to take to address these user support needs. Requirements identified by users must be serviced in the short-term if the college is not to end up paying more and perhaps suffering serious setbacks in the future. Not all two-year colleges and scholars seem to have recognized this critical need. For example, a 1996 book published by the American Council of Education, *Managing Higher Education as a Business* (Lenington), does not mention technology. Yet allocations for technology will absorb larger and larger segments of college budgets now and in the foreseeable future.

The review of the literature and the telephone interviews with college officials revealed that the following organizations fund technology support programs in community colleges: IBM Instructional Technology Transfer Centers (11 two-year colleges), Apple Computer, Department of Labor Grants, Title III Grants, state-funded curriculum development programs (i.e., North Carolina, Minnesota, and California), and the National Endowment for the Humanities.

Common funding patterns across states or localities do not seem to exist. Westbrook and Kerr (1996) note a broad range of funding strategies for technology in education, including donations from business and industry; cooperative arrangements with manufacturers and suppliers of hardware and software; designated allocations from the state; individual entrepreneurial efforts by administrators, faculty, and parents; and small-scale school fund-raising events such as bake sales or car washes. Reallocations of the colleges' budgets are also frequently used to access funds, albeit at the expense of other college priorities.

Mast (1997) reports that "according to a 1996 benchmark study by the Financial Executives Institute and The Hackett Group, information technology costs–including labor and outsourcing–consume 2.2 percent of the average company's revenue" (p. 17). Although we did not obtain the percent of budget expenditures for technology from college respondents, a comparison of the current expenditure ratios for the nation's two-year institutions would be interesting.

Another consideration (Westbrook & Kerr, 1996) is the question of how to handle purchases and manage the planning and accounting for technology within the college or university structure. Traditionally, college budgets have not included designated line items for technology. Rather, educators have included costs under categories such as instructional supplies, instructional equipment, or administrative support. This makes comparison of expenses and sources impossible, a problem for suppliers, and also a problem for institutional planning and management.

A third funding issue (Westbrook & Kerr, 1996) relates to the effects of technology funding on access and equity: "The diversity of funding patterns, diffuseness of the budgetary data, and concerns about equity and access all make it difficult for us to perceive a significant issue that has yet to be thoughtfully addressed in American education: the recapitalization of schools as workplaces for students and teachers." They continue the argument:

> We must reconceive in a fundamental way our basic notions of what schools are, and thus also of how we think about funding schools. The amounts that schools now typically pay for instructional materials will be completely inadequate to provide

schools with the level of technology that many educators, policymakers, employers, and parents see as desirable. Perhaps most significantly, if we have only weakly managed to figure out how to provide these kinds of resources to schools on a one-time basis, then we have not even begun to think about how to do so in a way that continues over time, that sees the regular recapitalization of the educational workplace as a normal and expected expenditure. And determining the size and possible distribution of the needed resources is in fact the easy part of this calculation; the hard part is deciding if the large costs involved are really worth it, whether they add sufficiently to the educational enterprise to warrant our making the investment. This . . . is where the debates about school finance and the nature of education must come face to face with our social and political structure for thinking and deciding about. (Westbrook & Kerr, 1996, p. 51)

Colleges must also consider long-range planning and budgeting. West (1996) makes an interesting comparison:

We have to compare both the initial investments of each system and the ongoing operational costs. I cannot cite specific data, but intuitively I have to believe that over time a network infrastructure will be demonstrably less expensive than building and maintaining a traditional campus plant. For instance, we estimate that it would take $650 million of capital funds to construct a new campus for 15,000 students. For the same amount we can build out the networking infrastructure of our 22 campuses and provide a network with sufficient capability to handle the interactive video, high speed data and voice necessary to share instruction and information resources. To accomplish this trade-off we would need to have an average 5 percent increase in each campus' enrollment within existing resources. (p. 11)

Another approach to consider is using existing technology to reduce costs: "The Internet has the potential to encourage significant cost savings and the potential to generate new revenue sources . . . [could] realize a savings in terms of physical resources, instructional resources, or both" (Freund, 1996, p. 7). The Web, used properly and judiciously, can provide many instructional resources that might be otherwise unavailable.

While faculty attendance at professional conferences is often not possible due to limited funding, participation in virtual sharing is free or inexpensive. Participating in a discipline-specific listserv, for example, puts the faculty member in the company of experts and students in the field who share their experiences, research, and opinions on particular topics. The faculty member can participate whenever he or she has access to the Internet.

Software and professional publications appropriate to specific disciplines are increasingly available on the Internet; however, training in the use of search engines is required. As Freund (1996, p. 9) notes, "the resources of the Internet are different from those of today's libraries in that library collections have been well indexed by professionals." On the other hand, publications indexed in libraries, particularly books, experience a content time lag. One downside of relying on print media is that change in all spheres is continuous and fast. By the time books are printed and distributed, the information is often out of date.

The Best of the Best: A Proposed Model for Faculty Development and User Support for Instructional Technology

Drawing on the experiences, programs, and services of the colleges featured in this chapter, we have constructed a prototype program and present a list of suggestions to be considered when developing or enhancing community college instructional technology programs, services, and support. Many colleges must approach improvement in instructional technology in small steps; each institution must fashion its own collegewide technology plan, specific to its needs.

We will first present an overview of this model approach and suggest responsibilities that should be assigned to an oversight group. We will then suggest programs and services for colleges to consider offering, as they are able, for instructional technology faculty development and instructional technology user support. The model is not meant to be a rigid "must do" archetype; rather, we developed it to stimulate thought and discussion.

We suggest that a multiple-year institutional instructional technology plan be developed, and then updated annually. Input should be secured from faculty, administrators, representatives of instructional programs, experts in instructional technology, students, and stakeholders such as trustees, employers, and accreditation agencies. A call for suggestions and recommendations for specific goals and objectives should then go out to instructional areas, departments, and faculty. We suggest that priorities be set with some attention to the expected annual budget, but not restricted by that figure, as funding may become available through grants, donations, or both. The finished plan, including goals, objectives, and priorities must include human resources personnel and equipment purchases, upgrades, and maintenance. The plan should guide the grant-seeking activities prioritized by the college's development office. Significant college constituencies should be presented with the institutional instructional technology plan and assistance requested in securing grants, equipment, and donations. For example, employers are often willing to supply equipment if the college will offer training in the use of the equipment.

The institutional instructional technology plan must be fluid. If a significant grant is available for priority number four and priorities two and three have not yet been implemented, the college may decide to implement priority four and work on two and three later. Technologies and circumstances are constantly changing, so plans and personnel must be responsive to new opportunities that are consistent with the college mission.

Oversight Group

An oversight group or structure should be established, with membership consisting of those most involved with developing the instructional technology plan. This group may be the president's cabinet or a group of other representatives designated specifically to develop and monitor the plan. Suggested activities and responsibilities for such a group are listed below.

1. Coordinate and monitor the institutional instructional technology plan.
2. Review and recommend priorities for purchasing hardware and software.
3. Make decisions or recommendations to the board regarding distance education.

4. Make decisions regarding the establishment of technologically equipped classrooms or alternatives such as mobile technology stations.

5. Commission the design and implementation of a faculty instructional technology development plan. Each faculty member and the appropriate managers should annually put in writing an instructional technology development plan. The institution might decide to require several core workshops for all employees, then encourage elective training to complement the individual faculty member's plan. Metropolitan Community College (NE) offers an impressive array of training opportunities; those required of all employees include *TeamWork at MCC, Vision and Transformational Change,* and *Ethics of Choice.*

6. Define the meaning of user support. In this chapter, we have separated the faculty development function from user support. In some institutions, another distinction may make more sense. Johnson County Community College has chosen to channel its resources through administrative computer support, network services, and academic computer services.

7. Work to develop incentives for faculty who are actively integrating technology in their classrooms. Release time, stipends, paid sabbatical semesters, paid internships, other additional technological equipment, or financial support to attend instructional technology conferences could be considered. Consider awarding each faculty member a desktop computer and printer or other needed technological hardware or software upon completion of a core of instructional technology courses.

8. Create and implement lobbying plans to inform state legislators of community college instructional technology funding needs.

9. Monitor the institution's ongoing search for external funding.

10. Develop, review, and recommend board policy for technology related issues such as copyrights, ethical matters, and faculty load for distance education courses.

11. Encourage classroom assessment conducted by faculty to compare student learning outcomes in classes using instructional technology approaches and in classes without instructional technology tools and approaches.

12. Participate in other activities as determined by the institution.

We have focused in this chapter on *faculty development for instructional technology* and *user support services* for those learning about or using instructional technology. Faculty development cannot and should not always be considered separate from user support. However, we have created two suggestion lists for clarity of communication: one for faculty development and one for providing user support services. The suggestions are offered with the full realization that colleges operate under different circumstances. The following lists are designed to encourage discussion.

Faculty Development Components

1. Strongly encourage the college community to include considerations for faculty development when the collegewide technology plan is created or updated.
2. Support and encourage "for faculty, by faculty" programs for instructional technology.
3. Routinely identify training priority in key areas:
   a. basic skills
   b. advanced computer maintenance
   c. finding useful online resources
   d. discovering online instructional skills (e.g., chat rooms, sending class assignments in as attachments)
   e. use of computer media skills (e.g., graphics, animation, sound, video)
   f. creating presentations using technology
   g. authoring
   h. classroom assessment and evaluation
   i. classroom instruction skills
   j. distance education skills
4. Evaluate and encourage the use of appropriate commercial instructional multimedia materials.
5. When off-the-shelf products are not available, support an integrated approach to developing multimedia curricula by providing training, consultation, research, and support services for faculty.
6. Develop and offer faculty training in instruction designed specifically to enhance student learning and student success.

7. Develop training materials on topics such as digitizing and distributing information over the Web.
8. Provide faculty with opportunities to propose instructional technology projects that, if selected, will be supported with institutional resources. Glendale Community College's Innovation Center encourages multimedia, database, and publishing projects, and Johnson County Community College has a program that supports faculty instructional computing projects.
9. Provide faculty access to a media development center of instructional technology tools.
10. Facilitate development of interactive media and instructional computing projects. Johnson County Community College's Web Wizard workshop is designed to train faculty to develop and maintain their own Web pages, create components for technologically-enhanced classrooms, and provide assistance with the development of online courses.

User Support Services

Ideally, colleges support the faculty development and user support functions equally; in reality, however, colleges sometimes place more emphasis on faculty development than they do on user support. Because user support is essential when faculty are implementing strategies they have learned through faculty development, the two functions are vitally connected. Several strategies are available to promote user support and thereby enhance faculty development outcomes:

1. Explore and test new technologies.
2. Explore and test mechanisms for the creation and distribution of digital video and live feeds across the Web.
3. Explore and test the use of Web-based forms, database access, testing, forums, and interactivity for instructional applications.
4. Continue to upgrade and acquire appropriate instructionally related hardware and software.
5. Provide prompt troubleshooting services for hardware and software problems.
6. Evaluate the development and use of a suite of tools, utilities, and personal storage space for faculty use via a network.

7. Develop, maintain, and support technologically-enhanced classrooms.
8. Provide technical support for distance education programs.
9. If faculty agree, consider supporting the development of a "student desktop." At Fayetteville Technical Community College, the student desktop enables learners to view syllabi, participate in chat room discussions, ask for instructor assistance, receive and return assignments, or receive announcements.
10. Consider which organizational unit should be responsible for equipment maintenance contracts. If this responsibility is not assigned to the instructional technology user support area, consider naming a representative from user support to the unit charged with this responsibility.
11. Maintain student and faculty labs and faculty desktop computers.
12. Explore middleware tools such as Java, Javascript, CGI, Perl that can generate code for Internet-based instruction projects.
13. Determine the most efficient and effective organization chart and distribution of staff responsibilities between and among administrative computer, academic computer, and network services.
14. Classrooms dedicated to incorporating technology into instruction are needed. Consider an alternative nicknamed a COW (Henderson, 1996), a wheeled cart that contains equipment such as a computer with CD-ROM drive, laser disc player, audio speakers, and projection system. Such a cart could be reserved and moved easily to different classrooms.
15. Faculty need good communication with technology support staff to remain informed about the kinds of support that are available and how support may be accessed.
16. User support personnel can offer faculty training in solving hardware and software problems, thereby making users increasingly self-sufficient.

Conclusions

If you get ahead in this world, kid,
don't ever take no for an answer. Get it?
-P. Gallico, *Three Legends*

Persistence on the part of important college constituencies is a requirement for developing and enhancing community college instructional technology programs. When it comes to integrating technology, community colleges must never take "no" for an answer; they must instead find another way. Integrating this attitude into the culture of an institution is important to the success of instructional technology faculty development and user support programs, and to the collegewide technology program. At the same time, though, a word of caution:

We must remember that technology is simply a means to an end and that the faculty, departmental, and institutional goals and objectives with regard to students and teaching must be the focal point of our efforts. It is essential to find ways to bring faculty, administrators, and computer services personnel together to discuss problems in implementation. The idea is to insure that educational innovations are not divorced from strategic planning and technical support. (Noblitt, 1997, p. 39)

As West (1996, p. 11) notes, "The use of technology, and planning for it, is more a process than a destination or single outcome." It is a collegewide process that requires people to plan, persist, and then prevail. Community colleges may not always seem to be walking a little faster, but many are moving ahead at a steady pace and with a determined and persistent drive. With a long-term commitment to instructional technology and its contribution to student success, these colleges are figuring out how to keep the porpoise from treading on their tails.

References

Alvarez, L. R. (1996, May/June). "Technology, Electricity and Running Water." In Educom Review Staff, *Why technology? Educom Review*, 31(3), 1-3. Available: www.educom.edu/Web/pubs/pubHomeFrame.html.

Bacon, J. (1997, October). The Web Wizard Workshop: The Compressed Version. Preconference session presented at the League for Innovationin the Community College Conference on Information Technology, Atlanta, GA.

Barone, C. A. (1996, May/June). "Full Speed Ahead-With Caution." In Educom Review Staff, *Why technology? Educom Review*, 31(3), 3-5. Available: www.educom.edu/Web/pubs/pubHomeFrame.html.

Carroll, L. (1865). *Alice's Adventures in Wonderland*. In E. M. Beck (Ed.), (1980). *Bartlett's Familiar Quotations*. Boston, MA: Little, Brown and Company.

Community College League of California (1996). "Preparing to Serve the Student of the Future: A Planning Resource Report." Sacramento, CA: Community College League of California. (ERIC Document Reproduction No. ED 395 606).

Freund, R. (1996). "Community Colleges and the Virtual Community. One of a Number of Essays by Fellows in the Mid-Career Fellowship Program at Princeton University." (ERIC Document Reproduction No. ED 397 871).

Gallico, P. (1996). *Three Legends: The Snow Goose, the Small Miracle, Ludmilla*. Garden City, NY: Doubleday.

Henderson, J., Neibling, J., & Degner, A. (1996, November). "Bits, Bytes, and Bricks....The Impact of Technology on Classroom Architecture." Paper presented at the League for Innovation in Community College Conference, Atlanta, GA. (ERIC Document Reproduction No. ED 402 972).

Lenington, R. L. (1996). *Managing Higher Education as a Business*. Phoenix, AZ: Oryx Press.

Luskin, B. J. (1997). "The Best Time to Plant a Tree was Twenty-Five Years Ago." *Technological Horizons in Education (T.H.E.) Journal*, 24(11), 81-83.

Mast, C. (1997, March). "Managing in the Digital Age," *Kellogg*, 5(1), 16-20.

Noblitt, J. S. (1997). "Making Ends Meet: A Faculty Perspective on Computing and Scholarship." *Educom Review*, 32(3), 38-43.

Office of Technology Assessment (1989). *Linking for Learning: A New Course for Education*. Congress of the U.S. (ERIC Document Reproduction No. ED 310 765).

Webb, K. (1976). Ashputtel (pp. 153-160) in *Grimm's Fairy Tales*. Auckland, New Zealand: Penguin Books (NZ) Ltd. (Original published 1823).

West, T. W. (1996). "Leveraging Technology." In Educom Review Staff, *Why Technology? Educom Review*, 31(3), 10-12. Available: www.educom.edu/Web/pubs/pubHomeFrame.html.

Westbrook, K. C., & Kerr, S. T. (1996). "Funding Educational Technology: Patterns, Plans, and Models." In S. T. Kerr (Ed.), *Technology and the Future of Schooling* (pp. 49-72). Ninety-Fifth Yearbook of the National Society for the Study of Education, Part II. Chicago, IL: The University of Chicago Press.

Appendix A

Two-Page Fax Survey

A League for Innovation
Information Technology Staff Development Survey

Dear Staff Development Officer,

In preparation for a chapter on *faculty development for instructional technology* that will be included in the League's next book, *Information Technology in the Community College: The Big Picture*, I am requesting your help. The data you provide will become part of this comprehensive work on technology faculty development programs, services, and activities. If information about your institution is included in the chapter, it will be with your review and approval. Please fill out and return this **FAX SURVEY** in the next few days to XXXXXXX at (000) 000-0000 (fax). Thank you!

1. Our college is (circle one):   rural   suburban   urban
2. The student FTE for FY 96-97 was: _____.
3. Our institution's annual budget for FY 96-97 was: _____.
4. Our college provides training and/or development opportunities for faculty (circle YES or NO):

a. in computer-based instruction: drill	YES	NO
tutorials	YES	NO
simulations	YES	NO
b. regarding technology-driven equipment used in vocational technical courses (electronics, CAD/CAM, etc.)	YES	NO
c. in distance education: correspondence	YES	NO
curriculum development	YES	NO
instructional strategies	YES	NO
2-way audio-video	YES	NO
2-way audio/1-way video	YES	NO
World Wide Web (WWW): synchronous	YES	NO
asynchronous	YES	NO
audiographics	YES	NO
CU-See Me/Videoconferencing	YES	NO
d. in the use of the Internet for instructional purposes	YES	NO
e. on classroom management tools, such as grade books	YES	NO
f. on tool software (other than word processing, spreadsheet, database)		
graphics	YES	NO
video editing	YES	NO
desktop publishing	YES	NO
presentation software	YES	NO
hypermedia	YES	NO
g. in visual media production: photography	YES	NO
video recording	YES	NO
video editing	YES	NO
television production	YES	NO
h. in faculty use of CD ROM presentations	YES	NO
i. regarding the development of CD ROM presentations	YES	NO
j. in the use of animation in instructional presentations	YES	NO
k. in the use of online video	YES	NO
l. in automedia: audio recording	YES	NO
m. in the use of virtual laboratories (in chemistry, biology, etc.)	YES	NO
n. in the use of Listservs for instructional purposes	YES	NO

o. in the use of LCDs/Video Data Projection   YES   NO
p. in the use of automated assessment   YES   NO
q. in the development of home pages on the World Wide Web   YES   NO
r. in the use of home pages   YES   NO
s. in the use of "online" editing techniques   YES   NO
t. in the instructional use of asynchronous environment
    for faculty and students   YES   NO
u. in the use of electronic library or other databases   YES   NO
v. in the use of "chat" rooms   YES   NO
w. in telecommunications: E-mail   YES   NO
                                        Internet   YES   NO
                                        LAN/WAN   YES   NO

x. other: _____

        _____

5. Please write in the name, address, phone, and e-mail (or fax) of the individual who filled out this survey:

6. Does your college have an organized faculty development program?   YES   NO

7. Please print this information about the **person most knowledgeable** about the <u>faculty development programs and activities</u> available at your institution: **name, title, your college name, full college address & zip, phone, e-mail, and fax**:

8. If your institution has at least one individual responsible for providing <u>user support</u> to faculty working with technology, please print this information below: **name, title, your college name, full college address & zip, phone, e-mail, and fax**:

9. List here the two colleges you believe have the <u>best faculty development for technology</u> programs or activities in North America. Feel free to include your own.

A. _____
     College Name   Contact Person   City/ State
     Phone/E-mail/Fax

B. _____
     College Name   Contact Person   City/ State
     Phone/E-mail/Fax

*Please Fax the completed survey to XXXXXXXXX at (000) 000-0000
On behalf of the League for Innovation in the Community College, thank you for your time.
If you have any questions regarding this survey you can e-mail XXXXXXXXX at
XXXXX@XXXXXX.XX.XXX

Appendix B
Definitions of Terms Used in the
Faculty Development for Instructional Technology Survey

1997
Lynn Sullivan Taber[6]

A. Computer-Based Instruction (CBI):

i. **drill**–usually used to reinforce a lesson already presented to the student. Manual equivalents include flash cards and work sheets. Most commonly used in math, language skills, grammar, and spelling. Often used in special education classrooms (Picciano, 1994).

ii. **tutorials**–"one-to-one method of instruction in which decisions made by the tutor (live, text, computer, or expert system) are programmed in advance by means of carefully selected, structured instructions, is individually paced, requires active learner response and provides immediate feedback" (Reigeluth & Miller, 1997, p. 28). Often used to teach a person something new, such as software purchased for a computer.

iii. **simulations**–"an abstraction or simplification of some specific real-life situation, process, or task" (Reigeluth & Miller, 1997, p.28). The goal of the software is to recreate real-life situations on a computer. Students interact with the computer simulation, influencing decisions and outcomes. Examples of subject matter that might benefit from this tool: chemistry, historical events, automotive mechanics, construction (Picciano, 1994).

B. **technology-driven equipment** used in vocational/technical courses; examples are CAD or CAM: computer assisted design and computer assisted manufacturing.

C. **distance education**–A "strategy for providing instruction to learners who are geographically separate from their teachers. . . It is the design of

---

[6] *With great appreciation to Terri Boyer and Drs. Marsh, McFadden, Price, and Rice, faculty in the University of Alabama Instructional Technology program, for their expert assistance in compiling this list.*

the software, the organization of the delivery, and the built-in interaction and feedback that make [distance education] a unique application of technology in education" (Ely, 1997, pp. 16-17).

In the *two-way approach* to distance education, the equipment infrastructure may involve "a typical broadband cable distance learning environment using two-way, multiple-sites. Video and audio are communicated via a common broadband coaxial cable to/from each site. In this arrangement, each site has its own one-to-many TV channel (video and audio) that every other site in the network can access. Because every site must have as many monitors as there are sites in the mix, three to four active sites represent a practical limit" (Holmes & Wenrich, 1997, p. 142).

Another approach involves *one-way transmission.* "The medium is communicated in only one direction and is broadcast simultaneously to any number of other sites capable of receiving the transmission. Learners at all remote sites can observe (see and hear) the instructor; however, the instructor cannot see or interact with any students at the various sites" (Holmes & Wenrich, 1997, p. 142).

Distance education may occur using vehicles other than television, including computer-based instruction.

> i. **correspondence**–lessons are distributed, communication is done, and student assignments are returned via videos, U.S. mail, e-mail, or fax.

> ii. **curriculum development**–development of curriculum for distance education media involves different considerations than those required for classroom teaching. Doctoral programs are now offered in instructional development using technology because the principles, techniques, and tools have changed so dramatically.

> iii. **instructional strategies**–instructional strategies are designed specifically for different distance education delivery systems. For example, distance education through television or satellite linkups requires far more visuals than needed in a traditional classroom setting. Also, a variety of strategies becomes important in order to hold attention. Some would say that ALL classrooms would benefit from applying some of the strategies used with distance education.

iv. **2-way audio-video**–this is instruction taking place when the teacher and the students are in two different physical locations at the same time. Instructor and students are able to hear and see one another.

v. **2-way audio/1-way video**–this is instruction taking place when the teacher and the students are in two different physical locations at the same time. Instructors and students are able to hear one another, but only the students can see the instructor. The teacher cannot see the students.

vi. **World Wide Web**–(the WWW, W3, or the Web) The World Wide Web may be defined as a "hypertext-based document retrieval system" (Pfaffenberger as cited in Hackbarth (1997, p 110.). It "has become the Internet user's navigational tool of choice because it is. . . the simplest way that has yet been devised to get around on the Net" (Chamberlain & Mitchell, 1997, p. 1, Lesson 26).

   a. **synchronous**–the teacher and the students experience the media or the transmission simultaneously. Examples include Internet relay chat and CU-See Me Videoconferencing through the Web (not satellite).

   b. **asynchronous**–This term describes how a computer may transmit data to other computers. "A method of data communication in which the transmission of bits of data isn't synchronized by a clock signal, but is accomplished by sending the bits one after another, with a start bit and a stop bit to mark the beginning and end, respectively, of each data unit" (Que Corporation, 1995, p. 34).

vii. **audiographics**–Some colleges "deliver courses from one campus to another via telephone lines and computer networks. Participants in the classroom are able to communicate interactively with their instructor using microphones and view course material presented graphically via a computer. A site facilitator assists students with equipment and ensures they have appropriate course material, assignments, etc. The instructor leads the discussion for the course at all sites and handles all evaluation" (www.mohawkc.on.ca/dept/disted/ audgraph.html).

viii. **CU-SeeMe Videoconferencing**–production of live interactive video events on the Net. Live video, plus audio, text, and graphics, can be fed to viewers with the proper software. Viewers can participate. New software on the market adds color video; whiteboard, phone book, incoming-call alert; conference management; video and audio controls; support for Windows 95; NT and Web browser and tech support. Users can hold "point-to-point" conversations between two sites; group conferences for collaborative work; or perform "Webcasting" where participants receive video, audio, text, and graphics, but cannot send (Webreview.com/96/09/27/addict/index.html).

D. **the use of the Internet for instructional purposes**–helping students discover what is available through the Internet, how to find it, and incorporating the use of the Internet into student assignments.

E. **instructional technology classroom management tools**–grade book and attendance record software are examples of such tools.

F. **tool software** (basic tool software includes word processing, spreadsheets, and databases).

i. **graphics**–software to create graphics and place them in documents.

ii. **video editing**–software that enables computer-aided editing of videos.

iii. **desktop publishing**–software that permits the production of documents that combine word processing and graphics. One example of such a software tool is Pagemaker.

iv. **presentation software**–software capable of creating graphics and print, in color or black and white, that can be projected onto a screen or a wall in a classroom or lecture hall. When this software is the only medium used (and the appropriate hardware is in place) there is no requirement for transparencies or printed materials, although these software packages do permit the production of both. Microsoft's PowerPoint is one example of such a software.

v. **hypermedia**–an educational technology that is also sometimes referred to as courseware. Hypermedia involve both linking and timing, a combination of hypertext linking and a synchronization factor. "Graphics and sound which allow pictures, text, and audio to be presented from one document" (Chamberlain & Mitchell, 1997, p. 2, Lesson 26).

G. **visual media production**:

i. **photography**–learning to take photographs, using the proper equipment, that will be inserted into a multimedia program.

ii. **video recording**–learning to use video equipment to take "moving pictures" that will be inserted into a multimedia program.

iii. **video editing**–learning to use editing equipment to select or deselect scenes from the video tape so that it is appropriate for the intended instructional use.

iv. **television production**–the ability to "put together," from start to finish, a program that will be filmed for distribution for educational purposes. Includes scripting, props, setting scenes, filming, editing, etc.

H. **the use of CD-ROM presentations**–"Acronym for compact disk-read only memory, a read only optical storage technology that uses compact disks. CD-ROMs can store up to 650M of data. CD-ROM technology was originally used for encyclopedias, dictionaries, and software libraries, but now they often are used in multimedia applications" (Que Corporation, 1995, p. 78). A CD-ROM "machine" plays multimedia programs from a compact disc, usually in color. Multimedia programs may be any mixture of media, such as synchronization of time-based media, particularly video and sound.

I. **the production of CD-ROM presentations**–CD-ROM consists of hardware and software and is another communication medium. "CD-ROM drives are used in 37 percent of the public schools, accounting for more than 15 million students in the United States" (Hayes as cited in Ely, 1997, p. 16). Faculty can learn to produce their own CD-ROM presentations designed for a specific purpose.

J. **the use of simulation in instructional presentations**–software packages provide visual, motion, tactile, and/or acoustic cues to simulate various operations. For example, architectural design in three dimensions, or "virtual" surgery that appears real and provides opportunities for student interaction. Student interactions can have different outcomes. Simulations are used as learning tools and as part of student assessment. Flight simulators reproduce conditions a pilot might encounter, and the simulators are used for flight training and pilot assessment.

K. **the use of online video**–online video involves the merging of computer and video technology. Online video can be linear or nonlinear. The source of linear video is tape; the source of nonlinear is the hard disk. Faculty can use online video segments to augment the instructional process, often using these segments as part of a longer computer presentation.

L. **in audio media: audio recording**–ability to make audio tapes appropriate for instructional use either as stand-alone aids, or as part of multimedia presentations. Generally these recordings are of short length and can be excerpts from commercial tapes, student projects, interviews, etc.

M. **the use of virtual labs (in chemistry, biology, etc.)**–students and instructors can simulate chemistry experiments or dissections for biology using software designed for this purpose. This technology reduces the need for lab equipment, improves safety conditions, and impacts the learning process. Definitive research findings are not yet available that confirm exactly how learning processes and outcomes are affected.

N. **the use of LISTSERVs for instructional purposes**–LISTSERVs support distribution, discussion, and file exchange among people joined together online by their shared interest in a particular topic (Chamberlain & Mitchell, 1997). Students can participate actively in a LISTSERV by contributing their resources, opinions, or questions. LISTSERVs are developed for use with e-mail software.

O. **the use of LCDs/Video Data Projection equipment**–LCD stands for liquid crystal display and is "a low-power display technology used in laptop computers and small, battery-powered electronic devices such as meters, testing equipment, and digital watches" (Que Corporation, 1995, p. 296). Video Data Projection equipment is hardware that plugs into a PC and projects images onto a screen. The production of transparencies is eliminated, thereby reducing the time needed to produce a usable program.

P. **the use of automated assessment**–Automated assessment is being used as an online vehicle to respond to students' papers and exams, store grades, or as assist with teacher evaluation systems.

Q. **the development of home pages on the World Wide Web**–design and creation of a working home page.

R. **the use of home pages**–"a home page is roughly analogous to a gopher root menu or a table of contents. . . [and] provides links to the collection of online materials the site distributes. . . it is the welcome mat and the front door" (Chamberlain & Mitchell, 1997, p. 1 of Lesson 27) and it uses hypertext.

S. **the use of online editing techniques**–involves use of computer-based editing systems. Special effects or special manipulations (such as coloring, diffusion, and grain filters) may be utilized. Online video images are generally much better than those generated offline.

T. **the instructional use of asynchronous environments for faculty and students**–instructional strategies using, for example, e-mail, MIME, or video mail, as tools to assist in reaching instructional objectives.

U. **the use of electronic libraries or other databases**–instructional strategies that students use to locate databases and libraries on the Internet. Increasingly, journals and other publications are available for reading and printing through the Internet.

V. **the use of "chat" rooms**–instructional strategies requiring students to log on to a "room" or a location on the Web where people are invited to talk with one another (through their keyboards) about a particular topic. Students in a U.S. classroom could "talk with" students in a classroom in Great Britain, for example, to compare their educational experiences and their cultures.

W. **telecommunications**:

i. **e-mail**–electronic mail. Allows people on networks to communicate with those on other networks. Provides the ability to compose, send, and receive messages quickly and without regard to time zones or office hours. Examples of e-mail educational uses: exchange information, communicate ideas, discuss issues, share files, and review and edit manuscripts. E-mail also supports LISTSERVs and gives access to telnet, file transfer protocol (ftp), and gopher (all Internet protocols) (Chamberlain & Mitchell, 1997).

ii. **Internet**–"is...a vibrant, living Web of interconnecting strands or links crisscrossing the entire globe and providing multiple avenues to information on a scale never before known" (Ely, 1997, p.3). "The Internet is defined as a 'system of linked computer networks, worldwide in scope, that facilitates data communication services such as remote login, file transfers, electronic mail, and distributed news groups" (Pfaffenberger as cited in Hackbarth, 1997, p. 110). "A 'network of networks', connecting a growing number of regional sites to an intercontinental electronic grid that today encompasses. . . 13.4 million individual servers in more than 100 countries" (Chamberlain & Mitchell, 1997, p. 1 of Lesson 2).

iii. **LAN/WAN**

LAN–a local area network (LAN) connects computing equipment. A communication medium linked by high-performance cables. LANs vary greatly in size and complexity, but are generally limited to two-mile distances. Access to a LAN means that users can share expensive peripherals, software, and communication. A LAN draws on a file server–a storage unit. For example, users on a network may be able to share the software PowerPoint to make color graphic presentations for use in the classroom (Ely, 1997).

WAN–wide area networks (WANs). "A network that uses high-speed, long-distance communications networks or satellites to connect computers over distances greater than those traversed by LANs" (Que Corporation, 1995, p. 557).

Related Definitions and Concepts

browsers–There are two types. First, there are graphical browsers (GUI for graphical user interface). Mosaic, the original GUI browser is no longer in development. Explorer and Netscape are now competing for the #1 spot. Explorer and Netscape software are available on the Internet free of charge for educational sites and personal use (noncommercial). The second type, text-based browsers (such as Lynx or Charlotte), usually use hypertext links. The user selects items using the cursor or directional keys. (Chamberlain & Mitchell, 1997).

digital–The technology most commonly used to transmit cellular calls is known as analog. Through analog transmission, your voice is actually carried on the airwaves. Pure digital transmission, on the other hand, handles phone calls as a stream of digital bytes, the same way a computer handles data. Like the video disc, the CD is a digital recording made and read by a laser beam. Digital technologies provide the following:
1. the ability to encode a great quantity of data in numeric, verbal, and iconic forms;
2. discs highly resistant to damage;
3. random and rapid access information;
4. freedom from background noises; and
5. durable discs. (Negroponte, 1995)

hypertext–text with links among the components. This makes it possible to click on a highlighted word and, through a link, be taken to a separate screen that usually tells more about the word or phrase the user clicked. Allows you to jump from one document to another.

HTML–"Hypertext Markup Language (HTML) contains codes that tell Web browsers what typeface to use and how to format it. Most browsers can also display digitized pictures, so that a well-written HTML document appears as an illustrated page (Chamberlain & Mitchell, 1997).

Internet Protocols–software designed for use on the Internet to accomplish specific tasks. For example, *ftp* is a "file transfer protocol" capable of transferring files from one computer address to another; *gopher* searches just against document titles; and *http* searches the full text of documents.

satellite dish–can be used to uplink or downlink programs broadcast from long distances. "Quality Education Data reports that 10 percent of elementary schools, 22 percent of middle/junior high schools, and 37 percent of high schools had satellite dishes in 1994-1995" (QED as cited in Ely, 1997, p.16).

uplink–refers to the process of connecting to a satellite from a production site in order to send information or a program to another site. The receiving site must have a satellite capable of "downlinking" in order to receive the information or program.

upload–refers to the ability to send information in a file up to a server. When individuals would like to receive the file, they "download" the file to their computer.

URL–stands for "Universal Resource Locator" and acts as a unique address on the global Internet.

video disc–A communication medium that is a close relative of CD Rom, requires hardware and software, and is in the laser disc family. Allows "interactive educational programs with audio and visual capabilities. Film sequences can be stored less expensively on video discs than on computer disks" (Ely, 1997, p. 16).

Virtual Reality (VR)–"The idea behind Virtual Reality is to deliver a sense of 'being there' by giving at least the eye what it would have received if it were there, and more important, to have the image change instantly as you change your point of view" (Negroponte, 1995, p. 117). Typically the individual wears a helmet with displays (one for each eye) in a set of goggles. As wearers move their heads, the images are so rapidly updated that wearers feel they are making those changes by their movement. In some VR set-ups, individuals wear gloves that allow the person to "reach into" the scene and open doors or manipulate objects. "The range of potential applications includes architecture, where VR systems will allow architects to present clients with three-dimensional VR "walkthroughs" of proposed structures; and physicians will be able to try out new surgical techniques within three-dimensional, simulated 'patients'"(Que Corporation, 1995, p. 548).

WWW Browser or Engine–"A Web browser runs on your computer and acts as a graphical interface between you and the Web. When you click on a link, it issues the necessary commands to request data from other computers, then interprets whatever comes back" (Chamberlain & Mitchell, p. 1, Lesson 27.) "A program that runs on an Internet-connected computer and provides access to the riches of the World Wide Web (WWW). Web browsers are of two kinds: text-only browsers and graphical Web browsers such as NCSA Mosaic and Netscape Navigator. Graphical browsers are preferable because you can see in-line images, fonts, and document layouts" (Que Corporation, 1995, pp 553-554).

Technology Definition References

Chamberlain, E., & Mitchell, M. (1997). BCK2SKOL: *A New Class on the Net for Librarians with Little or No Experience.* Available: Web.csd.sc.edu/bck2skol/fall/lesson2.html.

Ely, D.P. (1997). Trends in Educational Technology 1995. In R.M. Branch, M. Branch, & B.B. Minor, with D. Ely (Eds.), *Educational Media and Technology Yearbook,* Vol. 22 (pp. 2-23). Englewood, CO: Librarians Unlimited.

Hackbarth, S. (1997). Web-Based Learning in the Context of K-12 Schooling. In R.M. Branch, M. Branch, & B.B. Minor, with D. Ely (Eds.), *Educational Media and Technology Yearbook,* Vol. 22 (pp. 109-131). Englewood, CO: Librarians Unlimited.

Holmes, G.A., & Wenrich, J. (1997). Revisiting Cable TV in the Classroom. In R.M. Branch, M. Branch, & B.B. Minor, with D. Ely (Eds.), *Educational Media and Technology Yearbook,* Vol. 22 (pp. 138-144). Englewood, CO: Librarians Unlimited.

Negroponte, N. (1995). *Being Digital.* New York: Alfred A. Knopf.

Office of Technology Assessment. (1989). *Linking for Learning: A New Course for Education.* Congress of the U.S. (ERIC Document Reproduction No. 310 765).

Picciano, A. G. (1994). *Computers in the Schools: A Guide to Planning and Administration.* New York: Merrill.

Que Corporation (1995). *Que's Computer and Internet Dictionary* (6th ed.). Indianapolis, IN: Que Corporation.

Reigeluth, C.M., & Miller, L.M. (1997). A New Paradigm of ISD? In R.M. Branch, M. Branch, & B.B. Minor, with D. Ely (eds.), *Educational Media and Technology Yearbook,* Vol. 22 (pp. 24-35). Englewood, CO: Librarians Unlimited.

Appendix C

E-Mail Survey to Colleges Indicating User Support Services Available

1. Name of person responding to this survey:
2. College name and address:
3. Phone: 4. E-mail: 5. Fax:
6. Do you offer user support specifically for faculty who are using instructional technology?
7. Describe the components and activities of your user support programs and services:
    a. Technical support for hardware and software
    b. Application training is virtually nonexistent, most is done through trial and error or the faculty member or support staff member taking a course on the specific area.
8. In what specific ways could your user support program be improved:
    a.
    b.
9. What obstacles do you face when you attempt to make these program improvements?
10. Describe your ideal user support program for faculty who are using instructional technology:
11. What is the title of the individual to whom the user support person(s) report?
12. What FTE of the faculty or staff are dedicated to user support for faculty using instructional technology?
13. What percent of the user support person(s)' time is spent on user support for the faculty using instructional technology?
14. Please rank your perception of the adequacy of user support for faculty and instructional technology at your institution:
    (Very Poor) 1   2   3   4   5   6   7   8   9   10 (Outstanding)

CHAPTER 7

INTO THE BREACH:
A NATIONAL STUDY OF COMPUTERS
AND THE "AT RISK"

Laurence F. Johnson

Author's Note: The study described in this chapter was conducted over a period of two and one-half years between 1994 and mid-1996 and remains the largest study of computer use in community colleges ever conducted in terms of the advance of information technology and its application in community colleges. Nevertheless, much has happened in the years since the study concluded, and the reader may well wonder if the findings are still relevant given the rush of change in this arena. The Internet, for example, has taken a dramatic hold on our collective consciousness, to the point where now every evening one can see multimillion-dollar ad campaigns for websites on the national television networks. The use of computers, burgeoning in 1996, has continued to explode, and in 1999, for the first time, more computers were sold worldwide than television sets.

As computers have become more and more ubiquitous, they have become a part of almost every curriculum, and, in this context, an interesting trend has emerged. The importance of basic computer skills for success in college-level coursework has come to be a given, and more and more colleges are now offering developmental coursework to provide students the basic computer skills they will need to be successful in their mainstream coursework. Far from rendering the study irrelevant, however, the events of the ensuing three years have reaffirmed the overall findings of the study, especially the implications of the study for practitioners. The overriding conclusions of the study–that factors such as the role and attitude of the teacher, the quality of support for students within the lab, and the value and relevance of the computer activities to the class play much more important roles in student success than the particular choice of software or technology to be used–remain just as true today and have been validated by experience.

At the same time, it should be noted that even with the power of the Internet and the many advances that it has propelled, there are still no "magic bullets." Developmental students, whether taught by traditional means or with technological tools, still come to college with significant academic problems and support needs. A successful approach to using computer- or Internet-assisted learning activities for developmental students will recognize this and ensure mechanisms are in place that provide the structure and support these students require. Attention to these details will have a far greater impact on retention and success rates than will the use of any particular technology or software tool.

The most important finding of the study continues to merit our attention: developmental students can learn using computers. The vast majority are satisfied and comfortable with using computers and would enroll in a class using computers again. Like their mainstream counterparts, developmental students see the wide-ranging impact of technology in our society and recognize that they must learn to use it if they are to be successful. Exposing them to technological tools adds value to the learning process in ways that go beyond the learning objectives and activities of the class.

Although community colleges are faced with a seemingly unending flood of underprepared students, state and local pressure is mounting to cut resources allocated to developmental education in states across the country. In this atmosphere, technology has been heralded as an answer to streamlining and adding efficiency to developmental efforts, but little has been done to document the value and outcomes of computer-assisted instruction for developmental students, and little is known about the factors influencing success in computer-assisted developmental coursework. This two and a half year study involved nine community colleges, four disciplines and two special programs, 49 faculty, and 2,381 students in an exploration of the relationship between student outcomes in developmental courses and a variety of factors, including (a) student demographics, attitudes, and academic history, (b) unique aspects of the instructional software used in the developmental programs, (c) the instructional approaches used by developmental faculty, and (d) characteristics of the computer lab environment.

Since the first community colleges were founded at the turn of the century, these institutions have been viewed as a "second chance" for adults to learn what they could not or did not learn in the public schools. As enrollments rose with the emerging baby boom, an increasing number of students entered with severe deficiencies in basic reading and math skills. By the late sixties, half of any community college freshman class was found to be deficient in essential academic skills (Roueche, 1968).

Bolstered by an increasing national focus on the competitiveness of America's work force, addressing the needs of the underprepared student remains one of the most pressing issues facing community colleges today. California community colleges, for example, spent $300 million in 1993-94 on remedial activities–11 percent of the total budget for community colleges statewide (Irving, 1996). The doggedness of the underprepared student issue is remarkable, and legislators are increasingly concerned about underprepared college students.

More than half of all community college students lack the skills for college-level work (McCabe, 1988); in urban institutions, the proportion of underprepared students can be as high as 75 to 95 percent (Richardson & Elliot, 1994). Nonetheless, despite the great numbers of students in need, developmental education programs in community colleges are under siege. California, Texas, and Florida lead the nation in reevaluating, reassessing, and possibly revoking remedial education efforts in higher education (Katsinas, 1994). State accountability and institutional effectiveness mandates of the 1990s are evidence of the growing discontent and perceived failure of public education efforts (Green & Gilbert, 1995).

The challenge to community colleges is to continue somehow to meet the needs of the large population of underprepared students with fewer and fewer college resources–and at the same time, answer the increased pressures to document and measure success. Parnell (1994) asserts that not only does the at-risk population entering the open door of community colleges face an uncertain future, but the nation's future as a progressive society is also at risk. The realities of changing demographics, increasing populations of the academically underprepared, and growing disparities among wage earners are serious issues for community colleges, and are made no less so by tremendous advances in information technology that widen the gap between the skilled and the unskilled. While a select cadre of students is entering higher education with the advantage of years of experience and familiarity with technology tools (Wilson, 1994), this advantage is not shared by those traditionally underserved in education. More than 60 percent of the American population has no exposure, experience, or access to computer-assisted technology (Hancock & Wingert, 1995).

Driven by the great difference in technological skills in the population and an increased focus on these approaches as possible cost-saving strategies, there is a growing debate on the effectiveness of computer-assisted instruction and how and if it contributes to academic success. Between 1988 and 1992, several meta-analyses of empirical research on the effectiveness of computer applications in schools were published. These studies focused on different time periods, educational levels, and computer applications, but in each of the studies, students who received assistance from computers generally learned more in classes, remembered longer, and spent less instructional time learning their lessons (Kulik, 1991; Liao & Bright, 1991; Ryan 1991). A more recent meta-analysis of thirty-six independent studies showed that computer applications have a positive effect on students' academic achievement from elementary schools through college and university level curricula (Khalili & Shashanni, 1994). Unfortunately, almost no research has been conducted to determine the effectiveness of computer-assisted approaches for developmental students in community colleges; as a result, little is known about the benefits of these approaches for the developmental population.

Purpose of the Study

In the fall of 1993, in response to the need for research into the effectiveness of computer-assisted instruction for developmental students, an invitation was made to a number of community colleges using computer-assisted instructional techniques in their developmental programs to participate in a broad-based national study of the issue. Nine colleges met the criteria for participation and a meeting of the campus-based project directors was held in January 1994 to begin planning for the project. A pilot of the research instrumentation was conducted in the fall term of 1994. Data collection began in the spring term of 1995 and continued through the fall.

The purpose of the study was twofold: 1) to identify and describe effective instructional models of computer-assisted instruction for each of the developmental disciplines; and 2) to identify student characteristics that contribute to or impede student success in computer-assisted developmental coursework.

Participants

The nine colleges involved in the study represented seven states and included four urban colleges, two suburban colleges, and three rural or small colleges (Figure 7A). Their student populations totaled 83,519 students. Developmental populations ranged from 4 to 83 percent of the enrollments in each institution. The colleges were: Central Arizona College, Coolidge, Arizona; Central Florida Community College, Ocala, Florida; The Community College of Denver, Denver, Colorado; Cuyahoga Community College, Cleveland, Ohio; El Centro College, Dallas, Texas; El Paso Community College, El Paso, Texas; Kingwood Community College, Kingwood, Texas; Miramar College, San Diego, California; and Santa Fe Community College, Santa Fe, New Mexico.

Figure 7A. Project Participants

College	Faculty	Class Sections	Students in the Study	Total Developmental Population	Total Student Population	Setting	Remediation Required
Central Arizona	6	7	130	287	7,148	Rural	N
Central Florida	12	15	404	1,065	6,105	Rural	N
Cuyahoga	3	6	88	3,424	21,608	Urban	N
Denver	3	6	319	5,523	6,661	Urban	Y
El Centro	5	7	439	1,502	4,349	Urban	Y
El Paso	5	6	95	10,537	20,162	Urban	Y
Kingwood	12	13	561	1,206	3,494	Suburban	Y
Miramar	2	3	274	982	8,310	Suburban	N
Santa Fe	1	1	71	676	5,682	Rural	N
Total	49	64	2,381	25,202	83,519		

The 49 participating faculty provided access to 64 classes for the study, including 17 writing classes, 18 math classes, 15 reading classes, 3 English as a Second Language (ESL) classes, and 11 developmental classes of other types. All students in these classes were provided with a description of the purposes and goals of the study; 2,381 students signed an informed consent form and are included in the reported results.

Of the students who agreed to participate in the study, 665 were enrolled in writing, 877 in math, 564 in reading, 108 in ESL, and 167 in other developmental classes. The average age of these students was 25.8 years and 66 percent were female; 44 percent identified their ethnic group as Anglo, 21 percent as Hispanic, 25 percent as African American, 7 percent as Asian or Pacific Islander, and 3 percent as Other. Some 22 percent were repeating the course, 6 percent for the second time or more.

Almost half of the students were continuing studies from the previous term, but 20 percent–a fifth–had been out of school for three years or more.

Grade point averages for students participating in the study were comparable to the average for all developmental students across the colleges: 2.44 on a 4-point scale for students in reading courses (compared to 2.41), 2.32 for writing courses (compared to 2.36), and 2.36 for math courses (compared to 2.38). Drop rates for the classes included in the investigation were 16.7 percent for students in reading courses, 25.6 percent for writing courses, and 23.8 percent for math courses.

Methodology

The purpose of the study, as noted earlier, was twofold: 1) to identify and describe effective instructional models of computer-assisted instruction for each of the developmental disciplines; and 2) to identify student characteristics that contribute to or impede student success in computer-assisted developmental coursework. To accomplish the first purpose, a multiple analysis of variance was performed on a random subset of 800 cases to determine if a significant difference could be found between the colleges and instructional programs involved in the study, with student grades and persistence as the dependent variables and discipline and institution as the independent variables. Age, gender, ethnicity, and four groups of variables from the student surveys (ability and comfort with computers, orientation toward using computers, academic history, and attitudes) were included in the model as covariates to control for the effects of these factors.

To aid in understanding the differences between college programs and to help identify the most effective instructional approaches, a summary sheet was prepared for each developmental discipline by college that included a range of information from each of the data sets, including course grade point average, average course persistence, and noncomputerized instructional strategies used in classes, as well as factors such as whether the computer activities were a formal part of the class, if the teacher was present when the computer activities took place, the presence of support staff or tutors, and the fit of the overall learning objectives with the software. Also included in the analysis were written reports from faculty and lab supervisors that addressed lab structure and philosophy issues, methods of instructional delivery, the correlation between instructional software and existing curricula, student attributes, and the relationship between time in the lab and other class activities.

To address the second purpose, frequencies and correlations were calculated on student responses to a 13-question survey. (A principal components analysis of the survey responses revealed that four factors accounted for 67 percent of the variance. These were ability and comfort with computers, orientation toward using computers, academic history, and attitudes.) A discriminant function analysis (DFA) was then run on the entire set of 22 variables to determine factors influencing persistence and academic success. In the DFA, a random sample of cases was selected and two sets of analyses were run for each outcome variable. The first required all variables to enter into the model at once, to ensure that the control variables were taken into account. Then the process was rerun, allowing a stepwise procedure, based on the minimization of Wilkes' lambda. The results of these analyses were then crossvalidated against the remaining cases to establish the consistency of the prediction models.

Findings

The overall findings related to the first purpose of the study (to identify and describe effective instructional models of computer-assisted instruction) are detailed in the subsection below. The findings related to the second purpose of the study (to identify student characteristics that contribute to or impede success) follow. The third subsection of the findings presents snapshots of 14 successful developmental programs which detail important programmatic characteristics that emerged in the analysis of individual programs. A final subsection provides a summary of the key findings.

Instructional Models

A random subset of 800 cases was used to determine if a significant difference could be found between the colleges and instructional programs involved in the study, with student grades and persistence as the dependent variables and discipline and institution as the independent variables. As noted previously, age, gender, ethnicity, and the four dimensions that emerged from the student surveys (ability and comfort with computers, orientation toward using computers, academic history, and attitudes) were included in the model as covariates to control for the effects of these factors. The multivariate analysis of variance found significant differences between colleges and between disciplines on the outcomes of student grades and persistence, and within colleges by discipline. Details of the multivariate analysis of variance are presented in Figures 7B through 7E.

Figure 7B. Multivariate Tests of Significance Between Colleges
(S = 2, M = 2 1/2 , N = 376 1/2)

Test	Value	Approx. F	Hypoth. DF	Error DF	Significance
Pillais	.06771	3.31145	16.00	1512.00	.000
Hotellings	.07059	3.32664	16.00	1508.00	.000
Wilks	.93321	3.31906	16.00	1510.00	.000

Figure 7C. Multivariate Tests of Significance Between Disciplines
(S = 2, M = 1/2 , N = 376 1/2)

Test	Value	Approx. F	Hypoth. DF	Error DF	Significance
Pillais	.03679	3.54198	8.00	1512.00	.000
Hotellings	.03751	3.53503	8.00	1508.00	.000
Wilks	.96353	3.53851	8.00	1510.00	.000

Figure 7D. Multivariate Tests of Significance for Disciplines Within Colleges
(S = 2, M = 8 , N = 376 1/2)

Test	Value	Approx. F	Hypoth. DF	Error DF	Significance
Pillais	.16712	3.62793	38.00	1512.00	.000
Hotellings	.18731	3.71659	38.00	1508.00	.000
Wilks	.83796	3.67230	38.00	1510.00	.000

Figure 7E. Results of Univariate F-Tests

Effect/Dependent Variable	F	Significance	DF
Between Colleges			
Grades	4.14573	.000	8,756
Persistence	4.85592	.000	8,756
Between Disciplines			
Grades	3.40614	.009	4,756
Persistence	4.09466	.003	4,756
Disciplines within Colleges			
Grades	2.83652	.000	19,756
Persistence	1.65610	.039	19,756

Because most colleges in the study used very similar sets of software (within disciplines), and because all the participating programs used an integrated learning system (ILS[1]) for many class activities, these results suggest that the manner in which computer activities are integrated into the class is a critical factor in the success of students in the program. (Summaries and descriptions of the most successful approaches by discipline are provided later in the chapter.)

Figures 7F and 7G, which provide the results of a regression analysis between the covariates and the two dependent variables, show the relative influence of each of the covariates on these outcomes. The lack of significant relationships between the covariates and the dependent variables provide additional evidence that the differences in grades and persistence rates between colleges and disciplines are largely due to factors related to the instructional approaches and the ways in which the courses were offered and are not attributable to the various student characteristics which the covariates attempted to measure.

Indeed, a wide variety of instructional approaches were revealed by the surveys and written reports of the instructors, with considerable variation even between faculty on a single campus. In general, however, it

---

[1] *An integrated learning system (ILS) is a type of sophisticated computer program that generally includes a comprehensive set of instructional activities and an instructional management system. The management system allows the student's progress through the materials to be governed in a variety of ways. Most integrated learning systems also include some mechanism for assessment and/or placement within the set of instructional activities, and a process for determining if individual learning objectives have been met.*

Figure 7F. Regression Analysis; Grade as Dependent Variable

Covariate	B	Beta	Std. Err.	t-Value	Sig. of t
Age	.00983	.04228	.009	1.111	.267
Ethnicity					
Anglo	-1.28225	-.32791	1.867	-.687	.492
Asian	-1.19837	-.11358	1.906	-.629	.530
Black	-1.11380	-.25032	1.864	-.597	.550
Hispanic	-1.24639	-.27400	1.874	-.665	.506
Other	-1.19605	-.10733	1.907	-.627	.531
Gender	-.02950	-.00713	.148	-.200	.842
Ability and Comfort with Computers	-.01627	-.00697	.090	-.181	.857
Orientation to Computer Use	-.17610	-.05751	.139	-1.267	.206
Academic History	.07432	.03252	.084	.884	.377
Attitude	.19934	.09358	.103	1.944	.052

appears that faculty who attended the computer lab with their students were more satisfied with the appropriateness of the software and were more knowledgeable users. The sites with the strongest indicators of satisfaction among faculty and students had a clear service orientation within the lab and actively involved lab supervisors who contributed to the overall effort with training, classroom support, and problem resolution.

Most, but not all, faculty actively participated in computer lab activities. Some faculty held full class meetings in the lab, some held office hours in the lab, and others required students to work in the computer lab outside of normal class time. The amount of course time devoted to computer-assisted activities ranged from one to seven hours per week, and 10 to 75 percent of total class time was spent on lab-based work.

The most commonly used software package was an ILS, and instructors devised a number of unique applications using ILS software

Figure 7G. Regression Analysis; Persistence as Dependent Variable

Covariate	B	Beta	Std. Err.	t-Value	Sig. of t
Age	.00163	.05373	.001	1.407	.160
Ethnicity					
Anglo	.02525	.04948	.244	.103	.918
Asian	.04193	.03045	.249	.168	.867
Black	-.04524	-.07792	.244	-.185	.853
Hispanic	.01742	.02934	.245	.071	.943
Other	-.02937	-.02019	.250	-.118	.906
Gender	.03258	.06036	.019	1.686	.092
Ability and Comfort with Computers	.01350	.04432	.012	1.145	.252
Orientation to Computer Use	.02508	.06278	.018	1.378	.169
Academic History	-.00905	-.03035	.011	-.823	.411
Attitude	-.02373	-.08536	.013	-1.768	.078

and related materials. Faculty used ILS software as a key component in a number of cooperative learning endeavors, including collaborative writing and editing assignments, critical-thinking projects, and personal development activities.

Comprehensive orientation activities were closely associated with successful strategies; most colleges incorporated a formal orientation process into the first week's activities. The lab manager and/or tutors were introduced as part of the presentation, and students reported that this helped them become more familiar with the setting and more comfortable asking for assistance from lab staff. A clear association emerged between students' favorable perceptions of the appropriateness and capabilities of the computer activities and the presence of the instructor in the lab when assigned activities took place.

The role of the lab supervisor was complex at sites which expressed the highest levels of faculty satisfaction, with the lab supervisor functioning at various times as trainer, liaison, teacher-aide, and problem solver. Furthermore, lab supervisors developed sophisticated customized curricula for their ILS systems and helped to match course objectives to ILS lessons. These custom curricula were found very useful by faculty and were used in virtually all of the most successful approaches.

Student Characteristics

Students felt using the ILS system made learning the material easier; only 11 percent of students felt using the system made the courses harder. Most students (74 percent) felt their computer lessons were a good fit with other classwork, and 88 percent said they would enroll in a similar course again.

Over 70 percent had some typing skills before entering the course, and almost half of those felt their typing skills were very good. Nearly 60 percent of the students reported themselves comfortable with computers before the semester, but by midsemester 81 percent reported that they felt somewhat or very comfortable using computers. Seventy percent of students described themselves as having from "some" to "a lot" of computer experience before classes began.

Gender was significantly correlated with age and typing skills, indicating that on average, female students were older and better typists. Age was negatively correlated with all measures of computer experience and comfort. Older students were less experienced with computers, less comfortable using computers, and took longer to become comfortable with the system. On average, older students were returning to school after a break in their studies.

Student comfort with computers was associated with computer experience, the degree to which students thought computer skills were not important to use the software, and typing ability. Student comfort with the class was related to whether or not students thought the computer lessons "were a good fit" with other course work; a good fit was correlated with greater comfort in the class. Additionally, student comfort in the class was related to how students perceived the computer's effect on the course workload, with less perceived work relating to a greater degree of comfort.

The time it took a student to become comfortable using the computers was positively related to the student's age–indicating that older students may need additional time and support at the start of the semester. An inverse relationship was found between students' perception that computer lessons were important (i.e., a "good fit") and the time it took them to become comfortable using the system. If faculty stress the value of these lessons in class, the time required for students to become comfortable may be reduced.

In general, being a member of a minority group or female was associated with longer amounts of time to become comfortable in the lab. The degree to which students felt they might enroll again in a similar course was inversely related to the time they required to become comfortable. Students inclined to enroll again in a similar course, by and large, became comfortable more quickly.

To aid in understanding these descriptive and correlational findings about students, a discriminant function analysis was conducted to determine key factors influencing persistence and academic success. (Discriminant function analysis is a classification algorithm that combines variables to build statistical models of the outcome variables.) Five student characteristics were found to form significantly predictive models of each of these outcomes. The factors are listed in Figure 7H in decreasing order of their standardized discriminant function coefficients, which can be used to determine the relative importance of each of the factors.

The five factors that emerged in the academic success analysis correctly predicted success 65.43 percent of the time in the calibration sample. On crossvalidation, the correct classification rate degraded only slightly, and the model was found to explain 4.44 percent of the variance in academic success ($F=19.0541$). The five factors that comprised the persistence analysis correctly predicted success 72.6 percent of the time in the calibration sample. On crossvalidation, the correct classification rate degraded only slightly, and the model was found to explain 3.93 percent of the variance in academic success ($F=16.752$).

Two of the factors that emerged in the academic success analysis are surprising. A common perception among faculty is that typing or keyboarding skills are an important prerequisite for computer-assisted

Figure 7H. Discriminant Factors Ranked by Standardized Coefficients

Characteristics Predictive of Success	Characteristics Predictive of Persistence
1) Relatively lower levels of typing skills	1) Computer lessons considered a good fit
2) Somewhat experienced using computers	2) Being male
3) Workload considered similar to other courses	3) Feel computers make work easier
4) Being male	4) Comfortable with the system by midterm
5) Relatively longer time to become comfortable using the system	5) Workload considered similar to other courses

study. These results do not support that view, and indeed prior typing skills were found to be negatively related to success. Students who take a relatively longer time to become comfortable with the system appear to enjoy a higher rate of success than those who adjust to the system more quickly. This is also counter to conventional wisdom, and may indicate that these students are in fact delving deeper into the system than those reporting quicker adjustment periods.

The emergence of a gender-related factor in both analyses can be attributed to the fact that more males than females in the study reported having experience with computers before the course began. The remaining student characteristics associated with success and persistence include several factors that can be influenced by the teacher. A student's perception of whether or not computer lessons are a good fit with the learning objectives of the course is often based on comments or attitudes expressed by the instructor. Similarly, teacher comments and attitudes can influence how a student feels about the rigor of the work on the computer in comparison to other activities or other courses.

Successful Instructional Models

Data on individual programs were collected from institutional records (student grades and persistence rates for each course), as well as a series of written reports and survey data from students, faculty, and lab supervisors. To aid in understanding the differences between college programs and to help identify the essential characteristics of the most effective instructional approaches, a summary sheet was prepared for each developmental discipline by college that included a range of information from each of the data sets–course grade point average,

average course persistence, and noncomputerized instructional strategies used in classes–as well as factors such as whether the computer activities were a formal part of the class, if the teacher was present when the computer activities took place, the presence of support staff or tutors, and the fit of the overall learning objectives with the software. Also included in the analysis were written reports from faculty and lab supervisors that addressed lab structure and philosophy issues, methods of instructional delivery, the correlation between instructional software and existing curricula, student attributes, and the relationship between time in the lab and other class activities. In general, three criteria were required for designation as a superior approach to computer-assisted instruction: 1) a persistence rate across the program of above 75 percent; 2) strong evidence of student satisfaction from the student survey results; and 3) written statements from faculty in their periodic reports that indicated the learning objectives addressed through computer-assisted activities were being met. In the final category of nontraditional developmental programs, the 75 percent benchmark for programwide persistence was relaxed to accommodate the unusual diversity of approaches within that category and to offset the small number of programs of these types included in the study.

Successful Strategies for Reading. The reading programs at Central Florida, Cuyahoga, El Centro, and El Paso were judged to be superior to other approaches (Figure 7I). Across these four programs, student persistence ranged from 78 to 95 percent. The proportion of the classes' total contact hours spent on computer activities was between one-third and two-thirds of the total class time, and students spent (on average) from 6.4 hours to 10.4 hours on the computers over the academic term. The instructors used computers to teach or reinforce about half of the learning objectives for the class, with the proportions ranging from 47 to 62 percent. In each of these programs, the following common elements of success were noted:

- Computer activities were a formal part of the class.
- A custom curriculum was used for ILS activities.
- Students received a comprehensive orientation to using the computers; to the operating system and computer software; to the lab resources, personnel, and policies; and to the class activities and grading.

- All used several instructional software packages, with the largest proportion of assignments devoted to the ILS System.

Figure 7I. Distinctions among Successful Reading Programs

College	Teacher attends lab?	Tutors available in the lab?	NON-ILS Strategies	Students per station	Other factors
Central Florida	Y	N	Lecture, group work, collabor- ative projects	2	Practice on other software encouraged, but not mandatory
Cuyahoga	N	N	Group work, collaborative projects, other software	1	Independent study
El Centro	Y	N	Lecture, group work	1	Used for TASP remediation
El Paso	Y	Y	Lecture, group work, other software	1	Large lab, with group and individual areas

Successful Strategies for Mathematics. The mathematics programs at Central Arizona, Central Florida, and Cuyahoga were judged to be superior to other approaches (Figure 7J). Across the three programs, student persistence ranged from 92 to 100 percent. The proportion of the classes' total contact hours spent on computer activities was between 37 and 55 percent of the total class time, and students spent (on average) from 6.4 hours to 10.4 hours on the computers over the academic term. The instructors used computers to teach or reinforce more than half of the learning objectives for the class, with the proportions ranging from 50 to 80 percent. In each of these programs, the following common elements of success were noted:

- Computer activities were a formal part of the class.
- A custom curriculum was used for ILS activities.
- Students received a comprehensive orientation to using the computers; to the operating system and computer software; to the lab resources, personnel, and policies; and to the class activities and grading.

- An ILS was the primary instructional software package available to students.

Figure 7J. Distinctions among Successful Mathematics Programs

College	Teacher attends lab?	Tutors available in the lab?	NON-ILS Strategies	Students per station	Other factors
Central Arizona	Y	Y	Lecture, group work, collaborative projects	1	Practice on other software encouraged, but not mandatory
Central Florida	Y	N	Lecture, other software	1	ILS workbooks are used for some homework
Cuyahoga	Y	N	Lecture, group work, other software	1	Practice on a variety of other software packages mandatory

Successful Strategies for Writing. The writing programs at Central Florida, Miramar, and Santa Fe were judged to be superior to other approaches (Figure 7K). Across the three programs, student persistence ranged from 88 to 100 percent. The proportion of the classes' total contact hours spent on computer activities was between 43 and 50 percent of the total class time, and students spent (on average) from 6.1 hours to 10.4 hours on the computers over the academic term. The instructors used computers to teach or reinforce more than half of the learning objectives for the class, with the proportions ranging from 50 to 60 percent. In each of these programs, the following common elements of success were noted:

- Teachers were actively involved in lab activities.
- Computer activities were a formal part of the class.
- A custom curriculum was used for ILS activities.
- Students received a comprehensive orientation to using the computers; to the operating system and computer software; to the lab resources, personnel, and policies; and to the class activities and grading.
- All used several instructional software packages, with the largest proportion of assignments devoted to the ILS System.

Figure 7K. Distinctions among Successful Writing Programs

College	Teacher attends lab?	Tutors available in the lab?	NON-ILS Strategies	Students per station	Other factors
Central Florida	Y	N	Lecture, group work, collaborative editing projects, other software	2	Used for CLAST remediation, keyboarding lessons encouraged
Miramar	Y	Y	Lecture, group work, collaborative editing projects, other software	1	Extensive use of tutors, individualized portfolios
Santa Fe	Y	Y	Lecture, group work, collaborative editing projects, other software	1	Used to satisfy required remediation

Successful Strategies for English as a Second Language. The ESL programs at Central Florida and El Paso were judged to be superior to other approaches (Figure 7L). In both programs, student persistence was a remarkable 100 percent. The proportion of the classes' total contact hours spent on computer activities was between 30 and 43 percent of the total class time and students spent (on average) from 7.8 hours to 10.4 hours on the computers over the academic term. The instructors used computers to teach or reinforce many of the learning objectives for the class (42 percent and 46 percent, respectively). In both programs, the following common elements of success were noted:

- Teachers were actively involved in lab activities.
- Computer activities were a formal part of the class.
- Bilingual tutors were available in the lab during class activities.
- A custom curriculum was used for ILS activities.
- Students received a comprehensive orientation to using the computers; to the operating system and computer software; to the lab resources, personnel, and policies; and to the class activities and grading.

- Classes used immersion projects and audio and video resources extensively.
- An ILS was the primary instructional software package available to students.

Figure 7L. Distinctions Between Successful ESL Programs

College	Teacher attends lab?	Tutors available in the lab?	NON-ILS Strategies	Students per station	Other factors
Central Florida	Y	Y	Lecture, group work, collaborative projects	2	Practice on other software encouraged, but not mandatory
El Paso	Y	Y	Lecture, group work, collaborative projects, other software	1	Large lab, with group and individual areas

Successful Strategies for Other Developmental Programs. Two colleges used computer-assisted approaches for nontraditional remediation (Figure 7M). At Kingwood College, students met TASP noncourse-based remediation requirements by self-remediating in the computer lab; 56 percent of students choosing this approach completed the semester successfully. The Community College of Denver used an ILS system in a required noncredit Basic Skills course as part of class and group work guided by a teacher; 100 percent of these students remained at the end of the semester. In both cases, other activities were available to the students, and students spent about half their time on computer activities. Students spent 13 hours (on average) using the ILS system over the academic term at the Community College of Denver. The instructors used the computers to teach or reinforce more than half of the learning objectives for the class, with the proportions ranging from 54 percent at Kingwood to 62 percent in Denver. The following common elements of success were noted:

- Computer activities were a formal part of the class.
- Classes did not use lectures in any significant manner.
- A custom curriculum was used for ILS activities.

- Students received a comprehensive orientation to using the computers, to the operating system and computer software, to the lab resources, personnel, and policies, and to the class activities and grading.
- An ILS was the primary instructional software package available to students.

Figure 7M. Distinctions between Other Successful Developmental Programs

College	Teacher attends lab?	Tutors available in the lab?	NON-ILS Strategies	Students per station	Other factors
Denver	Y	N	Group work, computer practice	2	Portfolio-based individualized study
Kingwood	N	N	Computer practice, other software	1	Independent study

Summary of Findings

A number of clear results emerged from this study of colleges' computer-assisted practices for developmental students. In interpreting these findings, it is important to note that the students involved in the study possessed very similar demographic characteristics (age, gender, and ethnicity) to developmental students in the aggregate across all nine of the colleges, and grade point averages were comparable between the computer-assisted classes and other developmental classes offered by the participating colleges. A summary of the key findings of this investigation follows:

- Significant differences were found in course outcomes for students between the nine colleges, between the five types of programs studied, as well as between disciplines within the colleges. Because this analysis controlled for the effects of a range of student-related factors, the implication of these findings is that the manner in which a college or program chooses to implement its computer-assisted activities has a clear impact on the outcomes of developmental students.

- Computer-assisted activities are most effective when included as a formal component of the course. The data on this point are clear. All of the most successful programs devoted at least one-third of allotted class time to work in the computer labs, and reported that computer-assisted learning objectives were achieved satisfactorily by students. In contrast, none of the programs which chose to "add on" the activities as out-of-class assignments or recommended additional activities found the computer-assisted learning objectives to have been met satisfactorily. In addition, student satisfaction with the computer-assisted activities was below the norm in these programs.

- Factors such as the role and attitude of the teacher, the quality of support for students within the lab, the nature of the computer activities within the class, and characteristics of the students themselves appear to play a more important role in student success than the choice of software to be used.

- Developmental programs that used computer software or an ILS system as one of several instructional strategies that also included group work, collaborative projects, and other more traditional approaches were found to be generally more successful than programs that relied on computer-assisted strategies alone.

- A clear association emerged between students' favorable perceptions of the appropriateness and capabilities of the computer activities and the presence of the instructor in the lab when assigned activities took place. Other key factors that emerged as common to successful programs were a comprehensive student orientation in the first week of classes and structuring the computer activities as a formal part of the class.

- Students were found generally to enjoy working with computers, and student characteristics commonly considered to be obstacles to success in computer-assisted instruction, such as the student's comfort level with computers and typing or keyboarding ability, appear to have little impact on student success. Most students (74 percent) felt their computer lessons were a good fit with other classwork, and 88 percent said they would enroll in a similar course again.

- Student characteristics associated with success and persistence included several factors that can be influenced by the teacher. A student's perception of whether or not computer lessons are a good fit with the learning objectives of the course, for example, appears to be based on comments or attitudes expressed by the instructor. Similarly, teacher comments and attitudes may influence how a student feels about the rigor of the work on the computer in comparison to other activities or other courses.

Recommendations for Practitioners

These findings suggest a number of recommendations for practitioners wishing to implement or improve the use of computer technology in developmental programs. While the results of this study clearly indicate that developmental students can effectively learn using computers–and that they can do so despite their lack of experience or training in technology–it is also clear that some colleges have been more successful in implementing computer-assisted learning in developmental programs than have others. The following recommendations are based on the factors that distinguished programs with high levels of success from those that were less successful:

There are no "magic bullets." Developmental students, whether taught by traditional means or with technological tools, still come to college with significant academic problems and support needs. A successful approach to using computer-assisted learning activities for developmental students will recognize this and ensure mechanisms are in place that provide the structure and support these students require. Attention to these details will have a far greater impact on retention and success rates than will the use of any particular software tool.

Computer-assisted strategies are not for every teacher. The quickest way to ensure that the computer activities will not be successful is to require all instructors to use them. Developmental students are acutely attuned to subtle signals or off-hand comments from the instructor about the value of the time they spend on a particular activity. It is vital that instructors using computer-assisted strategies spend the time required to familiarize themselves with the instructional material and to determine for themselves if the software is adequate to the task of achieving the learning outcomes expected of the activities.

The value of the computer activities must be clear. Computer-assisted learning activities for developmental students work best when formally integrated into the class, and with a clearly articulated rationale that explains their importance and value to the learning process for both the instructor and student. Assigning computer-based activities as out-of-class or optional exercises is a far less effective strategy.

An early orientation to the lab is critical. All of the most successful programs included a comprehensive orientation during the first week of classes that addressed using the computers; the operating system and computer software; the lab resources, personnel, and policies; and class activities and grading. Providing such an orientation early, especially during the first week of class, not only helps students to understand what it is they are being asked to do, it identifies the computer activities as an important aspect of the class experience during the time when students are most attuned to understanding what is expected of them.

The teacher should be available to students in the lab. The presence of the instructor during computer activities communicates volumes about the worth of the time spent by the student on the learning activity and provides an important human component to the learning experience. If the activity is not worth the instructor's time, students will feel their time is better spent elsewhere as well.

The computers must be given enough time to work. The most successful programs devoted at least one-third of class time to work in the computer lab. If the computer activities are to be successful in helping the students accomplish their learning objectives, enough time must be devoted to the task to ensure that students can use the technology to engage the material.

Developmental students can learn using computers. A final recommendation is targeted at dispelling the notion that, because of their lack of experience or skill with computers, developmental students are not up to the task. While this study uncovered differences among students' perceptions, attitudes, and backgrounds that affect their learning outcomes, the vast majority are satisfied and comfortable with using computers and would enroll in a class using computers again. Like their mainstream counterparts, developmental students see the wide-ranging impact of technology in our society and recognize that they must learn to use it if they are to be successful. Exposing them to technological tools adds value to the learning process in ways that go beyond the learning objectives and activities of the class.

Conclusion

The nine community colleges involved in this study are similar in many respects to other colleges across the country and face many of the same challenges in dealing with large numbers of developmental students. Significant differences were found in course outcomes for students between colleges as well as between disciplines within colleges. The effects of a range of student-related factors were statistically controlled in this analysis and most of the colleges involved in this study used very similar sets of computer software for each of the disciplines. The clear implication is that other factors–the role and attitude of the teacher, the quality of support for students within the lab, the nature of the computer activities within the class (formal versus informal), and characteristics of the students themselves–play a more important role in student success than the choice of software to be used. Unfortunately, in too many cases, these aspects of computer-assisted learning do not receive the same levels of thought and planning, nor is the debate over their importance as fierce, as attends the selection of one software package over another.

If the success of the developmental student is of primary importance, colleges should take special care to attend to the humanistic aspects of how they implement computer-assisted programs and aim to achieve a balance between "high-tech" and "high-touch." While developmental students can clearly benefit from computer-assisted activities, the use of computers alone does not address the affective and behavioral learning needs commonly associated with "at-risk" students.

A final conclusion is worthy of note. The ancillary benefits that accrue to students under the instructional models described in this study are remarkable in their own right. Computer-assisted developmental instruction targets those students who are least likely to have had experience with or access to technology. This study has demonstrated that they can nonetheless be successful using technology to learn. If such programs are expanded, they may serve to reduce the growing disparity between those who come to community colleges already well versed in technological skills and those increasingly disenfranchised students who have had little or no opportunity to develop those skills. The approaches described in this study, in addition to providing instruction in basic academic skills, also give developmental students valuable experience using technology–experience which they will carry forward into other courses, other programs, and ultimately the workplace.

Given the scale of the need for developmental education and the societal and institutional factors driving the integration of technology into instructional programs, the application of computer-assisted instruction to developmental education is an area ripe for further investigation. Much work remains to be done, not only in finding and describing effective models, but also in detailing the costs of such an endeavor and understanding the characteristics of learners that contribute to success. These findings are offered as a starting place for institutions wishing to better understand how to effectively implement computer-assisted developmental instruction.

A version of this chapter first appeared as Meeting the Challenge: Final Report of the Computer-Based Developmental Education Project, *A Report to Invest Learning Corporation from the League for Innovation in the Community College, by Larry Johnson and Stella Perez, Mission Viejo, CA: League for Innovation in the Community College, May, 1996. The study was supported by Invest Learning Corporation.*

References

Campbell, C. B. (1981). "A Supportive Services Program for Students with Predicted Low Academic Abilities: A Coordinated Approach." *Journal of College Student Personnel*, 22, 453-454.

Cope, R. G. (1978). "Why Students Stay, Why They Leave." In L. Noel (Ed.), *New Directions for Student Services: Vol. 3. Reducing the Dropout Rates* (pp. 1-11). San Francisco: Jossey-Bass.

Green, K. C. & Gilbert, S. W. (1995). "Great Expectations: Content, Communications, Productivity, and the Role of Information Technology in Higher Education." *Change*, 27(2), 8-18.

Hancock, L. & Wingert, P. (1995). "The Haves and the Have-Nots: Computer Gap." *Newsweek*, 83, 50-53.

Irving, C. (1996). "Drive for Standardized High School Testing." *Crosstalk*, 4(2), 1.

Katsinas, S. G. (1994). "Is the Open Door Closing?" *Community College Journal*, 64(5), 22-28.

Khalili, A. & Shashaani, L. (1994). "The Effectiveness of Computer Applications: A Meta-Analysis." *Journal of Research on Computing in Education*. 27(1), 49- 61.

Kraetsch, G. A. (1980). "The Role of the Community College in the Basic Skills Movement." *Community College Review*, 8, 18-23.

Kulik, C. C., & Kulik J. A. (1991). "Effectiveness of Computer-Based Instruction: An Updated Analysis." *Computers in Human Behavior*, 7, 75-94.

Liao, Y. C., & Bright, G. W. (1991). "Effects of Computer Programming on Cognitive Outcomes: A Meta-Analysis." *Journal of Educational Computing Research*, 7(3), 251-268.

McCabe, R. H. (1988). The Educational Program of the American Community College: A Transition. In J. S. Eaton (Ed.), *Colleges of Choice*. New York: ACE/Macmillan.

Moore, W., Jr. (1976). *Community College Response to the High-Risk Student: A Critical Reappraisal*. ERIC Clearinghouse for Junior Colleges, Horizon Series. Washington, DC: American Association of Community and Junior Colleges.

Parnell, D. (1994). *Dateline 2000: The New Higher Education Agenda*. Washington, DC: Community College Press.

Roueche, J. E. (1968). *Salvage, Redirection, or Custody?* Washington, DC: American Association of Junior Colleges.

Roueche, J. E. (Ed.). (1977). *New Directions for Higher Education: Vol 20. Increasing Basic Skills by Developmental Studies*. San Francisco: Jossey-Bass.

Roueche, S. D., & Roueche, J. E. (1993). *Between a Rock and a Hard Place: The At-Risk Student in the Open-Door College*. Washington, DC: Community College Press.

Ryan, A. (1991). "Meta-Analysis of Achievement Effects of Micro Computer Applications in Elementary Schools." *Educational Administration Quarterly*, 27(2), 161-184.

Weber, J. (1985). "Thoughts and Actions on Student Retention." *Innovation Abstracts*, 7(30), 1-2.

Wiener, S. P. (1984). "Through the Cracks." *Community, Technical, and Junior College Journal*, 55(4), 52-54.

Wilson, B. J. (1994). "Technology and Higher Education: In Search of Progress in Human Learning." *Educational Record*, 75(3), 6-9.

CHAPTER 8

THE EVOLUTION OF DISTANCE EDUCATION

Judy Lever-Duffy

Distance education, alternative learning, distributed learning, open learning, virtual instruction–these educational "buzz words" all refer to the delivery of instruction to students remote from their teacher, separated by time, location, or both. For the purpose of this chapter, "distance education" will be used to refer to both the historical and the more recent collection of instructional delivery methodologies that serve as alternatives to classroom-based instruction. Distance education may not be the most descriptive term, but it is indeed the most common.

From Chautauqua's correspondence courses to current courses via the Web, educators have attempted to deliver content to students, regardless of where those students reside. Initial barriers were actual physical distances between teacher and student. Contemporary barriers may include not only these same physical distances, but also time constraints on individuals juggling the demands of modern life. Today's technological, demographic, and societal shifts conspire to increase the demand for lifelong education and training, and at the same time require that educational delivery formats be increasingly flexible and accessible (MacBrayne, 1995).

A review of the evolution of distance education reveals that two goals appear to have driven the changes in distance delivery. The first goal is the desire to improve access to instruction for students unable travel to a campus. This goal has been achieved through the many distance delivery formats historically and currently implemented. The second, and perhaps more critical, goal is to ensure that the instruction delivered across distances is as rich a growth experience as that delivered in the traditional classroom. Such richness is the consequence of quality along three dimensions. The first dimension is quality of instruction in terms of pedagogy. Distance instruction must be equal to on-site instruction in the breadth of content and in the effectiveness of the teaching methodology. The second dimension is the quality of the interaction between faculty and student. In a classroom, a unique rapport is established among the participants in the teaching and learning process. If the faculty member is highly skilled in the art of teaching, sharing beyond content ensues. This relationship adds richness to both the learning and the teaching experiences. The final dimension is the quality of interaction among peers. Few who have facilitated a lively class discussion would deny the contribution of this type of interaction to learning. Not only does peer-to-peer interaction add new and unique threads to the fabric of the learning experience, it also creates new opportunities for students to establish personal connections to the content and to their peers.

These driving forces behind distance education's evolutionary development are illustrated in Figure 8A. With these forces delineated, the history of distance delivery can be more easily reviewed.

Figure 8A. Distance Education Goals

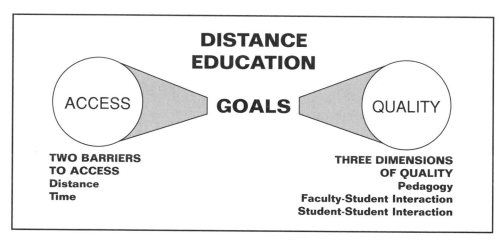

A Historical Perspective

The foundation of contemporary distance education programs is the correspondence course. This format focused on the initial goal of distance education, the desire to improve access to instruction. Beginning in Sweden as early as 1833 and in England dating back to 1840, instruction through the post offered courses of study for composition and shorthand. By 1873, correspondence study had crossed the Atlantic to Boston with the founding of the Society to Encourage Studies at Home. This initial distance education effort attracted more than 10,000 students of the classical curriculum (Hanson et al., 1997).

The first U.S. distance delivered academic degree was authorized by New York state through the Chautauqua College of Liberal Arts. To complete Chautauqua programs, students were required to participate in a combination of summer institutes and correspondence courses. At that time, confidence in this new methodology was so great that those involved in this early movement thought it likely to expand until it became more successful than traditionally delivered classroom-based courses (Hanson et al., 1997)

Correspondence courses and degree programs continued to develop in both Europe and the U.S. Notable in the states were the University of Chicago's University Extension division and the University of Wisconsin's Farmer's Institutes, the basis of Wisconsin's University Extension division. All of the correspondence courses during this early period revolved around print materials distributed and returned via mail. Interaction time between student and faculty was limited by the speed at which the mail moved; peer-to-peer interaction was nonexistent. As cumbersome and slow as this methodology may seem to Information Age distance educators and students, correspondence courses still thrive in the U.S. today, particularly as commercial home study courses. Print remains the primary delivery medium for the correspondence approach, although interaction may now be supplemented by telephone, fax, and modem. Many higher education institutions use the descriptor "independent study" when referring to the correspondence-style distance delivery format (Moore, Kearsley, & Scriven, 1996).

The integration of technology into the correspondence format moved distance education up to the next rung of its evolutionary ladder. With the advent of radio and television, distance educators were able to augment delivery through broadcasting. In the 1920s, radio stations were constructed at educational institutions, and as early as 1930, experimental television teaching programs were produced. By the 1950s, college credit courses were offered via broadcast television (Hanson et al.). The integration of broadcast technology increased access and to some extent addressed pedagogical quality issues. Teachers became active participants in the teaching and learning process, and the teacher-directed instruction once presented in the classroom now became available via technology. However, the addition of broadcast technology to distance delivery did little to improve the quality of interaction. Students remained passive recipients of teacher-centered instruction. The mailing of print materials to accompany broadcasts was a primary component of this technology-enhanced correspondence-type course, and student response via mail continued as the primary mode of communication between teacher and student.

In the 1970s, with the advent of the Public Broadcasting Service (PBS), the Instructional Television Fixed Service (ITFS), and cable television, distance education took another upward step. With these technology options, the cost of television-based distance education decreased while access increased. The application of this technology allowed more distance education programs to use limited broadcast to achieve their access goals. Further, with local broadcast, initiation and implementation of instructional programming became easier to control and manage. To maximize the quality of instruction, broadcast-quality instructional productions with carefully prepared printed support materials were produced by a number of institutions. These videos and supplementary print materials not only were used by the institution, but also were sold to other institutions for distribution via local limited broadcast systems. Such high-quality productions, packaged with appropriate curricula, came to be known as telecourses. However, this improvement to distance delivery still did not address issue of the quality of interaction. Using the telecourse approach to distance, students remained primarily passive recipients of instruction in potentially isolated learning environments. Instruction continued to be teacher-centered, that is, focused on the presentation of materials by the instructor without regard to responses by the students receiving the instruction. Some telecourse-based distance education programs did integrate the use of telephone, fax, and mail to promote faster and more responsive communication between instructor and students. However, these methods of interaction did little to provide the same quality of faculty-to-student interaction as might be found in the classroom. Further, telecourse students often had little or no contact with their peers.

During the mid-1970s, some distance education programs added satellite-delivered instructional television to the repertoire of delivery technology. This technology offered broader distribution of instruction across larger distances. Further, when combined with telephone and fax access, real-time interaction became possible. Thus the teleconference emerged as a distance delivery tool. This was a major advance for distance education in that groups would gather for televised delivery and could interact with the instructors via telephone or fax during the broadcast. And, since students gathered in a single, if distant, location, they could interact among themselves. The teleconference added the technology necessary to provide faculty-to-student interaction and the aggregation necessary to enable peer-to-peer interaction. Teleconferences added quality to distance interaction as a less passive form of distance education became possible.

Along with expanding the choices of delivery media, distance education was evolving in terms of the types of institutions delivering it. Prior to the 1960s, distance education was primarily an outreach program of traditional institutions. In the 1960s and 1970s however, open universities formed in South Africa and in England. Dedicated to distance delivery, these institutions gave credibility to distance education by offering full degree programs and advanced courses. Further, they provided models for the development of similar institutions internationally. The Open University model provided the general population with open access to higher education. It also added new components to distance teaching, including regional study centers and tutors, further reducing the isolation and passivity that characterized correspondence courses (Moore, Kearsley, & Scrivens, 1996).

With the advent of microcomputing in the late 1970s and early 1980s, distance education capabilities moved forward in their potential and their evolution. As microcomputing and its delivery counterpart, telecommunications, became commonplace in the 1980s and 1990s, their application to distance education expanded. Audio, video, and text (multimedia) in an interactive format was made possible via computer disks, CD-ROMs, and local and wide-area networking. Real-time (synchronous) and time-shifted (asynchronous) communications via telecommunications and network connections made the student isolation from faculty and peers so often associated with distance education relatively easy to overcome. Computer technology provided the interactive capabilities necessary to achieve both access to and quality of instruction along all dimensions. And, with the potential for massive interconnection offered by the Internet and the emerging technology associated with it, distance education may well evolve into models less like those that have come before and more like those appropriate to the 21st Century. Inexpensive, readily available microcomputing and telecomputing have made computer-mediated instructional delivery a driving force in the evolution of distance education.

Distance Education Today

Distance delivery of instruction has evolved consistently with the delivery technology options available to distance educators. Advances in technology have made the delivery of information and instruction more accessible and interaction more immediate. They have enhanced the quality of distance interaction and extended it to include the peer-to-peer interaction previously only available in the classroom. The distance delivery technology available today continues to extend the capabilities of the instructional environment to maximize the learning experience for distance students. With the implementation of these technology options, the need to aggregate people before teaching them has disappeared (MacBrayne, 1995).

Technology and Distance Delivery

Clearly, the emergence of new, innovative technology options has altered distance education, but this technology-centered view of the evolution of distance education, however accurate, raises some concerns among many distance educators. Distance education programs have too often been constructed around a technology rather than around the instruction that technology is intended to deliver. Too often, an institution either has or acquires a given technology and then engages in the creation of a distance education program based on that technology. The technology becomes a solution in search of a problem (Sedlak and Cartwright, 1997). This techno-centric approach results in technology driving instruction rather than instruction driving the selection of appropriate technology. Such a technology-driven approach to distance education is likely to result in methodologies that may not be appropriate for students, content, or teaching styles, and may well result in too great an investment in quickly dated delivery approaches. Willis (1993) advocates an integrative approach to selecting distance delivery technology to ensure that no single medium dominates instruction in an institution's distance education program. Today, the integrative approach appears to be prevailing. Many institutions that previously focused on a single delivery technology are reevaluating that position and broadening their technology options.

A New Paradigm for Distance Delivery

Technology itself is not the only focal point for change in distance education. A quiet revolution has underscored the technology-based evolution that is under way. A transformational, although less conspicuous, outcome of technology-enhanced distance delivery is a steady paradigm shift from faculty-driven instruction to faculty-facilitation of instruction. This movement from the instructor as "sage on the stage" to "guide on the side" has initiated a rethinking of the design and methodology of distance delivered curriculum. For those distance educators able to avail themselves of some of the newer delivery options, surprising and innovative changes to methodology become possible. The new technology options offer creative faculty opportunities to design strategies that provide interaction and communication between and among students. Because these technology options and resultant strategies offer students much of the interaction they previously might have experienced only in a conventional classroom, they add a richness and depth to the distance learning environment. A shift of focus away from the classroom-based model to a model based on open access to information and facilitation of new ways of learning becomes possible (Hopey & Ginsburg, 1996).

Gates (1996) suggests that information technology will open new and different opportunities for learning. Technology will humanize the distance education environment by overcoming isolation and facilitating collaboration. Donahoe (1995) suggests that new distance education methodologies will enable learning communities, enhance communication, promote interaction among diverse populations, and take learners beyond the limits of the classroom. Clearly, educators have just begun to explore the possibilities created through the application of emerging distance delivery technology and methodologies. Like many higher education institutions, community colleges are on the brink of discovering where this new paradigm might lead.

Approaches to Distance Education

The technology used to deliver instruction at a distance initially defined distance education as implemented by an institution. Today, however, so many technology options are used in so many unique and creative ways that classifying distance education programs in terms of the technology they incorporate is no longer easy or appropriate. Programs are better defined in terms of the manner in which delivery of content and opportunity for interaction are made possible. All distance education programs provide access to the instructional event to students remote from their instructor. The question, then, is how any given program offers students the opportunity to access instruction and to interact with the instructor and with their peers. The terms synchronous and asynchronous distance delivery accurately describe an institution's choice of approach to the delivery of education to distant students.

Synchronous Distance Delivery

Synchronous delivery is time-bound delivery of the instructional event. Students and instructor meet together at a given time to participate in the teaching and learning process and to interact with each other. On campus, this event typically takes place in a single designated location, the traditional classroom. At a distance, the event may take place at numerous locations, but students and instructor participate in the event at the same time. The instructor may conduct a conference call with a small group of participants, each in a different city; groups in different places may meet together by participating in a live teleconference with an instructor; or students may join an instructor in a live chat room on the Internet. The common quality in these examples is that the instruction is synchronized, that is, it occurs simultaneously for all participants. Location does not hinder instruction and may not impact interaction. Students and faculty may be distant from one another, but the time frame in which the instruction occurs is the same for all.

The advantage of synchronous distance delivery is that it maximizes opportunities for real-time interaction. If the students and faculty are all available at the same time, technology can provide ways to overcome the distances that separate them. Live interaction is possible by telephone, fax, computer, compressed video, or other telecommunications systems. The benefits of this type of interaction are the spontaneity of the interaction, the free flow of ideas, and the potential for communication.

The disadvantages of synchronous distance delivery include many of the same difficulties found in a traditional classroom. Most obviously, the instruction is time-bound. That is, students who are unable to participate at the designated time miss the instructional event and the benefits of participation. Further, even for those who are able to attend, live interaction may not be as participatory as it initially seems. In the traditional classroom or the synchronous distance experience, the shy or self-conscious student may not actively participate. He or she may assume a passive role, following the interaction but remaining outside of it. The opportunity for interaction may be present, but interaction itself may not be a reality for all students.

Asynchronous Distance Delivery

Asynchronous distance delivery is time-shifted instruction delivered without regard to location. Asynchronous instruction may occur on or off the campus, with faculty and students partaking of instructional components or opportunities for interaction at times convenient to them. The faculty member may use video or audio technology to store a lecture for access by students when their schedules permit. Students may use electronic mail or conference to work cooperatively on an assignment or project. Student voice mail may provide for time-shifted group discussion. The key element in asynchronous delivery is that faculty and students share an instructional environment in which they can access the components they need when they need them. Many technology options facilitate this approach to distance delivery. Traditional distance technology applications, including print, video tape, and audio tape, make possible asynchronous delivery of content. New distance delivery options, such as electronic conferencing, e-mail, and Web pages, make asynchronous interaction possible.

The obvious advantage of asynchronous distance delivery is the improved ability to fit teaching and learning into a hectic life schedule, but other advantages exist as well. For the shy student, the semi-anonymity provided through asynchronous interaction devoid of visual cues and body language may provide a comfortable environment in which to participate. Further, the delay in responding to a question posed by an instructor or peer may give the more thoughtful and careful student sufficient opportunity to frame a response. For such students, asynchronous interaction takes the pressure and immediacy out of interaction and provides a learning environment better suited to their personal preferences. Berge and Collins (1995) suggest that for some students, the freedom to explore alternatives provided by computer-mediated delivery enhances the development of their own personal style of learning.

As with every methodology, asynchronous delivery has its share of disadvantages. For some students, the experience of face-to-face interaction is a critical component in the learning process. They need the visual cues, classroom rituals, and spontaneity of discussion to become engaged in the process and expand their level of understanding (Billings, 1996). Others simply need the structure of a given time and place for learning to stay on track, organized, and focused (Threlkeld and Brzoska, 1994). Some students find the technology necessary for effective asynchronous interaction challenging to use. Effective use of asynchronous delivery must address this need and provide adequate technical support and training for such students (Willis, 1993).

Toward an Ideal Delivery System

An institution engaged in distance delivery or contemplating the creation of a distance education program must make a series of significant decisions in order to create an effective structure. Distance delivery technology requires a substantial investment in terms of acquisition, installation, training, and support. Facilities may need to be planned, created, or remodeled. Carefully planned synchronous or asynchronous curricula must be developed, often with the substantial use of faculty time and effort. Institutions are fully aware of the costly implication of errors in dealing with any of these factors. The decisions are complex, intricately interconnected, and difficult to embrace. It is no wonder that often a distance delivery system decision finally focuses on the simplest of all components of the process, the delivery technology itself.

Some would argue that it is easier to come to a decision about a given technology and then build a distance education program around it. This approach, though tempting, is simplistic and is unlikely to move the institution toward its ideal. Willis (1995) states that "the key to effective distance education is focusing on the needs of the learner, the requirements of the content, and the constraints faced by the teacher before selecting a delivery system" (p.2). Since each institution serves its own audience, focuses upon both general and highly specialized content, and employs diverse faculty, each institution needs to examine its internal and external environments before making any significant distance education decisions (Albrecht and Bardsley, 1994).

Bates (1995) suggests that a framework for making decisions is necessary to avoid the three common decision-making scenarios frequently hindering the move towards the ideal. These three scenarios include the doing nothing is safer scenario; the sympathetic anarchy scenario, in which enthusiasts are encouraged to use whatever they have or can get; and the single medium mania scenario, in which a single technology adopted.

The ideal distance delivery system for an institution may be synchronous, asynchronous, or a hybrid of both. As Willis (1995) suggests, specific instructional and institutional factors impact the selection of an appropriate approach. Once the approach is decided, the technology options can be explored, evaluated, and selected. Typically, careful planning will result in an integrative approach supported by a media mix created specifically for the institution and its clients. The ideal delivery system, therefore, is customized for the students and faculty who use it and the institution that supports it. Careful and strategic decision making is clearly necessary in the implementation of a new or expanded distance education program; the one-size-fits-all response is both inappropriate and incorrect. Moving toward an ideal system requires that the institution fully examine and articulate its own needs.

Current Distance Education Programs

With little doubt, alternatives to traditional systems are needed and distance delivery is one of the most explored alternative systems to date. Chute (1996) suggests that educational institutions can no longer keep up with skills obsolescence. A just-in-time approach is needed to prepare learners for the demands of the 21st Century workplace. Green and Gilbert

(1996) state that changing demographics demonstrate an increase in the number of students who will benefit from distance education. Day (1996) projects that up to 75 percent of the existing workforce will require significant job retraining in the next five years. Martorella (1996) suggests that as currently constituted, educational delivery systems will outdistance available resources in the struggle to prepare their constituencies for the future. A review of current practices and approaches reveals that a variety of distance education options are being used.

Model Practices and Approaches

Gates (1996) notes that by 1996, half of all higher education institutions offered a formal distance education program. Lever-Duffy, Lemke, and Johnson (1996) collected examples of model distance education programs among community colleges. The sixteen colleges judged to be examples of multiple approach model programs are summarized in Figure 8B.

This sample of model practices makes clear that current approaches and uses of technology in community colleges span the distance education continuum from synchronous to asynchronous and from print to the Internet. However, a trend toward increased asynchronous, online instruction exists. In a 1991 survey of community college distance education programs (Lever), an average of only 12 percent identified some type of online delivery as a component of their programs. Just 5 years later, 81 percent of the new sample (right) had added this component. No doubt, as technology evolves and community college students increase their access to it, online and similar delivery approaches will continue to expand. Of note, also, is the continuing use of old technology in distance delivery, despite the growing use of emerging technology. As Berge and Collins (1995) suggest, older technology options are augmented by newer ones rather than replaced by them.

Distance Technology Overview

Barbrow, Jeong, and Parks (1996) suggest that when selecting appropriate distance technology, the overriding concern should be to consider technology options that will create equitable and effective teaching and learning systems. Major (1995) projects further integration of voice, data, and video technology in service to and in support of changing instruction.

Figure 8B. Model Community College Distance Education Programs Summary of Approaches and Technology Employed

Institution	Synchronous (S) Asynchronous (A) Hybrid (H)	Print	Audio	Phone/ Fax	Video	Compr. Video	Comp. Mediated	Online
Austin Community College	H	✔		✔	✔		✔	✔
Chattanooga State Technical Community College	A	✔			✔			✔
Chemeteka Community College	H	✔	✔		✔			✔
Dallas Community College District	H	✔	✔	✔	✔			✔
Florida Community College at Jacksonville	A	✔	✔	✔	✔			✔
Genessee Community College	H	✔	✔	✔	✔		✔	✔
Kirkwood Community College	S	✔	✔		✔	✔		
Miami-Dade Community College	H	✔	✔	✔	✔	✔	✔	✔
Northern Virginia Community College	H	✔	✔	✔	✔	✔	✔	✔
Northwestern Michigan College	S	✔	✔		✔	✔		
Rio Salado College	H	✔	✔	✔	✔	✔		✔
San Diego City College	H	✔		✔				
Sinclair Community College	H	✔	✔	✔	✔			✔
Tarrant County Community College	H	✔	✔	✔	✔		✔	✔
University College of the Cariboo	H	✔		✔	✔			✔
Washtenaw Community College	H	✔		✔	✔	✔		✔

Hopey and Ginsburg (1996) note that the emergence of new technology will further enable the shift of focus from delivery of classroom-type instruction to the facilitation of new ways of learning. Technology clearly enables delivery while impacting the very nature of the materials delivered.

The assortment of distance delivery technology options available at most institutions has emerged over time. Older technology may at one time have been the core delivery technology but now serves as only one of multiple delivery options. Some older technology options have been designated to serve other instructional methodologies, while others have been upgraded for new applications. Few have been abandoned. The community college that is currently engaged in distance delivery or that is seeking to establish a distance program must critically examine its current technological resources and carefully plan for the acquisition of future technology consistent with the instructional goals of its distance education program. Figure 8C summarizes the application of and requirements for many of the distance education technology options in place today.

Relationship Between Delivery Technology and Instruction

Technology enables and supports instructional events. If one of the primary goals of distance education is to ensure that the instructional quality at a distance equals or exceeds that which occurs in the classroom, then distance technology must directly contribute to the achievement of this goal. In Figure 8D (p. 268), a summary diagram demonstrates the relationship between traditional and distance methodologies and the various distance technology options that enable them. As illustrated in Figure 8D, most traditional classroom strategies can be replicated at a distance via the application of appropriate technology. Faculty instructional choices and potential strategies are not limited by the spatial or temporal distances faced by instructor and student. Rather, they are changed in terms of the methodology and technological support necessary to achieve them. Teaching and learning at a distance do not need to be instructionally inferior if the innovative application of technology is encouraged and supported.

The Future of Distance Education

When Green and Gilbert (1997) reviewed the implementation cycle of corporations and nonprofit organizations and applied it to information

Figure 8C. Applications and Requirements for Current Distance Education Technology Options

Technology	Application *Approach*	Institutional Requirements	User Requirements
Print	Communication of course information and content *Useful for both synchronous and asynchronous approaches*	Ability to create, reproduce, and distribute hard copy	Ability to receive or pick up materials
Audio Broadcast	Radio broadcast of content best communicated via audio (e.g. lectures, music, languages, poetry, drama) *Primarily synchronous*	Ability to broadcast live or via tape to local and/or distance audience	Ability to receive broadcast
Audio Tape	Easy and inexpensive way to distribute lectures or other audio based instruction *Useful for both synchronous and asynchronous approaches*	Ability to record, edit, dub, and distribute audio cassettes	Ability to playback audio cassettes
Telephone	Provides interaction between faculty and student or student and peers; may also use for short instructional components or communication of course information *Use for both synchronous and asynchronous approaches*	Private telephone access for faculty, long distance capabilities	Access to telephone
Phone Conference	Provides group interaction between faculty and small group of students or student and peers; useful for small group activities and short lectures or communication of course information *Primarily synchronous*	Minimum: telephone system with conferencing capabilities, preferred system offers a phone bridge with a single access number to call to participate	Access to telephone
Voice Mail	Provides asynchronous opportunities for interaction between faculty and student(s) or student and peers; useful for short instructional components or communication of course information *Useful for asynchronous approaches*	Voice mail system providing student voice mail boxes	Access to telephone

Technology	Application *Approach*	Institutional Requirements	User Requirements
Fax	Supports written interaction between faculty and student or student and peers; useful for written instructional components or communication of course information *Useful for both synchronous and asynchronous approaches*	Phone lines and fax machines at teaching locations and/or faculty offices	Access to telephone line and fax machine
Video Broadcast	Television broadcast or cablecast of instructional content best communicated via combined audio and visual media *Primarily synchronous*	Ability to produce and broadcast live or recorded video	Access to TV and broadcast signals
Video Tape	Recorded instructional content best communicated via combined audio and visual media *Useful for both synchronous and asynchronous approaches*	Ability to produce, record, edit, dub, and distribute video tapes	Access to TV and VCR
Compressed Video	Two-way live video and audio transmission of traditional classroom setting; next evolution may include participation from individual workstations *Primarily synchronous*	Compressed video equipment at send and all receive sites; high speed communication lines between sites	Ability to get to compressed video classroom
Computer Software	Computer-based instructional software to demonstrate content, tutor, and/or build skills *Primarily asynchronous*	Ability to buy software licenses or design, produce, and distribute instructional software on disk, CD-ROM, or via networking	Access to compatible hardware
Electronic Mail	Computer groupware provides written one-to-one, time-shifted interaction between faculty and student or student and peers; useful for short instructional components or communication of course information *Useful for both synchronous and asynchronous approaches*	Electronic mail server with mail boxes for faculty and students	Access to computer, modem, and network

Technology	Application *Approach*	Institutional Requirements	User Requirements
Electronic Conferencing	Computer groupware provides one-to-many time-shifted written interaction among members of an instructional unit (faculty and students); useful for short instructional components or communication of course information *Useful for both synchronous and asynchronous approaches*	Electronic conferencing software and server accessible via network or modem	Access to computer, modem, and network
Chat Rooms	Computer groupware provides real time written interaction among members of an instructional unit (faculty and students); allows for an on-screen communication space in which real-time written interaction is displayed; useful for short instructional components or communication of course information *Primarily synchronous*	Chat room software and server accessible via network or modem	Access to computer, modem, and network
Web Pages	Internet-based World Wide Web site graphically presents a course; can be designed to communicate course information and content, connect to Internet resources, provide access to above network-based resources, offer multimedia instruction *Primarily asynchronous*	Web server, access to the Internet; ability to program, create, and maintain Web pages; ability to manage a website	Access to computer, modem, and the Internet
Network/Internet Instructional Systems	Internet or network based integrated instructional system provides the facility to put all aspects of a course online including text, video, audio, chat, e-mail, conferencing, Internet access, and assessment *Primarily asynchronous*	Ability to maintain instructional system server; wide area network; access to Internet; ability to create and maintain instructionally appropriate components; ability to manage and maintain system and hardware	Access to computer, modem, and the Internet or network
Audio graphics Conferencing	Combination of telephone interaction and real-time computer-based communication of visuals; useful for voice instruction supported by real-time interactive visuals *Primarily synchronous*	Telephone access; hardware and software for audio graphic conferencing; additional phone line to connect computer component	Compatible hardware and software; access to phone and additional line

Figure 8D. Traditional and Distance Instructional Strategies and their Enabling Technologies

Traditional Strategies	Enabling Technologies	Possible D.E. Strategies
Lecture		Instructor's Lectures via Videotape, Audiotape, or Phone Conference; Off-campus "Expert" Presentations; Guest Speakers (taped or live)
Reading: Text/Supplements		Hard Copy; Online; Audiotape Books
Library Research		Public/School Libraries; Online Libraries; Telephone/ Fax Reference Services
Written Responses/ Papers		Computer-Assisted Writing; Shared Hard Copy; Class Publications
Class Discussions		Small Group Phone Conferences; Electronic Conferences; ListServs/E-mail; Fax Forward
Class Demonstrations		At-Home Kits; Open "Labs"; Activity Directions Using Common Materials
Learning Groups		Seminars; Skill Workshops; Electronic Chat Groups; Conference Calls; Phone "Buddies"
Audio and Video Supplements		Faculty Prepared A/V; Commercially Prepared A/V; Student Prepared A/V; TV/Radio Broadcast
Oral Presentations		Simulations and Dramatizations; Individual Performances; Group Performances; Conference Calls; Taped Presentations
Field Experience		Interviews; Observations; Visitations and Tours; Service Learning Experiences
Collaborative Learning		Phone "Buddies"; Conferencing/Chat Groups; Chain Letters; Conference Calls

COMPUTER   FAX   DISK   TEXT   PHONE   A/V TAPE   MAIL   HARD COPY   COMMON MATERIALS   IN PERSON   NETWORKS technology in higher education, they identified four stages of the cycle. These include Stage 0, during which some planning, investment, and experimentation takes place; Stage 1, during which some capital investment has occurred that enables the institution to accomplish a task never before attempted and to make modest gain towards its achievement; Stage 2, during which investment and capacity continues to grow and new functions are implemented; and Stage 3, during which the organization achieves new levels of efficiency and effectiveness and is in fact no longer the same institution that it was when it started the cycle. Green and Gilbert (1997) note that regarding information technology, most colleges are somewhere in Stage 1.

When this cyclical review is applied to distance education, the situation is even more critical. Some community colleges are firmly entrenched in Stage 0 or Stage 1; others have progressed to Stage 2. There is little doubt that the society these institutions serve continues to be transformed into a fragmented one (Martovella, 1996) that is moving away from collecting individuals at designated locations for activities. The new emphasis is on decentralization, smaller institutional units, and unique learning communities (Donahoe, 1995). To serve this changing constituency, community colleges must begin to address new roles and instructional alternatives.

Day (1996) states that in 1950, 60 percent of the available jobs were unskilled, but by 1991, only 35 percent of the jobs were unskilled. In contrast, in both 1950 and 1991, professional level jobs stayed at a steady 20 percent of all available jobs. The projection for 2000 is that available unskilled jobs will shrink to just 15 percent of available jobs, while professional jobs will continue to remain at 20 percent. Further, up to 75 percent of the existing workforce will require significant retraining over the next five years. The role of the community college in training the current and future skilled workforce is clear. The question remains one of how it can be done with limited community college resources and limited availability of learners who have personal and work responsibilities. Distance education offers at minimum a partial solution to this challenge and at best an opportunity for seamless and effective lifelong learning options.

Many issues in distance delivery still need to be addressed. Significant academic as well as technological controversy must be researched, evaluated, and appropriately resolved. Community colleges need to plan carefully and strategically for distance delivery initiatives and evolve into Stage 3 institutions that offer targeted and appropriate instruction in new and effective ways. Partnerships and collaborations such as the Western Governor's Virtual University and the Asynchronous Learning Network (ALN) demonstration projects funded by the Alfred P. Sloan Foundation need to be carefully examined and reviewed. Such leading edge efforts serve as models for community colleges regardless of the evolutionary stage in which they currently reside. For all community colleges, the opportunities are as limitless as the need.

The future of distance education is not to surpass mainstream education. It is instead to become mainstream education. Distance education will have arrived when it is no longer a segregated, unusual, or innovative learning option, but is instead as common a component of an institution's course offerings as is an evening class. Distance education has not yet become what it will be for community colleges and the students they serve, but there is little doubt that just-in-time, targeted, accessible, customized, technology-enabled instruction must be as significant an objective for community colleges as it is for training units in major corporations and state legislatures concerned about training America's workforce. Distance education will become the source of educational opportunity across local, regional, state, and national boundaries. It will target niche learners and the general population alike. It will ultimately offer learners an interconnected system of learning and training opportunities with community colleges serving as regional hubs in a national and international network. Future iterations of today's embryonic distance education programs will fulfill the promise of extending the learning environment to ensure that every learner can engage education any time, any place, via any path, and at any pace he or she might need. Distance education, alternative learning, distributed learning, open learning, virtual instruction, or whatever term best serves, is the beginning of an instructional evolution fueled by a technological revolution we have only just begun to experience. The future of distance education is not in question, but its final shape and form remain to be determined. However distance education ultimately presents itself, community colleges, with their responsiveness to the needs of their constituents, are no doubt positioned to be the leaders of 21st Century instructional delivery.

References

Albrecht, R. & Bardsley, G. (1994). Strategic Planning and Academic Planning for Distance Education. In B. Willis (Ed.), *Distance Education: Strategies and Tools*, (68-86), Englewood Cliffs, NJ: Educational Technology.

Barbrow, E. P., Jeong, M., & Parks, S. C. (1996). "Computer Experiences and Attitudes of Students and Preceptors in Distance Education." *Journal of the American Dietetic Association*, 96(12), 1280.

Berge, Z. & Collins, M. (1995). "Computer Mediated Communication and the Online Classroom in Distance Learning." Available: sunsite.unc.edu/cmc/mag/1995/apr/berge.html [June 9, 1997].

Bates, A.W. (1995). *Technology, Open Learning, and Distance Education*. London: Routledge.

Billings, D. M. (1996). "Distance Education: Adapting Courses." *Computers in Nursing*, 14(5), 260.

Campbell, P. B. & Storo, J. (1996). "Reducing the Distance: Equity Issues in Distance Learning in Public Education." *Journal of Science Education and Technology*, 5(4), 285-295.

Carey, D. A. (1996). "Distancing Your College Courses." *Planning for Higher Education*, 24(4), 5-13.

Chute, A. G., Hancock, B. W. & Balthazar, L. B. (1991). "Distance Education Futures: Information Needs and Technology Options." Available: www.lucent.com/cedl/distance.html [June 9, 1997].

Donahoe, S. S. (1995). "Using Distance Learning and Telecommunications to Develop Strategies for Communication for Widely Diverse Populations." Unpublished information analysis.

Day, P. R. (1996). "Responding to the Challenge of Workforce and Economic Development: The Role of America's Community Colleges." American Association of Community Colleges White Paper.

Dede, C. (1996). "The Evolution of Distance Education: Emerging Technology and Distributed Learning." *American Journal of Distance Education*, 10(2), 4-36.

Froke, M. (1994). "A Vision and Promise: Distance Education at Penn State, Part 2. Policy and Organization." *Journal of Continuing Higher Education*, 42(3), 16-23.

Gates, B. (1996). "Linked Up for Learning." *Educational Record*, 66(4), 34-41.

Green, K. C. & Gilbert, S. W. (1995). "Great Expectations: Content, Communications, Productivity and the Role of Information Technology in Higher Education." *Change*, 22(2), 8-18.

Hanson, D., Maushak, N. J., Schlosser, C. A., Anderson, M. L., Sorensen, C., & Simonson, M. (1997). *Distance Education: Review of the Literature* (2nd ed.). Washington DC: Association for Education Communications and Technology.

Hopey, C. E. & Ginsburg, L. (1996). "Distance Learning and New Technology. You Can't Predict the Future But You Can Plan for It." *Adult Learning*, 8(1), 22-23.

Johnstone, S. M. & Krauth, B. (1996). "Balancing Quality and Access: Some Principles for Good Practice for the Virtual University." *Change*, 28(2), 38-41.

Lever, J. (1991). *Distance Education Resource Guide*. Mission Viejo, CA: League for Innovation in the Community College.

Lever-Duffy, J., Lemke, R., and Johnson, L. (1996). *Learning Without Limits: Model Distance Education Programs in Community Colleges*. Mission Viejo, CA: League for Innovation in the Community College.

MacBrayne, P. S. (1995). "Rural Adults in Community College Distance Education: What Motivates Them to Enroll." *New Directions for Community Colleges*, 23(2), 85-93.

Major, H. (1995). "Teaching for Learning . . . At a Distance." *Michigan Community College Journal*, 1(1), 49-60.

Marsden, R. (1996). "Time, Space, and Distance Education." *Distance Education*, 17(2), 222.

Martorella, P. H. (1996). "The Degathering of Society: Implications for Technology and Educators." *NASSP Bulletin*, 80(582), 34-41.

Miller, L. G., Hyatt, S. Y., Brennan, J., Betani, R., & Trevor, T. (1996). "Overcoming Barriers for 'Niche' Learners through Distance Learning." Unpublished conference paper.

Moore, M. G., Kearsley, G., & Scriven, B. (1996). "Distance Education: A Systems View." *Distance Education*, 17(2), 412.

Moss, P. (1997). "The Evolution of Policy and Practice: Telecom-Based Instruction in Oklahoma." *Technological Horizons in Education (T.H.E.) Journal*, 24(9), 58-60.

Ranall, B., Bishop, J., & Caudle, K. (1996). "A Marketing Approach to Distance Education Technology: A Statewide Survey." *Community College Review*, 23(4), 15.

Sedlak, R. A. & Cartwright, P. G. (1997). "Two Approaches to Distance Education: Lessons Learned." *Change*, 29(1), 54.

Threlkeld, R. & Brzoska, K. (1994). Research in Distance Education. In B. Willis (Ed.), *Distance Education: Strategies and Tools* (pp. 41-67). Englewood Cliffs, NJ: Educational Technology.

Tulloch, J. (1996). "Seven Principles for Good Practice in Distance Learning." Unpublished conference paper.

Willis, B. (1993). *Distance Education: A Practical Guide*. Englewood Cliffs, NJ: Educational Technology.

Willis, B. (1996). *Distance Education: An Overview*. Available: www.uidaho.edu/evo/dist1.html#delivery [June 9, 1997].

Wolcott, L. L. (1996). "Distant, But Not Distanced: A Learner-Centered Approach to Distance Education." *TechTrends*, 41(5), 23.

CHAPTER 9

ON THE MOVING ROCK WE STAND: TECHNOLOGY AND TRANSITION

Steven Lee Johnson and Conferlete Carney

The important waves of technological change are those that fundamentally alter the place of technology in our lives. What matters is not technology itself, but its relationship to us.
— Weiser and Brown, 1997, p. 75

The challenges that accompany managing major information technology transitions include countless factors–expected and unexpected–that can cause a major technology project to fail. Budget, time, performance, acceptance, or any combination of these measures of success can stall a major technology initiative. Ironically, of the many factors affecting technology project success, only a few are related to the innate capability or functioning of the technology itself. Typically, the roots of most technology successes and problems are not within the direct control of the chief technology officer or the technology staff. The technology staff swims, and sometimes sinks, while towing major technology initiatives through a sea of overall college politics, social and work customs, finances, state and federal policies, organizational structures, and other factors outside the daily operations of the technology department. This is not to imply that technology transition success does not require tremendous technical skill from a good many people, because it does. However, technology transition success also requires that technology leaders have the inclination and ability to understand the culture of the college and to partner with influential nontechnology administrators to gain continuous support and resources. We believe that this simple, yet powerful, principle is key to approaching and managing major technology transitions successfully.

In addition, managing major technology projects requires detailed planning and careful execution of the plan. This chapter provides ideas intended to contribute to better planning and execution of technology-based change. Though good luck may also be a requirement for the success of major technology projects, we believe that, more often than not, luck will find those who plan and execute well. Planning and executing are predicated on the ability to understand the culture, politics, and organizational behavior of the particular college and the ability to partner with key administrators outside of the technology department.

Five concepts and assumptions are key to this chapter:

- Major technology transitions are in fact organizational transitions. On a simple level, technology transitions are all about computers, software, networks, and technology staffing; however, at a more significant level, such transitions are actually more about institutional policies, types of services offered, costs and budgets, collegewide workflow and work behaviors, staff workload, and outcomes. These transitions are all about changing at least part of *what* is done in a college, *how* it is done, *when* is it done, *who* does it, *who pays* for it, and *what* the outcomes are.

- Managing organizational change is paramount to success in technology planning and execution. Effective technology leaders recognize the critical relationship between change and technology, and they work to develop and apply their skills in organizational change management.

- The priorities, goals, and actions of the technology department as a functional area should be aligned with the priorities and goals of the executive administrators and their respective functional areas.

- Managing organizational change requires recognizing and working with both the formal and informal cultures of the college.

- The fields of strategy development, organizational change, and process reengineering provide relevant insights into the problems and challenges associated with developing and implementing major technology transitions.

From our premise that many conceptual, organizational, and technical skill sets are needed for successfully managing major technology transitions, we present several interrelated concepts within this chapter. First, we set the stage with an exploration of two sets of significant changes that influence college management in the age of technology: shifts in society at large and shifts in technology itself. Next, we argue that college leaders need to be both technologically and politically astute. We surveyed technology professionals and share findings that reveal perceptions of unrealistic expectations regarding technology management in a number of institutions. Since we talk in terms of change at the organizational level, we present a model for understanding and analyzing an organization and we offer a straightforward, three-step process for managing major organizational changes. Next, we summarize the models we favor for developing an information technology strategy, and we share specific pitfalls to avoid when managing major technology and organizational transitions. Finally, we present a potpourri of tips and considerations that we have found useful in our fifty combined years of project and organizational management.

The Times They Are A-Changing

The effect of technology on our organizations is pervasive, a fact that is often underestimated within traditional thinking, despite all the attention on technology in recent years. It is now inconceivable to think in terms of major technological change without considering the major areas of the organization where technology resides (Bysinger & Knight, 1996). It is likewise inconceivable to consider organizational change without factoring in possible technological changes. Although it is still somewhat useful and necessary to maintain that managing technology is different and apart from managing the college in general, the line is blurring. Note, for example, the steady increase in the number of technology managers who sit at the executive level of the college rather than in mid-management. As information technology continues to permeate organizations at all levels, we must strengthen links between technology management and general college leadership. As Boar (1994) argues, the degree to which the culture of technology management aligns with general organizational leadership will no doubt be the degree to which we are effectively using technology. This potential alignment of technology and culture may be a factor in determining the degree to which our colleges reach their fullest potential as foundational institutions of society.

When addressing technology issues, we must deal with college change on two levels: the general level of the organization and the specialized level of technology. On the broad, primary level of management, we must understand the larger societal and other external factors that affect the college. On the secondary level of information technology, we must understand the changes driven by the many new technical tools, applications, platforms, and systems available to us. The changes occurring at both levels are significant enough to be viewed as paradigm shifts, and each of these shifts, though different phenomena, is interactive. In the following paragraphs, we present our current understanding of each of these two shifts.

Changes in College Operating Environments

In response to the changing nature of the global economy and other societal transitions, a general paradigm shift has affected virtually all organizations. During the past decade, phrases such as strategic planning, businesses processing, reengineering, "right-sizing," doing more with less, "working smarter not harder," continuously improving processes, and judging effectiveness in terms of outcomes have been used to describe this continuing movement within the major organizations of our society (Aburdene and Naisbitt, 1990; Drucker, 1989; Peters, 1992; Porter, 1990). This paradigm shift also involves the movement calling for more efficient operations, more creativity, customer-centered approaches, and mass customization. Community colleges must face all these issues and more. Colleges generally are affected by additional sector-specific nuances in the form of performance-based funding and outcomes-based quality assessment as described in Roueche, Roueche, and Johnson (1997). Additionally, in the spirit of "placing the customer first," O'Banion (1997) argues for realignment in colleges "to place the student first" through learner-centered instruction and student services (p. 22). To begin to comprehend managing major technology and organizational transitions, we are challenged to understand the overall shifting of the society in which our colleges operate. As one organization among many in a global community, the individual college negotiates with and adapts to a changing external operating environment.

Specific Changes Facing Community Colleges

A national survey of community college CEOs by the League for Innovation in the Community College (Milliron & Miles, see Chapter 1) found seven key issues facing community colleges. These seven issues represent general paradigm shifts in the college operating environment, each with significant ramifications for information technology management:

1. *Enrollment Pressures.* General enrollment in community colleges will increase over the next decade as will the diversity of the students enrolling.
2. *Turnover Waves.* The rate of faculty, administrator, and staff retirement will increase. More college employees are expected to retire in the next ten years than have done so in the previous twenty years.
3. *Technology Transitions.* The general trend toward increased use of technology will accelerate. Training faculty in technology will remain a major issue. The cost of obtaining and maintaining technology will be a major issue for governing boards and legislatures. New instructional delivery methods will increasingly be based on information technology.
4. *Partnership Programs.* Developing training partnerships with local corporations will become increasingly important. Welfare reform will necessitate stronger links with local social service agencies. Partnerships with K-12 schools and transfer institutions will be fostered.
5. *At-Risk Access.* As a larger proportion of the population seeks higher education, the need for basic skills training and developmental education will continue to grow.
6. *Accountability Mandates.* Legislatures will continue to call for greater accountability from colleges. Funding will increasingly be tied in some way to performance indicators. The need for good data collection and analysis will become increasingly important.
7. *The Learning Revolution.* Colleges will become more learner centered. Options for alternative learning times, places, and methods will increase, and many of these will involve information technology.

Technology Level Changes Facing Colleges

As we move from the level of general changes affecting colleges to a level more specifically focused on technology issues, we also find major paradigm shifts: "Just as the organizational structures, business environments, and old world order are being drastically altered by ongoing global changes, the first era of information technology is experiencing a similar fate" (Tapscott & Caston, 1993, p. 13). Boar (1994) provides an apt metaphor for this change, stating that "the information technology field has gone from being a still life painting to being a splatter painting" (p. 53). The quiet, predictable, and orderly picture has become dynamic, chaotic, and much less certain.

Though it is difficult to determine exactly what is emerging from the whirlwind of technology developments, several general directions are emerging (Lorin, 1996; Tapscott & Caston, 1993). These technology shifts are not minor enhancements or slight alterations to older technology; they have widespread ramifications regarding what can be done with technology and how those activities will be done. Figure 9A outlines eight critical changes identified by Tapscott and Caston (1993) that benchmark the shift from what they call the Era I technology paradigm of the past 30 years to the emerging Era II technology paradigm.

The previous era of one big central computer doing most of the work in an organization is rapidly vanishing. Increasingly, the total computing enterprise consists of diverse computers of different sizes, functions and "personalities" that must work together to address the needs of the organization. The client/server relationship among machines is continuing to expand and mature. To support this multiple computer model of distributed computing, software systems will also continue to mature. Within this new paradigm, a minimal cost of changing platforms must be achieved by allowing software to be both easily and quickly scalable (i.e., able to be used concurrently by thousands of users) and portable (i.e., easily modified to work on a totally different type of hardware).

This technology paradigm shift points not only to a different form of information processing technology, but also to increasingly higher levels of processed information. Another general characteristic of the emerging technology paradigm is access to information that is not restricted by technical limitations and boundaries (Gates, 1999). Within the constraints of law and policy, college students and staff, for example, will be able to access any information at any time and across any platform. A wider variety of information will be available than has been in the past, and it will be displayed in easily understandable graphical modes. The

Figure 9A. Eight Critical Technology Shifts Adapted from Tapscott and Caston (1993)

Shift 1. From Traditional Semiconductors to Microprocessor-Based Systems
The computer on a chip is now dominating the older mainframe style semiconductor-based architecture.

Shift 2. From Host-Based to Network-Based Systems
The large central host mainframe is giving way to numerous computers of various sizes cooperating over a network.

Shift 3. From Vendor Proprietary Software to Open Software Standards
This is a move away from the old model of one vendor making software that worked only on that vendor's computer. When a new computer was purchased, software had to be rewritten at great cost. By 1992, every major computer vendor had adopted open system standards as the main approach to technology.

Shift 4. From Single to Multimedia
In the previous era, voice, data, and video had to be managed by different technologies. As standards for digital information and for digitizing information increase, one set of equipment will manage these different forms of information.

Shift 5. From Account Control to Vendor-Customer Partnerships Based on Free Will
In the first era, vendors controlled the customer's destiny. Commitment to a vendor meant total commitment to a system with few options. On the plus side, system integration was the vendor's problem. Now that multiple vendors provide various components within a larger system, the customer is responsible for making the system work.

Shift 6. Software Development from Craft to Factory
Most software development jobs were custom jobs. When software broke, the person who developed it would likely have to fix it. Now standard tools and components are developing that make software development more consistent and reliable.

Shift 7: From Alphanumeric to Graphical, Multiform User Interface
The days of green screens and cryptic messages are waning. Interfaces that simulate multiple types of communications and analysis tools are continuing to develop.

Shift 8: From Stand-Alone to Integrated Software Applications
In Era II, the focus is on integrating and sharing information easily among functional areas. Using common data files eases the burden of assuring data compatibility and consistency. Using common end-user and technical-user interfaces lowers the overall learning curve and decreases mistakes when jumping from one system to another.

continued development of document sharing and multimedia applications will contribute to enhanced information, and electronic data storage, retrieval, and network transport systems will be expected to handle more and more unstructured information such as video and audio. We can expect that technology tools, systems, and workers will continue to proliferate.

As we conclude this look at the shifting paradigms affecting colleges, we offer one caveat: experience has shown that making predictions related to technology is a daunting factor in management. Denning and Metcalfe (1997) remind us that history proves how notoriously bad even the greatest minds of the technological age have been at predicting the technological future. For example, IBM leader Thomas Watson is reputed to have argued that a maximum of five large computers would ultimately serve all the computing needs of the United States. Other technology leaders argued that there would never be a reason or a market for home computers. The list of erroneous technology-related predictions is quite long, but one thing appears certain: information technology, already a seemingly boundless entity, will continue to grow and change at an unprecedented rate (Boar, 1994). The many technologies already available to us for selection and integration into a coherent whole are multiplying, and the technical competencies and organizational cultures that sustained our colleges in the past are rapidly becoming dated.

Needed: Broadly Thinking Technicians and Technologically Savvy Leaders

The rapid widespread societal changes related to technology are too extensive to be managed by isolated technology departments staffed by specialists working apart from the mainstream of our colleges. Our primary challenge is not managing technology hardware and software. Instead, the major challenge we face is managing our organizations in the age of technology (Johnson, 1997). Major technology transitions go hand in hand with major shifts in organizational culture, formal policies and processes, staff skill sets, and fiscal structure. We contend that technology transitions, especially the major ones, are also organizational transitions since they are accompanied by shifts in instructional services and business operations. Our premise is that information technology is becoming so deeply embedded within our colleges that close working relationships between technology managers and college leaders have become essential.

Tight coupling between the mindset and behavior of the college's executive leaders and the technology managers is key. The technology manager must be ambidextrous, striving both to be a competent technology specialist and to understand general organizational leadership issues. Similarly, the college leader needs the skills of an organizational generalist combined with a deep understanding of specific technology issues. If major technology transitions are to become effective organizational transitions, then organizational leaders and technology managers must be closely aligned and cooperate at multiple levels. Above all, the technology management perspective must be merged with the larger vision of organizational leadership to provide broad-minded, relevant solutions to the needs of the organization.

We contend that, to be effective, technology managers and general college leaders alike should share the essential characteristics of information technology leaders as proposed by Lorin (1996). Lorin argues that leaders must understand the nature of technologies in which they invest. This understanding comes from knowing what the technologies are, what they do, how they compare to one another, and which dominate the industry. They must also understand the current state of the art, knowing both the pros and cons of various technology options. They also need to have a feel for the next probable stage of technology transition and for the costs associated with it. The knowledge and skills common to most competent technology managers may be new to many general executives.

Conversely, some technology managers may lack important knowledge and skills common to competent administrators. Effective technology management calls for technologists to have a broader conceptual framework than they would typically master working only in technology areas. They need to understand the interrelated elements of the systems that make up the larger organization, including the social, legal, political, and fiscal aspects of the college. The ability to identify potential problems with technology is critical, as is the skill to estimate the rate of transfer and acceptance of technology into the larger organization. Ultimately, effective technology managers need political power and an understanding of key leadership concepts that may impact major technology transitions, such as organizational culture and change.

Unrealistic Technology Expectations within the College

We have argued that technology management and overall college management should be relatively tightly coupled, that technological change of any significance is also organizational change, that many factors cause both technological and organizational changes in our colleges, and that college leaders need to be technologically savvy organizational generalists. These arguments are supported by findings from a study of community college technology professionals.

To better understand the attitudes toward major technology projects in colleges, we conducted a survey of technology professionals at eight selected community colleges in six states to assess their perceptions about technology management, their role in the institution, and attitudes of their nontechnical colleagues. The sample size was very small (n=114) and the methodology was fairly informal; however, a review of the findings with the technology staff at our college revealed emphatic agreement with our survey findings. The eight technology staff members at our college who participated in the follow-up focus group have a variety of career experiences in different types of organizations, a factor that we believe lends depth and credibility to their perspectives.

Technology professionals responding to our survey indicated that their nontechnical colleagues have unrealistic expectations regarding the costs, time, and effort required to implement major technology transitions. This finding seems particularly important since such expectations determine the intensity of focus, support, and effort that the college community brings to bear on technology projects.

The technical staff focus group identified several tendencies among their nontechnology colleagues related to unrealistic expectations:

- Many nontechnical colleagues are not aware of the true complexity of modern information systems and so underestimate the amount of work required to implement and to maintain such systems.
- Nontechnical colleagues often lack a "big picture" perspective of major technology systems and understand only the portion they work with on a regular basis.
- Nontechnical colleagues are often unaware of the total costs of implementation and ownership of a complex system. Costs often overlooked include resources needed to support the infrastructure, to train the technical staff and users, to recruit and hire new technical staff to support new technology, to handle system failures and other inefficiencies that occur during system changes and conversions, and to pay annual system maintenance fees.

- Nontechnical colleagues tend to apply their understanding of simple, single-user office software or off-the-shelf office productivity software with the much more complex, enterprise-level, multiuser, multisite, multiplatform computer systems. Nontechnical staff may not realize that installing an upgrade to a favorite PC address book database application is not the same as upgrading a central set of programs used simultaneously by dozens or even hundreds of people.

The technical staff in our focus group identified five factors that may contribute to these widespread misperceptions about technology on the part of nontechnical employees:

- Technology vendors, salespersons, and external consultants many times persuasively illustrate the potential benefits of their products without disclosing or even knowing the full cost and time for integrating these products in a work setting or of long-term ownership. Complex technology products are less like commodities purchased in a department store that you take home and plug in than unfinished kits that need to be assembled and modified for practical use. There is a natural and understood tendency in the sales process to emphasize a product's potential and minimize the liabilities. Additionally, technology salespeople typically have little practical knowledge of a particular college's organizational culture, structure, and history, all of which influence the management of technology in the institution.
- College technology staff typically do not have the resources to fully analyze a major technology transition proposal as presented to them by a manager of a functional area. Time and staff limitations too often hamper the development of a full and realistic estimate of the time and costs associated with a new proposal that might counteract any overly optimistic expectations painted by the external salespeople and the internal champions of a technology project.
- Sometimes college leaders are overly optimistic when determining a "go live" date and a maximum budget amount for a technology project. Deadlines are important to overall organizational planning, but may have little relevance to the actual technical and budgetary requirements of the full organizational transition required by the technology project.

- The college technology staff, with a strong collective desire to be seen as cooperative and responsive to the college community at large, might also tend to be overly optimistic, not wanting to be seen as the bearers of unfavorable news related to major technology transitions.
- The college technology staff might not have the expertise needed to develop accurate estimates of the resources needed to deploy a particular technology transition. Project management experience and skills, especially as they relate to new technology, are not necessarily found within the ranks of internal staff.

Finally, the technical staff focus group offered three recommendations to help reduce the problems associated with planning and implementing major technology transitions:

- More college administrators need to gain direct experience in managing major technology transitions so they are better prepared to contribute to the development and critique of realistic technology proposals and plans. In addition to understanding the overall effects of major technology projects, administrators should understand the culture of the college and how to support the slow and costly process of cultural change.
- Technology staff need strong technology leaders who have experience in technology project cost and work estimation, project management, internal marketing, and organizational politics.
- The college needs to develop a technology vision and plan that incorporates multiple perspectives and contributes to the overall mission of the college. The plan should promote strategic technology use and restrict the natural tendency of a few strong departments or individuals to dominate decision-making or to select pet projects that consume resources needed for the overall institution.

Although this study did not include the perspectives of nontechnical employees, we believe the technical staff's comments reveal concerns worthy of attention from administrators who are leading their colleges through technology and, therefore, organizational transitions. Clearly, further study is needed to explore the perceptions of nontechnical faculty and to examine the perspectives of other nontechnical faculty. Nevertheless, these findings bolster our key premise that technology directors and senior administrators need to work closely together as technology changes are considered and implemented. The following sections describe an organizational model that college and technology leaders can use to approach technology management strategically in a shifting college environment.

Why Such a Fuss When Making Changes? The Organizational Model

Major technology decisions and transitions attract the attention of the entire college. Some groups are pleased; others are not pleased. The key to managing these competing views is to embed technology plans and practices solidly into the mission, plans, and practices of the college. But a clear picture of how a technology initiative might fit into the complex college organization is sometimes elusive. Tushman and O'Reilly (1997) provide an organizational model that can be used to strategically analyze the interaction an implications of a technology initiative on the overall institution. This model divides the organization (the total college) into four broad, interrelated areas:

1. the college's critical tasks (the things that are done)
2. the college culture (the beliefs, working atmosphere, history)
3. the formal organization (the rules, policies, formal reporting relationships, and formal offices and office holders)
4. the people it employs (the various skills represented among personnel)

These four areas interact dynamically with each other, and help a college create its identity. The assumption of this model is that the four organizational areas must be in balance with one another to produce the desired mission-critical outcomes. The leaders are responsible for maintaining the balance needed for a college to fulfill its mission.[†] Tushman and O'Reilly (1997) propose a 3-tiered analysis of these four components of the organization.

[†] For additional explanations of how this model has been used in the analysis of community college work, see Johnson (1997), who explained the use of the Tushman-O'Reilly model in technology leadership in community colleges. See also Milliron and Leach (1997), who proposed this model to frame and process strategic responses to the critical issues facing community colleges.

Analysis One: Know Your College's Potential and Deficiencies

Tushman and O'Reilly (1997) argue that a systematic analysis of an organization should begin with assessment of the organization's critical opportunities and problems. This process entails identifying and defining current deficiencies in performance that could cause the organization to miss future opportunities; these problems and opportunities are framed in terms of *performance* and *opportunity* gaps. For example, a *performance gap* exists if community college preengineering students are not provided with adequate technical training in computer-aided design, training they will ultimately need as they transfer to engineering programs at senior institutions. An *opportunity gap* can be illustrated by the case of a network design. Imagine a computer network that satisfies today's modest data communications needs of e-mail and small file transfer. No performance gaps exist at this level of use, but the same network may not support interactive audio and video for desktop computers when these features become practical to offer. In this case, an opportunity gap eventually leads to a performance gap. Identifying the gaps and understanding their causes provide the foundation and direction for the next two stages of strategic processing.

Analysis Two: Know the Critical Work and Workflow

The next step in the organizational analysis is that of analyzing and describing in detail the critical tasks and processes used to produce the desired outcomes. For example, computerized academic placement testing might be reviewed from the perspective of a technology-related service. Following a systematic process, the tasks necessary for providing student advising through computerized testing would be broken down into discrete steps and tasks. This critical task decomposition should result in a full understanding of the process: identifying tasks necessary for achieving the desired outcomes, assigning tasks, determining methods and locations for completing tasks, and establishing a timeline for completion of tasks. Along with a more complete understanding of the tasks should come a better opportunity to understand why and where problems arise in a particular service, as well as where gaps may exist that could cause the organization to miss future opportunities to provide better service.

Analysis Three: Know the Balance of the Organization

This third step in the process is the estimation of the organizational congruence and balance among the four previously described areas of the organization. The balance among the critical tasks, informal culture, formal organization, and skill sets of employees can be analyzed and understood in light of the expected outcomes, the particular gap(s) one wants to close, and possible future opportunities. Realignment, a practice basic to the application of strategic planning in technology (Boar, 1994), of these areas in relation to each other and to the external environment is critical to success. Looking again at the example of computerized college placement testing, one might find that realignments may close performance gaps in that area. For example, remodeling the structure of the testing center or changing its hours of operation would be a formal organizational realignment. Hiring a technician to maintain the otherwise unreliable technology is a realignment of personnel. Relocating the testing center closer to other student services to improve informal communications between functional areas is an organizational culture realignment. Such tactics might, in our hypothetical example, provide improved services, close performance gaps, and position the college for future opportunities.

Application of the Tushman and O'Reilly model to a technology initiative can help ensure the strategic integrity of the college when facing major technology changes. As noted previously, the growing influence of technology on our institutions has transformed technology changes, which in the past were specialized self-contained transitions, into major organizational changes. Technology and change have become almost synonymous notions in community colleges, and the next two chapter sections offer insights into change management for college and technology leaders.

What We Know About Managing Change

It is well known that the introduction of IT can, in and of itself, cause tension and anxiety in an organization. Fear of technology, job displacement, job changes, and reorganization have been universally discussed. More recently, the cultural differences of the various units forced together by converging technologies are becoming more obvious.
-Woodsworth, 1991

College leaders aimed at innovation or improvement might sometimes wish the college worked like a machine with parts that can be changed at will, but we all know that making a major change is almost never so easy. Even with a good understanding of the college organization and adequate resources, changing the work behavior of groups and individuals is a challenging undertaking. Three major challenges must be managed during a major transition in a college.

The first challenge faced in implementing major transitions is the natural resistance to change. To many members of the college, change is inherently threatening. Some may fear the loss of identity and job security. Others may resent the added time and effort associated with the disruption of a major change. During transition phases of a major system change, there is typically much "double work."

The second challenge associated with major change is possible loss of organizational control. During a period of change, normal control systems like accurate financial reports or course management information can be disrupted, which can hamper control of key operations within the college. This makes the college vulnerable to a range of secondary problems, some conceivably quite serious, which might include audit criticisms and exceptions, harm to student progress, and a host of legal issues.

The third challenge is related to power in the form of personal influence and control of information and other resources. The balance of power held by individuals and groups can shift significantly with major transitions in the organization. Individuals and groups typically engage in active informal political action within a college to either resist or promote the change they believe is in their best interest. However, such "best interests" may be focused on goals such as less work, more pay, more influence over decisions and resources, better work schedules, more interesting colleagues, and more comfortable surroundings–outcomes that may not always be in the best interest of the college.

Managing a college during a major transition state is very different from managing in either the old state or the future state. The transition state of an organization is the "nether world" and requires special handling (Nadler, 1988). Information technology departments, for example, are often "caught in a squeeze" (Boar, 1994) because they must maintain the legacy systems that are currently running critical systems, while retraining and retooling to take advantage of new technologies. They are pressured to produce the same services within the same time frame while controlling costs, improving existing services, and dealing with resistance to change. According to Boar (1994), "When one compounds this situation by the business pressures and the threat of competition, it is obvious that the gifts offered by the enabling technologies have caught many information technology organizations unprepared" (p. 61).

A Three-Step Change Management Process

The problem of providing advice about change is not calling for change but selecting what to change to. Unless carefully designed, change can make things worse just as easily as it can make things better. Especially in an area like information technology, sooner or later, everything has only a past rather than a future.

(Boar, 1994, p. 2)

Nadler (1988) suggests a straightforward process for the management of organization and change that includes three steps we view as critical to strategic management of technology change in community colleges: (1) develop and communicate a clear image of the future; (2) identify and use organizational leverage points; and (3) address transactional elements of personnel, power, and resources.

The critical *first step* in a transition period is developing and communicating a clear image of the future. Anxiety-based resistance to change, or fear of the unknown, will diminish when those who are anxious about the unknown get a clear view of the vision of the leaders. A program of formal and informal communication methods used throughout the organization over a period of time assists in conveying the vision for the future of the organization.

Even with a clearly communicated vision, resistance will arise from those who do not accept the vision. To overcome such resistance and build organizational support for the change vision, the *second step* is to identify and use multiple leverage points in the organization. The true value of the Tushman and O'Reilly model (1997) is realized in this step in that the understanding of key components and issues of the college can direct leaders to valuable leverage points for advancing a change initiative. By understanding that the college is both formal and informal, with key task components involving various human skill sets, leaders can isolate policies, practices, and people having the greatest influence in the organization. The application of tactics across the leverage points in a manner consistent with the overall change yields the most effective results. Leverage points often include areas where rewards and punishments are applied and places where organizational realignment occurs. Changes in workflow associated with organizational change, for example, should be accompanied by changes in job descriptions; changes in job descriptions should be accompanied by changes in behavior that are the result of training. The leverage points are workflow, job descriptions, and training. All three leverage points should be managed and realigned with the overall transition needs in mind.

The *third step* in management of organizational change is addressing important transactional elements. A transition manager should be identified, and the position should come with the authority and resources necessary to effect change. The transition manager's budget should include funds for training, consulting, planning, and equipment. In addition, the transition manager should work from a plan designed to measure and shape performance, one which specifies benchmarks, performance standards, and the responsibilities of key individuals and groups. Finally, special organizational structures may need to be developed during the transition. Managing the process of change is frequently difficult within traditional organizational hierarchies (Nadler, 1988), so special task forces and experimental units often need to be formed for the transition period.

We realize that this three-step approach to organization change might be misconstrued as simplistic; however, Quinn (1988) argues that highly formalized approaches to long-range planning, goal generation, and strategic formulation are neither desirable nor effective: "[Effective leaders] artfully blend formal analysis, behavioral techniques, and power politics to bring about cohesive, step-by-step movement toward ends that are initially broadly conceived, but which are then constantly refined and reshaped as new information appears" (p. 733). This approach is termed "logical incrementalism" because awareness, commitment, and actions for change are built incrementally over time. The time can be greatly compressed if necessary, but the holistic, incremental steps remain the same.

Information Technology Strategy: Schools of Thought

Boar (1994) argues that technology leaders must achieve a state of strategic alignment between the entire organization and the IT department. Meeting this challenge requires major reengineering of the traditional community college technology department, which for the past 30 years typically has been only loosely or sporadically aligned with any strategic purpose other than to implement and support technology tools for the college. The problem is not one of reengineering or refocusing an existing alignment; it is a problem of constructing a strategic alignment for the first time.

Many differing schools of thought exist regarding the framework, attitude, and posture that should be taken when developing organizational strategy. Boar (1994) argues that the design approach, or rational school, predicated on deliberate forethought, experimentation, and design, is dominant. With the rational approach to strategy development, one approaches the unclear future through analysis, observation, and experiment. We favor this school of thought and use it both formally and informally in approaching strategic planning issues. In addition to the rational design school of thought, Boar (1994) outlines four other approaches to the development of organizational strategy:

1. *The Emergent Learning Approach.* In this view, strategy is derived from real life experiences. Strategy is a reaction to events that are analyzed to create a static account of those events and related factors. "A critic might take the view the emergent school formalizes the practice of 'muddling though'" (Boar, 1994, p. 11).
2. *The Interactive Approach.* This approach holds that since the external environment is in flux, and the future cannot be predicted, strategy must be done in real time. Just-in-time strategizing advocates reacting to each dynamic situation that arises. A critic might argue that this approach confuses broad strategic actions with day-to-day tactical actions.

3. *The Ready-Fire-Aim Approach.* The focus of this approach is action over planning in an effort to avoid "analysis paralysis." The emphasis is on the sheer numbers of active attempts, each an experiment among many to determine what actually works. A critic might argue that this approach suffers from a lack of stability and focus that comes from disciplined experimentation within the context of an overall guiding strategy.

4. *The Chaos Approach.* The basis of this approach can be found in popular interpretations of chaos theory. This school of thought has some fairly contradictory tenets, pitting the idea that life is a complex, nonlinear set of dynamic and unpredictable patterns against the idea that someday chaos theory will allow modeling and prediction of the seemingly unpredictable. This school of thought is relatively new, quite interesting, and still in the formative stage.

The purpose of an information technology strategy should be to align the technology department with the college as a whole, and this alignment can be via any of the approaches described. Each approach suggests that information technology departments can evolve to improve their effectiveness through process transformation. One approach we favor is Boar's (1994) five-stage model of information technology department

Figure 9B. Boar's (1994) Five Stage Model of Information Technology Department Alignment to the Overall Organization

Stage 1 Localized Exploitation
Technology is used to automate isolated functional areas and processes.

Stage 2 Internal Integration
Technology is used to build common systems across functional departments.

Stage 3 Business Process Redesign
Technology is used to build process-centric applications rather than function-centric applications.

Stage 4 Business Network Redesign
Technology is used to integrate major processes with suppliers and customers as one continuous system.

Stage 5 Business Scope Redefinition
Technology allows the organization to undertake novel initiatives, producing new services for new and existing customers.

alignment, based on the rational school of strategy development (Figure 9B). The model outlines an incremental approach to strategic management of technology which suggests that as the information technology department improves its state of alignment with the larger organization, it moves through recognizable stages of increasingly broad influence on overall college goals.

Conclusion: The Sum of Our Experiences

Changes in technology clearly require a response from the culture responsible for its acquisition, evolution, and use. Different organizations of different skill sets are required. Different metaphors and abstractions are needed to articulate system concepts and directions. Different working groups and group relations must be formed around technology as its own internal structure changes.

-Lorin, 1996, p. 20

Although we do not believe in simple recipes or magic formulas for managing, we have found during the course of the technology and organizational transitions we have experienced over our careers a few truisms and recommendations we think are worthy of sharing.

Many interesting, even awe-inspiring, technology-based solutions are searching for problems to solve. The technology world is a whirlwind of new products, many developed to solve a particular problem in some particular situation. Other products are developed on speculation that they will solve some problem that is not yet widely recognized. Clearly defining an organization's technology problems is a helpful way to avoid wasting resources by purchasing great solutions that do not match the problem.

Technology management is greatly enhanced by focusing on performance and opportunity gaps. First, understand the actual critical problems to be solved and the actual benefits to be expected by solving them. Then create and apply solutions, whether they are based on technology or on another approach. When a problem is understood and communicated, the technology vision is easier to define and helps combat resistance to change. When complex and prolonged technology transitions become clouded and confused, clarity in defining the problem is critical for retaining focus.

Specify the scope of a technology project at the beginning of the transition process and adjust as needed, but avoid "feature creep." As important as knowing why to start a technology transition process is defining the point at which it is finished. This product definition is a critical part of the planning process. The enemy of successful implementations is feature creep, the process that begins after the plans, the timeline, and the budgets are set. Feature creep occurs when typically well-meaning members of the organization begin to ask for one new feature or modification after another. The requests, small and harmless by themselves, begin to add up to a significant list. This process expands the scope of the project, and, if left unchecked, will outstrip resources, cause schedules to slip, and cause the project contributors to lose focus.

Resistance to change is pervasive and multiform. Do not underestimate the amount or the power of the resistance to change. Expect it from all quarters and from individuals whose reasons may be quite surprising. Learn to recognize the many faces of resistance. Open hostility to change is obvious, as is direct and open behavior focused on impeding the transition pathway. Much more challenging, however, are the passive aggressors who openly support the changes surrounding the technology transition but engage in quiet sabotage. Another face of resistance is that of the malicious compliers, who live up to the "letter" of the law related to change but do not apply the effort and initiative needed for the intended "spirit" of the change.

Committed support from the people in the organization who have the formal or the informal power to overcome resistance is critical. The best, most worthy technology project in the world will fail if the people who have formal and informal power do not support the change. These people can clear obstacles and provide resources that allow the transition to occur. If a commitment to the change initiative from these key organizational levers does not exist, then a major technology transition should not be attempted.

Major technology transitions require substantive participation from competent, knowledgeable individuals from numerous functional areas of the organization. Cross-functional teams are invaluable to the processes of planning and implementation. Given that technology transitions are transitions of processes, tasks, policies, culture, and people, it is essential to garner widespread involvement in the change initiative.

Understand the total cost of implementing any technology transition and the total cost of maintaining the new system once implemented. Miscalculating the costs of a major technology transition is easy. In part, this is because much of the focus in technology transitions is on the enabling technologies for end-users. However, behind the end-user technology is the need for adequate supporting infrastructure and technical personnel. Thus, the cost of the end-user technology is only a fraction of the total cost necessary to support that technology. In addition, new recurring costs related to maintaining a new system are likely.

Managing a technology-infused organization is not unlike standing on a moving rock. The base is solid, but it exists in a fluid space. Leaders can maneuver this unstable environment by maintaining focus on the fundamental goals of the organization and on ways to direct the dizzying transformation in technology transition toward achievement of those goals. In the community college, those goals are likely to be underscored by the need to use the best possible technology tools and strategies to fulfill the college mission. Strategically integrating technology management into the central core of community college operations while negotiating the mercurial landscape of technology transition in an era of resource limitations, social change, and accountability is not an easy endeavor. Boar (1994), though, reminds us of the value of this undertaking:

> Progress is possible only if there are people of action who have the courage to listen, reflect, discard, experiment, and finally trust their reason, their vision, and their instinct. Creative advances are always accompanied by a great outrage to some sacred custom, tradition, or belief; they are turbulent but exciting experiences. Do not be shy to confront the truth; change defaces what is, and what is will be staunchly defended. The mission of the IT strategist to reengineer the IT organization to reach a state of perfect strategic alignment with the business will not be easy, but will be valuable. (p. 3)

References

Aburdene, P., & Naisbitt, J. (1990). *Megatrends 2000: Ten New Directions for the 1990s.* New York: William Morrow & Company.

Boar, B. H. (1994). *Practical Steps for Aligning Information Technology with Business Strategy.* New York: John Wiley & Sons.

Bysinger, B., & Knight, K. (1996). *Investing in Information Technology: A Decision-Making Guide for Business and Technology Managers.* New York: Van Nostrand Reinhold.

Denning, P. J., & Metcalfe, R. M. (1997). *Beyond Calculation: The Next Fifty Years of Computing.* New York: Copernicus.

Drucker, P. F. (1989). *The New Realities in Government and Politics/in Economics and Business/in Society and World View.* New York: Harper and Row.

Gates, B. (1999). *Business as the Speed of Thought: Using a Digital Nervous System.* New York: Warner Books.

Johnson, S. L. (1997). "Community College Leadership in the Age of Technology." *Leadership Abstracts*, 10(5). Mission Viejo, CA: League for Innovation in the Community College.

Lorin, H. (1996). *Doing IT Right: Technology, Business and Risk of Computing.* Greenwich, CT: Manning.

Milliron, M. D., & Leach, E. R. (1997). "Community Colleges Winning through Innovation: Taking on the Changes and Choices of Leadership in Twenty-First Century." *Leadership Abstracts*, Special Edition. Mission Viejo, CA: League for Innovation in the Community College.

Nadler, D. A. (1988). Concepts for the Management of Organizational Change. In M. Tushman and W. Moore (Eds.), *Readings in the Management of Innovation.* New York: HarperBusiness.

O'Banion, T. (1997). *A Learning College for the 21ˢᵗ Century.* Published jointly by the American Association of Community Colleges and the American Council on Education. Phoenix, AZ: Oryx Press

Peters, T. (1992). *Liberation Management: Necessary Disorganization for the Nanosecond Nineties.* New York: Alfred A. Knopf.

Porter, M. (1990). *The Competitive Advantage of Nations.* New York: Free Press.

Quinn, J. B. (1988). Managing Strategic Change. In M. Tushman & W. Moore (Eds.), *Readings in the Management of Innovation.* New York: HarperBusiness.

Roueche, J. E., Johnson, L. F., Roueche, S.D. & Associates. (1997). *Embracing the Tiger: The Effectiveness Debate & the Community College.* Washington, DC: Community College Press.

Steele, L. W. (1989). *Managing Technology.* New York: McGraw-Hill.

Tapscott, D., & Caston, A. (1993). *Paradigm Shift: The New Promise of Information Technology.* New York: McGraw-Hill.

Tushman, M. L., & O'Reilly III, C. A. (1997). *Winning through Innovation: A Practical Guide to Leading Organizational Change and Renewal.* Boston: Harvard Business School Press.

Weiser, M., & Brown, J. S. (1997). The Coming Age of Calm Technology. In P. Denning & R. Metcalfe (Eds.), *Beyond Calculation: The Next Fifty Years of Computing.* New York: Copernicus.

Woodsworth, A. (1991). *Patterns and Options for Managing Information Technology on Campus.* Chicago: The American Library Association.

CHAPTER 10

SELLING THE SIZZLE: MARKETING COMMUNITY COLLEGES THROUGH INFORMATION TECHNOLOGY

Lawrence G. Miller, Paul Fuchcar, and David T. Harrison

"You better start swimmin' or you'll sink like a stone,
for the times, they are a-changin'"
-Bob Dylan

In the 50 years following Gutenberg's invention of the printing press, the cost of copying or storing written or coded information dropped one thousand-fold, making it possible to copy for a penny what once cost ten dollars. In the 25 years since the development of the microprocessor, the cost of copying or storing coded information has dropped ten million-fold and we can now copy for a penny what once cost $100,000 (Gibson, 1995). As developments in technology continue to make information more readily available, community colleges are finding the use of information technology–especially the Internet–in their marketing strategies an effective and inexpensive approach to selling themselves. Aware that competition for students and resources is increasing, community colleges are asking what levels of efficiency they can bring to these marketing efforts.

In an ironic twist, though, the very technologies community colleges embrace as marketing tools also represent a tremendous threat to these institutions. Brick and mortar and geographic convenience no longer provide the competitive advantage community colleges have always enjoyed. The barriers for entry into the learning market are now minimal, as online education and other alternative forms of delivery become widely accepted. Additionally, the emphasis now placed by employers and students on learning outcomes, such as acquired competencies and certifications, instead of on academic credentials opens the door further to private and for-profit firms to capture market share once owned by community colleges. More money is now spent on higher education outside of colleges and universities than inside them, and the percentage of postsecondary education delivered by colleges and universities is falling at an alarming rate (Cameron & Tschirhart, 1992).

While demographic projections point to a slow but steady increase in the college-eligible population, community colleges continue to suffer from flat enrollment in traditional credit programs. This comes at a time when the overall market for education and training services is growing. The demand for a skilled workforce and lifelong learning has never been higher. To reverse the trend of owning a smaller share of a growing market, community colleges must look to new methods to communicate their value.

Though marketing has been emphasized by many community colleges in recent years, in order for the colleges to compete effectively in the current environment, a strategic marketing approach is required. Even in the face of new and more intense competition, community colleges have distinct competitive advantages. A well-structured marketing plan will enable them to craft this message for many stakeholders. And although information technologies and the Internet have created this disruptive environment, they have also created limitless opportunities. By embracing these technologies in their marketing and business processes, community colleges can take full advantage of these new opportunities.

In today's networked world, marketing goes far beyond attracting new students to the campus. Marketing expert Philip Kotler (1999) draws an important distinction between yesterday's marketing strategy and that of today, stating, "Yesterday's marketers thought the most important skill was the ability to find new customers. . . . Today's consensus by marketers is the reverse. Keeping and growing customers is primary" (p. 121). This chapter describes the changing nature of markets in general due to emerging technologies, the opportunities and challenges of integrating these technologies into the marketing strategy, and the ways colleges can use these technologies to create an environment that fosters a sense of community–and customer loyalty–as a cornerstone for lifelong learning.

The Internet World

For good reason, the Internet and the World Wide Web have the attention of colleges and universities around the globe. The acceptance rate of these technologies is unprecedented, and they are rapidly and dramatically changing the way business is conducted. According to Deloitte & Touche (1999), it took the telephone 38 years to reach 10 million users, the fax machine 22 years, and the personal computer 7 years; it took the World Wide Web six months to reach 10 million users. Morgan Stanley's George Kelly emphasizes the Web's rapid growth, stating that "the Internet doubles in traffic every 100 days. There's nothing in the world except bacteria that grows that fast" (Deloitte & Touche, 1999). And while some still hold that the Internet is overhyped and will fade with time, Malcolm Frank (1997) believes the opposite is true, and that the Internet will have so great an impact that it will change the ways entire industries function. Despite the speed of the Internet and the "new rules" of the Web, though, common sense still applies. Organizations still must have the basics: customers, suppliers, employees, and a plan (Barker et al., 2000).

Marketing and Community Colleges

Dennis Johnson (1990), a marketing consultant who specializes in working with American community colleges, stresses that marketing has become a critical element for higher education:

There are those who will state that it is unethical or unnecessary to market a community college, and that it would be a waste of taxpayer and student funds. Nothing could be further from the truth. The question is not just one of who the community college may be now serving; it is, more importantly, who it may now be missing and not serving. . . . If marketing is understood as student-centered, and that the process includes and benefits everyone, it will not be seen as a threat, but rather as a tool of responsive management.

In a study of community college CEOs, Fuchcar (1999) found that presidents of community colleges recognized for their marketing prowess were eager to support and expand marketing efforts. His survey research also indicated that the two most common goals for marketing efforts were increased student enrollment and improving the image of the community college.

Using Technologies to Reach New Markets with New Products

Describing a marketing model with four components, Kotler (1999) notes that modern marketing aims to provide goods and services to specific segments of potential customers with (1) the product, (2) its pricing, (3) its place, and (4) the promotion of the goods and services provided. Importantly, Kotler emphasizes that the first three elements need to be understood fully before engaging in promotional activities. The infusion of information technology does not alter the basic model, but clearly new creative processes, products, and delivery systems can bring new opportunities.

Almost every community college has embraced the technology revolution in some way. Technology applications to enhance classroom instruction and stand-alone technology-based learning products, such as telecourses, teleconferencing, and multimedia production for CD-ROMs, have become common. Good teaching does not necessarily require technology, but the interest in technology-supported instruction is increasing, and in many cases it is improving teaching and learning. Through the use of information technology, traditional classroom teaching is enhanced and new products are developed for the marketplace.

The extension of the element of "place" through technology delivery has been equally profound. Distance learning has a lengthy history in American higher education, but the evolution of cost-effective delivery systems such as videotapes, CD-ROMs, and the World Wide Web has occurred rapidly. Educational services provided through technology have moved from the periphery of academic programs to the mainstream (Lever, Lemke, & Johnson, 1996).

The cost of technology and the effect on pricing are difficult to measure. In addition, most community colleges have limitations on pricing strategies because of their status as public agencies. However, it is safe to assume that information technologies may offer opportunities to contain costs or to expand services for the same costs.

Marketing and Technology-Based Promotion

Fuchcar (1999) found that colleges responding to a survey from the American Association of Community Colleges focused on four promotional delivery systems: print media, radio, websites, and television (Figure 10A).

Figure 10A. Promotional Delivery Systems

Media Used	% of Colleges Using Media (n=274)
Print Media	98
Radio	93
Websites	91
Television	72
Outdoor Display (Billboards)	33
Transit Display	12

(Fuchcar, 1999)

Clearly, many community colleges are using their websites as part of an overall promotion strategy. Moraine Valley Community College in Illinois maintains that its website must be consistent with all other "official publications." The site must "continue to reflect and represent the overall core values, mission, and image" of the college (D. Brooks, personal e-mail communication, February 2, 2000). Florida's Santa Fe Community College states that its website has parallel goals: to help recruit new students and interest casual Web users, and to better serve current students who have more specific needs (L. Keen, personal e-mail communication, January 20, 2000). Humber College in Toronto also sees the Web as an integral promotional tool for prospective students, receiving over 500,000 hits each month (K. Gataveckas, personal e-mail communication, January 31, 2000).

In her 1998 book *Customers.com*, Patricia Seybold describes five distinct stages of building an e-commerce organization:

1. Supplying organizational and product information
2. Providing customer support and enabling transactions
3. Supporting electronic transactions
4. Personalizing interactions with customers
5. Fostering community (p. 46)

Many community colleges are at the first stage in Seybold's model. This stage, which Seybold calls "brochureware," provides online information about the college, including such topics as its programs and courses, faculty, calendar, and schedules. Other institutions, like Moraine Valley, have gone a step further by allowing online registration and other transactions. In any case, the image projected by a college's website is not something taken lightly by leading institutions. As Santa Fe's design principles state, "whatever the medium, the message requires editorial direction in programming and content" (L. Keen, personal e-mail communication, January 24, 2000).

Because community colleges provide a broad range of services to many different stakeholders, developing a website that is meaningful and easy to use for all constituents is challenging. This is particularly complicated at a multicampus institution. Louis Murillo (L. Murillo, and K. Tow, personal e-mail communication, January 24, 2000) describes the challenges faced by the San Diego Community College District as the college system designed its site:

> There are current and potential students who may be looking for a variety of information from admissions criteria to courses available to fees and campus climate. But the district is also a major player in the community–a partner with business and industry, a provider of contract instruction, a source of cultural events, a fund raiser, an employer with jobs to fill and current employees to serve, and a large government entity with an obligation to provide the news media and public with information on governance, administration, and avenues for citizens' input. It became a chaotic jumble to try to address all these topics on a single home page.

Bo Peabody, Vice President of Network Strategy at Lycos, Inc., emphasizes the importance of a Web image reflecting an accurate message: "It's more important to show an image of what you've got instead of asking customers to guess. If you let them guess, they'll guess wrong" (Barker et al., 2000, p. 64).

New Technologies, New Habits, New Strategies

Each week during 1995, Americans spent 287 minutes consuming TV and video media, 116 minutes reading print media, 53 minutes using interactive media, and 161 minutes listening to audio media. Since consumers have a finite amount of time to consume media, adding new media alternatives to this mix will likely cannibalize existing media. Hence, the success of advertisers' new media strategies is subject to the number of those 1,000 minutes the consumer will commit to new media products (Fairfield Media Research, 1999).

These numbers certainly make the concerns of traditional entertainment venues such as television, print media, and motion pictures understandable. All indications are that these venues are losing their customers. In addition to a plethora of choices within a format–cable television, for example–the fastest growing threat is the World Wide Web. The *Graphic, Visualization, & Usability Center's (GVU) 10th WWW User Survey*, with more than 5,000 participants, reported the following daily or weekly use habits among respondents:

- 80 percent of survey respondents are on the Internet instead of watching TV
- 63 percent replace time on the telephone with the "Net"
- 48 percent replace reading with WWW time
- 43 percent spend time online instead of exercising
- 22 percent surf instead of going to the movies
- 22 percent use the Internet instead of going out/socializing (GVU, 1999)

Advantages of the Internet for Marketing

Author Larry Chase (1998, 1999) has written of the opportunities that Web-based marketing present. He suggests that typical television viewers need more than just a Web address to get them to turn off the tube, boot up the computer, dial up their Internet service provider, and fire up their Web browser to surf to a website shown in a TV spot. He suggests that companies lure consumers with promotions, cash-back giveaways, and information, and he predicts that companies' usage of Web addresses in TV ads might lead to an increase in the number of consumers who access the Web, especially with the advent of products like WebTV. As consumers are beginning to feel that the Internet provides products, services, or information they cannot get elsewhere, businesses are beginning to realize the importance and value of having a Web presence (Chase, 1998).

Design Considerations

Web development tools have evolved as rapidly as the Internet itself. Websites can be developed with very little technical savvy, and the very nature of the Internet provides little in the way of standardization. The development of a website typically involves trade-offs between creativity or attention-grabbing graphics and technical performance. What, then, makes a good website? Many experts unite around the idea that functionality and efficiency are paramount. James Cramer, co-founder of TheStreet.com, holds that "the look and feel of a site is meaningless. What matters is speed. People want to get in and get out. Until they get technology so that pictures and graphics don't delay load time, all pictures should be banned" (Barker et al., 2000, p. 60). Kathleen Eisenhardt (Barker et al., 2000) of Stanford agrees:

> Fancy graphics and animation don't buy you anything. There's a minimum level of slickness you want to see when you go to a site, and people will probably add those features as broadband becomes more common, but I expect you'll see a lot of diminishing returns as well (p. 60).

The tools are out there, but how they are used is what truly counts. Internet marketing guru Linda Cox (1999) colorfully states the real bottom line for a presence on the Web:

> It's okay to work in your underwear in your partially remodeled basement as long as everyone thinks you're in a suit in a high-rise on Success Avenue. It's NOT okay to broadcast your slovenly habits to the world at large via ill-formatted e-mail, poor spelling, sloppy grammar and inept punctuation. If every second line of your e-mail breaks after the first word, we're done.

Attracting Attention with Banners

Banners–graphic elements that appear on websites for the purpose of evoking an interactive mouse-click–are one of the basic advertising strategies for the Internet. Typically rectangular and often featuring animated graphics, banners generate "click-throughs," mouse clicks that take the Web surfer to a specific point where a targeted message is displayed. Banners can be particularly effective. A recent Andersen Consulting study concluded that experienced Web users in the U.S. are more likely to buy online from a company after exposure to banner ads than they are after exposure to traditional advertising (Hofman, 2000). Graduate students in the School of Business Administration at the University of Michigan discovered that the banner's location on the screen can be a powerful factor. Although banners are most commonly seen at the top of the page, this research found that a lower-right side banner placement proved to have a greater click-through rate by a factor of 228 percent (Sayers, 1999), something to consider when designing Web advertisements.

Not everyone agrees that banners are the right capture medium for everyone. In a roundtable discussion with other advertising agency CEOs, George Garrick stated:

> We have banners that have a .01 percent click rate, and we have banners that have a 20 percent click rate. And it's not because of where they're put and to whom they're shown. It's mostly because of what the banner says. It's a pretty well-established principle in direct marketing that something like 60 percent of an advertisement's effect is a function of the message and the creative rather than the media choice (Fourth Annual Advertising Roundtable, 1999).

Banners are not the only means of driving potential students to a college's website. In fact, many believe that traditional advertising is an important component in generating online activity. According to Siebel and House, "If you want to direct traffic to your site, you don't do it on the site" (Barker et al., 2000, p. 59). Peabody of Lycos agrees: "Off-line advertising is absolutely critical. . . . Traditional (organizations) going on the Web can use the advertising they already do" (Barker et al., 2000, p. 66).

Promoting a Web Presence with Newsgroups and Online Communities

Newsgroups, often called listservs, are an Internet exchange of information among individuals and groups, and they are available on a vast array of topics. Typically, people who are interested in a particular area read newsgroups devoted to that subject. Some newsgroups have specific protocols and procedures, so becoming familiar with the newsgroups and their cultures before making announcements on them is important. If a message does not meet a listserv's guidelines, it is likely to have a negative effect.

In many cases, newsgroups already exist to service very specific market segments. A college building a new academic program in Internet business should be able to locate listservs such as alt.ecommerce (www.deja.com/[ST_rn=if]/subng.xp?group=alt.ecommerce), read by only those with an interest in the subject. Subscribers can contribute valuable content, and the college Web address, included in the writer's signature file, will become known to a highly targeted group. Perhaps the best single source for educational newsgroups is the *Listservs for College Educators*, www.nhmccd.cc.tx.us/lrc/kc/edad-listserv.html. An excellent compendium can be found in *Catalyst: The Official LISTSERV Catalog* at www.lsoft.com/lists/listref.html.

Web marketer Larry Chase recommends listservs as one of the best-kept secrets of online advertising. Ads are inexpensive and production costs are minimal. Usually, sites with .edu or .org domains do not accept paid advertising; not all .coms do, either. The best strategy is to subscribe to listservs, understand their protocols and their audiences, and then determine the availability of advertising (Chase, 1999).

Seybold (1998) asserts that a strong Web presence and supporting processes can lead to unsurpassed customer loyalty. Through an ongoing Web-based interchange, the organization and the customer learn more and more about each other, creating the foundation for a more proactive, "intimate" relationship. This is Seybold's final stage of the e-commerce business model, which she calls "fostering community." Such a relationship can be established only when the Web is used to treat customers–or students–individually. She explains:

> You can plan your community initiatives at the outset, but you won't be ready to really foster community among your customers until you've built a high level of trust with each of them individually. That trust will come from paying attention to what they say and do and continuously improving their experience of doing business with you. (p. 344)

While many community colleges are not yet at this stage, Humber College has plans to get there. The college has created the position of Marketing Director with the intent of maximizing Humber's Web presence for "target marketing of specific products to specific customers on a mass-customized basis" (K. Gataveckas, personal e-mail communication, January 31, 2000).

Technology and Marketing Research

Increasingly, two-year institutions have relied on their institutional research operations to guide them toward quality standards such as accreditation criteria. Many community colleges have embraced measured criteria under the direction of institutional effectiveness or quality improvement. However, fewer colleges measure marketing effectiveness with the same zeal and sophistication that is employed in the sales-driven commercial world.

Perhaps a commendable but typical level of feedback research would be the efforts of Durham College (DC) in Oshawa, Ontario, where focus groups with secondary school students, guidance counselors, and DC students have led to significant positive changes in the college calendar. In DC's Program Review Model for Evaluation and Review, focus groups are used to obtain initial feedback, while surveys provide measures of attitudes toward programs, curricula, and instruction (Rahilly, 1992). While this kind of input from students is useful, it does not approach the customer intimacy model Seybold (1998) describes as possible through the Web.

Lodish and Reibstein (1986) suggest that information technologies and their application to marketing research have changed ways of conducting business. They explain that new ways to gather and analyze data allow marketers to determine the effects of individual elements of marketing such as pricing, advertising, and promotion. These Wharton School of Business researchers also suggest that the complexity of information generated through information technologies is of such a scale that market research analysis may be beyond the abilities and experiences of those who lack high-level training. In particular, they warn of the tendency to draw hasty conclusions about cause and effect (Lodish & Reibstein, 1986).

The Internet has further complicated the acquisition and analysis of customer trends, but it has created new market research opportunities as well. Buying patterns and preferences as well as movement through a site can be monitored and evaluated, and this information can enable decisions regarding the design of the site. Where are people spending their time? Where are they getting stuck? Additionally, personal market profiles are possible, enabling proactive marketing to individuals based on customized needs. Online retailers quickly provide additional buying suggestions to return customers based on historical purchases.

The ability to exploit technology fully for market research purposes lies in the organization's ability to implement and manage its information systems properly. While there is an encouraging trend among software vendors to incorporate marketing research capability into student information systems, such capabilities must be approached with caution. Integrating Web technologies with legacy systems can be very cumbersome. James Cramer warns, "A lot of the technology out there doesn't work well. Nobody admits it, because no one wants to tarnish the gloss that's on the Web" (Barker et al., 2000, p. 51). Dan Caulfield, CEO of Hire Quality Inc., advises that organizations making the jump to the Web should leave plenty of room for error: "Plan in time for technology that just doesn't go as smoothly as you'd like it to go" (Barker et al, 2000, p. 51). He maintains that a primary problem in innovating new technologies is that it takes much longer than it is supposed to.

New Expectations

The Information Age brings with it new expectations. For colleges, students and potential students are more likely to seek information and services through technology. The days of a campus information desk may not be over, but more and more learners will want to access information through technology rather than through site visits. With common use of the World Wide Web less than a decade old, colleges, like businesses, are wrestling with expectations of convenience, rapid response, accuracy, and interaction. In an article, "Have It Their Way," in *CIO Business Magazine*, John Edwards (1998) writes:

> The fast-paced, always-open nature of the Web has redefined customers' expectations for service. If a company's Web server is dishing up pages 24/7, customers want to know why they can't reach a service rep at 2 a.m. The Web never sleeps, so why should the customer service department.

With expectations come opportunities. Web and other technologies now allow service providers such as community colleges the ability to attract new customers and provide better services. As Edwards (1998) states, "New, sophisticated tools can help automate and streamline online customer service–as well as provide a larger menu of options." The opportunity also exists to direct actions from one technology system to another. For example, an effective Web page can spur a customer to the use of an automated telephone response system, such as telephone class registration or fee payment, or a call center operation. Edwards further suggests that information technology tools can be sorted on a continuum of customer interaction or gradient from least interactive, such as e-mail, to most interactive, such as chat sessions or live calls. He writes:

> The epitome of Web customer service is to have a seamless integration of multiple channels-all tied to your customer service database. Ultimately, the right services with the right integration can become a strategy for more than customer service-they can become a way to market new products and build your brand.

Further, the organizational disconnects and workarounds that are often overcome by individuals and manual processes will no longer be transparent to the customer who interacts online. Seybold (1998) warns that once organizations begin interacting with customers via their websites, customers will tell them exactly what they want and need. Organizations will quickly learn that the technology is a small part of the overall business model, and that existing enterprise systems and business processes must be streamlined from the customer's point of view. Customers will demand it. She writes:

> What your website highlights, in an unflattering way, is all the black holes that exist in your company's operations. Today you have people who know where the problems in your processes are. They do the workarounds. They fill in the gaps. They do their best to provide customers with seamless service. Yet behind the scenes there are usually a number of handoffs back and forth between departments; information is passed along verbally or informally. . . . Yet once customers begin interacting with you via the Web, that safety net falls away. Your company is left naked in front of its customers and channel partners. Every wrinkle shows; every blemish spoils the customer's ability to help herself to information and transactions. (p. 34)

Seybold summarizes the new expectations of customers like this:

> In the very near future, customers will expect you to know who they are and to deliver what they need. . . . Companies that identify and leverage customers will be the norm. Firms still selling product families (i.e., academic programs) to anonymous customers will be struggling to remain profitable. (p. 61)

Conclusion

The Digital Age brings a sense of excitement, continuous change, and connectivity. It also brings an environment of new competition, expectations, and opportunities. Community colleges will apply the tools of this information revolution toward fulfilling their mission to provide access to educational opportunities for all. Marketing has gained acceptance among community college leaders as a necessity of the times. Colleges can no longer afford to remain isolated, and technology allows them to connect not only to their communities, but also to the entire world. New products and services, new deliveries, and new cost efficiencies are worthy of promotion. To promote themselves in this new age of rapid change, community colleges should seize the moment and fully embrace the technologies that are available to them.

Community colleges should view this new environment as a call to action. The Learning Revolution provides opportunities for growth that community colleges have not seen in many years. Even though new competitors arrive on the scene daily, colleges can use emerging technologies to exploit their distinct competitive advantages, gaining new students while retaining current ones. By "selling the sizzle" through information technology, community college leaders can better position their institutions to succeed in an increasingly competitive market.

References

Barker, E., Borrego, A. M., & Hofman, M. (2000, February). "I Was Seduced by the Web Economy." *Inc.* p. 48.

Cameron, K. S. & Tschirhart, M. (1992). Postindustrial Environments and Organizational Effectiveness in Colleges and Universities. *Journal of Higher Education*, 63 (1), 87-108.

Chase, L. (1998). *Essential Business Tactics for the Web*. New York: Wiley Computer Publishing.

Chase, L. (1999, May). Six Tips for Attracting Traffic to Your Site. *Web Digest for Marketers*. Available: chaseonline.com/marketing/attractraffic.html.

Cox, L. (1999, June 29). 10 Great Myths of Internet Marketing. *Internet Day*. Available: www.internetday.com/archives/062999.html.

Deloitte & Touche (1999, December). The E-Business Economy: An Executive Perspective. Presented at the Business Leaders Forum. Dayton, Ohio.

Edwards, J. (1998, December). Have It Their Way. *CIO Web Business Magazine*. Available: www.cio.com/archive/120198_power.html.

Fairfield Media Research. *Media Consumption in America* (1999). Available: www.cybersurvey.com/mediaresearch/mediachoices.htm.

Fourth Annual Advertising Roundtable. (1999, June 7). *Internet World*.

Frank, M. (1997, May 15). "The Realities of Web-Based Electronic Commerce." *Strategy & Leadership*.

Fuchcar, P. L. (1999). *The Use of Marketing to Achieve Institutional Goals at Community Colleges*. Dissertation, University of Texas at Austin.

Gibson, S. (1995, May/June). "Getting Wired." *Sequence*, 30:3.

Graphic, Visualization, & Usability Center's (GVU) 10th WWW User Survey. (1999). Available: www.gvu.gatech.edu/user_surveys/survey-1998-10/.

Hofman, M. (2000, February). Dispatches from the Web Economy. *Inc.* Available: www.inc.com/incmagazine/article/1,3654,ART16849_CNT53, 00.html [August 11, 2000].

Johnson, D. (1990, May). Hi-Tech, Hi-Touch, Hi-Teach: Marketing for Community Colleges. Paper presented at the National Institute for Staff and Organizational Development (NISOD) Conference on Teaching and Leadership Excellence, Austin, TX.

Kotler, P. (1999). *Kotler on Marketing: How to Create, Win, and Dominate Markets.* New York: Free Press.

Lever-Duffy, J., Lemke, R. A., & Johnson, L. (Eds.) (1996). *Learning without Limits: Model Distance Learning Programs in Community Colleges.* Mission Viejo, CA: League for Innovation in the Community College.

Lodish, L. M, & Reibstein, D. (1986, January). "Keeping Informed: New Gold Mines and Minefields in Market Research," *Harvard Business Review,* 86(1), 168(8).

Sayers, C. (1999). Put 'Er There. *The ClickZ Network.* Available: www.clickz.com/index.shtml.

Seybold, P. (1998). *Customers.com.* San Francisco: Jossey-Bass.

CHAPTER 11

INTERNET VISION:
UNLEASHING THE POWER OF THE INTERNET
IN THE HIGHER EDUCATION ENTERPRISE

Mark David Milliron

The Internet Challenge

Eleanor Roosevelt stated that "the future belongs to those who believe in the beauty of their dreams." Buried deep in the rich history and traditions of higher education is the belief that its core mission is about reaching for dreams, preparing for the future, and challenging old assumptions. Community and technical colleges in particular have been called "dream catchers" and are argued to be well poised to help society reap the prosperity promised by the confluence of technology, education, and the economy (Davis & Wessel, 1997). However, no matter how motivational the modern community college movement may be, providing leadership for dream catcher institutions in the age of the Internet is becoming an increasingly harrowing experience.

The headline of the April 26, 1999, *USA Today* Money section sums up a key concern gripping college and university leaders as they step forward into the 21st Century: "Failure to Tangle with the Web May Jeopardize CEOs." The story boldly states that "CEOs are endangered if they lack an Internet vision," and documents how organizational leaders in various industries are scrambling to strategically integrate the power of the Internet into their enterprises. Compaq Computers, the world's largest manufacturer of personal computers, ousted its CEO with specific reference to his inability to "vision" how the Internet would change Compaq's business model in the years to come.

While these examples focus on business and industry, higher education leaders can relate to the pressure being felt by their peers outside of academia. Internet technologies are certainly impacting the higher education world, so much so that we have moved from the need simply for quality technology management to the imperative for visionary leadership in the Information Age. Leaders and teachers at almost all levels of the educational enterprise are having to develop plans for the thoughtful integration of key technologies–particularly the Internet.

In these fast-moving times, developing a vision for use of the Internet in the higher education enterprise is talked about more than tackled. However, if we look at how the Internet is being used in business and industry, and relate that to its already rapid integration into education, we can point to some key implications for community college leaders striving to formulate an "Internet Vision" for community college education. Please do not assume that with this progression of ideas I intend to advance a business metaphor in higher education. My approach is to see how broader societal trends and new technologies are being played out in the business and industry arena and then vision how these same trends and technologies may ultimately help us improve the way we connect with our students and communities.

Internet Vision in Business and Industry

In his 1995 book, *The Digital Economy: Peril in the Age of Networked Intelligence*, Don Tapscott asserts:

> Today we are witnessing the early, turbulent days of a revolution as significant as any other in human history. A new medium of human communications is emerging, one that may prove to surpass all previous revolutions–the printing press, the telephone, the television, the computer–in its impact on our economic and social life. (p. xiii)

Predictions like these that once rang with hyperbole are being answered by stunning facts about how Internet technologies are changing the way we work, play, and learn. It took only four years for the World Wide Web to be used regularly by more than a quarter of the U.S. population–a feat that took electricity 46 years, the telephone 35 years, the radio 22 years, the television 26 years, and the personal computer 16 years. When you consider that each of these technologies massively transformed industrialized nations over the span of their adoption, we can only ponder the impact of the short cycle of our Web embrace.

Here are some basic statistics that make the point that our adoption of Internet technologies is nothing short of staggering. More than 300 million people currently use the Internet worldwide, and its network traffic doubles every 100 days. E-commerce is exploding. More than $6.3 billion in travel bookings are expected from online sites this year, up from $1 billion just two years ago. According to ActivMedia Research, total consumer e-commerce hit $66 billion in 1999 and is expected to boom to $160 billion in 2000. The U.S. Commerce Department estimates that consumer e-commerce will reach $300 billion and business-to-business e-commerce $1.53 trillion by 2002. America Online (AOL) has grown to more than 20 million members, increasing more than 4 million members in the last year alone. AOL supports more than 1.1 million users at peak hours, boasts more than $10 million in e-commerce per month, and transfers more than 760 million messages daily–surpassing even the U.S. Postal Service in volume.

Digital Drivers

According to Tapscott's (1995) *The Digital Economy*, this explosion of Internet technologies has modified the business and industry landscape through a series of interrelated change drivers. The first and most fundamental factor is *digitization*, the ability to digitally transmit and store audio, video, and data. Digitization leads to increasingly fluid data use and sharing over the Internet and Intranets. The current drive is to digitize as much content as possible and make it available quickly and easily, and Internet technologies meet this need. The Internet and other Intranets have become key international digitized content pathways, allowing all forms of digitized content to be transported, stored, searched, displayed, and even consumed.

This ease of data transmission drives *disintermediation*, the elimination of the "middleperson." For example, when you can use the Internet to download your favorite movie directly to your TV, you will no longer need to go to your local video store. Traditional business models–particularly retail models–are turned on their head because of this trend. Producers of goods are no longer forced to use traditional retail "channels" to reach customers. Dell Computers is probably the most notable example of this trend. Dell shuns the retail market and champions selling "direct." You will never see a Dell computer in a CompUSA or a

Circuit City, but you can buy one 24 hours a day online. In an attempt to "reintermediate," some retailers are aggressively launching websites that directly compete with their own local stores. Others are simply reacting with fear and trying to limit Web access. For example, during Christmas 1999, some mall locations refused to allow their tenants to display advertising that directed shoppers to websites, for fear that it would reduce mall traffic.

Disintermediation puts companies closer to the consumer, but it also increases the expectation for *immediacy*. As consumers, we want products and services "on demand," "just in time," and "on our timeline." We have become increasingly impatient, especially about information. If we want to search for a new car, we will go online and fully expect to get immediate information about any model car we wish. If manufacturers have poor or "unfriendly" websites that do not provide immediate pricing, specification, or local showroom information, we instantly form negative impressions about them. Beyond information, we also expect almost immediate sales and service capacities.

These changes in data capacities and consumer expectations have companies focusing more on *workgroups* to effectively and easily share data, communicate, and make decisions to meet customer needs. And, as workgroups engage in these tasks, the technology supports *mobility*–bringing the work to the people through the Web, e-mail, voicemail, and fax. The capacity to disperse work to mobile employees is a complete shift from the Industrial Age where people moved to the cities because that was where the work was. The current trend is to outfit home offices for employees, an interesting digitally driven return to family. Finally, more often than not in large companies, these workgroups are linked *globally*, connecting employees in multiple countries who are working toward common goals.

Enterprise Resource Planning

Business leaders faced with these new economic drivers and the explosive growth of technology are hard-pressed to think broadly about how to bring their technological pieces together to rise to the challenge of today. Of course, the best of breed have taken on this challenge by improving current systems and engaging new strategies, serving customers and developing products in new and innovative ways.

For example, in recent years advances in software and Internet distribution have led to the development of more comprehensive and integrated Enterprise Resource Planning (ERP) systems. ERP systems are the large administrative systems that handle finance, human resources, supply-chain management, decision support, and business intelligence. Elements of these systems have been adapted for and are being applied in higher education as well. In education, the recent emphasis has been on developing institutional human resources, finance, and student systems that seamlessly share data and provide user-friendly interfaces for multiple audiences: administrators, faculty, staff, and students. Thanks to Internet technologies and more powerful databases, the promise of integrated and easily accessible ERP systems is now being realized.

Customer Relationship Management

Additionally, Internet technologies and services have spawned an aggressive push to fully develop and deploy a complement to ERP–the Customer Relationship Management (CRM) system. If you've ever met with a sales person, called an 800 number, or ordered merchandise on the Web, you have experienced pieces of CRM.

The goal of CRM is to integrate marketing, sales, and service with ERP systems to build a holistic customer relationship "from lead to loyalty." The system is so tightly connected that the business can meet customer needs seamlessly at any stage of the relationship with a wide array of options.

The standard integrated CRM (Figure 11A) package supports marketing, sales, and service on at least three levels: (1) in person, (2) on the telephone, and (3) over the Web. Using Internet technologies and robust databases to underpin both the ERP and CRM systems, businesses are able to provide an array of integrated services to today's consumer (e.g., a Web-enabled sales and service force, call centers, and Web stores).

In a relatively short period of time, we as consumers have come to expect CRM. For example, we expect our preferred airline to have a website where we can peruse and reserve flights online, an 800 number we can call if we have more detailed questions, and a counter in the airport staffed by knowledgeable agents who can answer our questions. If we have problems or questions about our reservations for our upcoming

Figure 11A. Customer Relationship Management Matrix

vacation, we expect to able to use the Web, phone the airline's call center, or visit their counter in person for help–whichever mode is most convenient to us at our moment of need.

Finally, because we indicated in our customer profile that we want to be notified about the airline's frequent flyer program, we expect to receive e-mail informing us about new promotions and free tickets for first-time enrollees. All of these interactions should be seamlessly supported by an integrated data system that keeps our information on file so we don't have to go through a customer history with each and every interaction.

Soon, net-to-phone discussions, one-touch video conferencing, digital personal service agents, and (a little down the road) holographic imaging, will further enhance and become standard elements of CRM. Each new innovation will further enable business and industry to build positive, long-term relationships with their customers. If we look back only ten years, we can see that the use of the Internet to enable ERP and CRM has certainly changed the ways businesses are operating and, more so, what we as consumers expect.

Internet Vision in Higher Education

Higher education is being influenced by and is quickly embracing Internet technologies as well. In the administrative and student service areas, almost every Request for Proposals (RFP) for major administrative systems released over the last three years has required that key functions are "Web-enabled." No college can responsibly plan for the upgrade or replacement of its key ERP systems without thoroughly examining how it will be able to be leverage the Internet to improve almost all business office and student service systems. Students and employees now have the same expectations regarding accessibility, interaction, service, and the operational systems of the college that they have for the other businesses they interact with every day.

The adoption in instruction is even more staggering. Kenneth Green's 1999 Campus Computing Survey released at the League for Innovation Conference on Information Technology in Chicago reveals that more than 50 percent of higher education classes use e-mail to connect students to faculty and students to students. This simple innovation has enabled more asynchronous interaction in instruction and opened up venues for communication that enable previously quiet students to be more open with their instructors. And, particularly for part-time instructors who have a difficult time holding or offering office hours, basic e-mail access brings them more directly into contact with their students outside of class.

The Campus Computing Survey also shows that more than 40 percent of courses nationwide use Internet resources. At St. Petersburg Junior College Clearwater Campus, for example, every instructor has the ability to have a "Web-enhanced" course, with the syllabus, additional readings, and other resources accessible via the college's website. These enhancements are particularly useful given that most surveys show that the average faculty member and student access the Internet at least once a day.

Finally, since 1994, the use of Internet tools to enable online learning has taken the distance learning field by storm. Every day we read of another "cyber" college or consortium of colleges that are "going virtual" to provide on-demand synchronous and asynchronous online instruction.

Given the resistance of higher education to prior technologies ranging from overheads to CD-ROMs, these developments are staggering. Most of the studies on innovation diffusion and technology from the 1970s and 1980s argued that after the "innovator" and "early adopter" camps crested their use of a technology around 15 percent, institutions of higher education were hard-pressed to promote more widespread acceptance of technology tools. Several causes traditionally have been offered to explain higher education's slow embrace of technology, ranging from a resistant culture to unwilling faculty to underprepared students to underfunded institutions.

This quick adoption of Internet-related technologies is not surprising, however, when you consider how effectively they connect students and faculty to educational content, rich context, and to each other, not to mention how readily they enable better service and support. In her 1999 League monograph, *Learning is About Making Connections*, K. Patricia Cross points out that research on learning from multiple fields demonstrates that quality education is about helping students make meaningful connections with content and with each other–neurological synaptic connections, cognitive schematic connections, socially constructed connections, and experiential connections. It seems that Internet tools have succeeded precisely because they have more quickly and easily made the connection to the core mission of higher education–learning–than had their technological predecessors.

The challenge now is to think holistically about higher education administrative systems, student services, and learning options. Indeed, Internet technologies can improve each of these areas individually. However, as has been seen in other sectors, there is greater promise in using the Internet to bring together long-separated processes and people to improve higher learning. A basic framework for exploring the Internet in your educational enterprise is to think about how this technology can help *operations, services,* and *learning*. By ensuring that your institution is developing an integrated infrastructure in each of these areas, you are positioning your college or university to get the most out of the technology infrastructure you want to support your core organizational mission, vision, and goals.

Internet Operations

To fully develop Internet operations, you must build your infrastructure on state-of-the-art core technology. Core technologies include database, data warehouse, and core network architecture. A recent move is for the major ERP and CRM systems that sit on top of this core technology to be Internet distributed, meaning they are always distributed via a Java-enabled browser, as opposed to the more traditional mainframe or client-server infrastructure. Client-server computing will still be used by some; however, even client-server advocates will be integrating elements of Internet distribution of their software and data.

With future applications based on an Internet distribution model, education leaders will have additional options for their operational infrastructure, including the newest wave of Application Service Providers (ASP). An ASP manages all server hardware, operational software, and system maintenance in a data center, significantly reducing the cost and complexity for institutions without the hardware or staff to support sophisticated systems. When an institution signs up with an ASP, faculty, staff, and students will access their human resource, finance, student, and learning systems via the Internet or an Intranet connection using a standard browser. Particularly for those institutions having a difficult time attracting and retaining top-quality technology workers, this model may become very attractive. Most studies indicate that the ASP model will have a lower total cost of ownership because of the economies of scale related to housing multiple databases and systems in a centralized, professionally maintained center. However, until ASPs show that they are stable and effective, their adoption in higher education may move ahead slowly.

Internet Services

Higher education leaders cannot hide from the reality that a new, more technology savvy set of employees and students is coming. New students with high expectations regarding technology have little patience for institutions that do not have a service infrastructure that includes the ability to access information, transact business, and receive services via the Internet, as well as the phone. A poor Internet/Web infrastructure will leave these students with a negative perception of your institution.

Moreover, as higher education institutions reel from the waves of retirements and turnover that are washing over us, we must also plan for and meet the needs of more technically oriented employees who have no interest in or reverence for the "way it's always been done." These employees will also expect top-quality technology to take on their instructional and service roles.

Thankfully, with the right Internet infrastructure, a college or university is able to more quickly create a service infrastructure that includes Web, phone, and personal options for general information, recruiting, admissions, registration, orientation, support services, bookstore, athletics, career services, and work study. Taking it one step further, you can help develop custom student services that link to the organizational database, enabling better service and support to the diverse students coming through your institution. This level of customization is often called a "portal strategy." A student's personal portal to your institution would be accessed through the Web and would tailor the information and services accessible to that student's profile. For example, if the student was a returning woman and your college had seminars available that week for this audience, that information would be "pushed" to her portal.

Regardless of the level of customization, visioning an Internet service system will be an increasingly important part of recruiting, retaining, and satisfying the dot.com students and employees in the community college for years to come.

Internet Learning

With the foundation of an Internet-based operations and service architecture, Internet learning can reach greater heights. The Internet and its associated technologies have inspired such unprecedented adoption because they quickly, easily, and more scalably increase an educator's capacity to help students make connections to content, context, and community, resulting in more powerful learning experiences overall. Improved communication, collaboration, presentation, production, and research are only a few of the core benefits. Student services and faculty–particularly part-time faculty–can work together more closely as they use integrated data systems and applications to wrap powerful support around each student. And instructors can take advantage of

Internet-based learning tools that enable everything from faculty-driven to student-driven, in-class to in-home learning.

This operations, service, and learning infrastructure leads to much the same hybrid Customer Relationship Model as is being seen in business and industry. In higher education it may be better termed Learner Relationship Management (LRM). Notwithstanding the limitations of any business metaphor in education–the process of learning being far more complex than a simple business transaction–the LRM concept could move us toward a more integrated educational infrastructure that supports robust interactions with students across multiple modalities (Figure 11B).

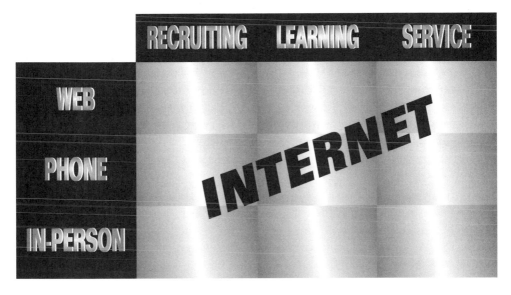

Figure 11B. Learner Relationship Management (LRM)

Clearly, students, faculty, staff, and communities are beginning to expect the outcomes this kind of Internet Vision provides. They expect to have a variety of options–Web, phone, or in-person–to check out programs and services; apply for admission; register for classes; take courses; reference syllabi; check grades; communicate with faculty, staff, or peers; and access state-of-the art research materials. Moreover, they expect all these services to be supported by an integrated data system that shares information seamlessly and securely.

Implications of Internet Vision in Higher Education

With these increased expectations comes the realization for today's educational leaders that developing, fostering, and maintaining a thriving academic community also means that they, too, will have to develop an Internet Vision. This vision must include technology infrastructures that transparently and seamlessly support the important mission and goals of higher education, allowing the rich interactions between educators and students to take precedence as they develop relationships with students "from leads to lifelong learners." As we move forward with efforts to unleash the power of the Internet in the higher education enterprise, however, we must consider key challenges, constituencies, and questions.

Key Challenges

First, Internet Vision is sweeping across the business world because it helps companies meet key challenges while achieving their core mission. Higher education will see this same effect. Internet Vision can help colleges and universities develop the kind of learning infrastructure that provides new options beyond the traditional time-bound, place-bound, role-bound, and bureaucracy-bound models of education.

Additionally, institutions will have the ability to handle the flood of new students slated to come into higher education over the next ten years, as well as the increasing number of returning and workforce development students. Also, as college and university faculty and staff retire, new employees will have a state-of-the-art service and learning infrastructure to walk into, not to mention new options for accessing information from home or on the road. Furthermore, institutions will be well positioned to partner with business and industry as they continue to advance with their use of Internet technologies. And, as state and federal policymakers call for more and more accountability data, institutions will be able to use business intelligence tools to quickly and easily gather process and outcomes data for use in internal decision making or external reporting.

Key Constituents

If we look at the likely results and expectations of Internet Vision in higher education, we can develop a good picture of what students, faculty, and administration will be seeing in the coming years. Students will have robust on- and off-campus access to college services and learning programs. They will have multiple modalities of communication and interaction with the institution, including Web, phone, and in-person. Moreover, students will have customized learning and service selections because they will be fully supported by an infrastructure that gives them access to more options. Ultimately, students will have choices galore. As more for-profit and aggressive colleges and universities continue to move into the online learning market, students will have the ability to choose from a wider array of education providers. Staying close to the learner and diversifying the learning options in this environment is an imperative.

Faculty, too, will have robust on- and off-campus access to college services and learning programs. Instructors will have a range of new learning tools with which to teach students. This does not mean that teaching and learning will be better necessarily–the Web clearly has the potential to make poor instruction that much more available. What it does mean is that the instructional tool kit will certainly be more complete. Faculty will have closer connections with student services because links between academic and administrative systems enable greater collaboration and support. Research, reference material, and student data will be much more readily available, and key grant projects will be much more manageable, enabling grant research to take precedence over grant management. Finally, Internet Vision will help faculty broaden their academic community to better serve local, regional, national, and international discipline and instructional groups.

An Internet Vision means that administration and support staff will also have robust on- and off-campus access to college services and learning programs. They will have a database and application suite that enables them to serve their institutions like never before. They will have powerful data systems to improve and track student, financial, and operational processes and outcomes. Their applications will be easily adaptable to meet the rapid changes in today's business processes and procedures. But, they, too, will be facing fierce competition. And, just as business and industry are discovering, without nimble ERP and CRM systems, they will be hard-pressed to continue to meet the changing needs of their learners and communities.

Key Questions

The continued expansion of Internet technologies is a given. Higher bandwidth, voice automation, and on-demand video will soon join the already existing innovations. As these and other technologies continue to change the way we work, play, and learn, higher education leaders must ask themselves these hard questions: (1) Is my institution taking advantage of Internet Vision? (2) How can my institution use Internet Vision to serve students, faculty, administration, alumni, and community better?

These are the sorts of questions that drove the *USA Today* story about CEOs grappling with the Internet. These are the sorts of questions that have driven the top companies using the Internet to take on their technology transformations and reap the rewards. These are the sorts of questions that must drive higher education leaders to think of new and innovative ways to use Internet technologies to meet the challenge of leadership and learning in the Information Age.

References

Cross, K. P. (1999). *Learning Is About Making Connections.* The Cross Papers Number 3. Mission Viejo, CA: League for Innovation in the Community College.

Green, K. C. (1999). *The 1999 National Survey of Information Technology in Higher Education.* Encino, CA: The Campus Computing Project.

O'Banion, T. (1997). *A Learning College for the 21st Century.* Published jointly by the American Association of Community Colleges and the American Council on Education. Phoenix, AZ: Oryx Press.

Tapscott, D. (Ed.). (1999). *Creating Value in the Network Economy.* Cambridge, MA: Harvard Business School Press.

Tapscott, D. (1995). *The Digital Economy: Promise and Peril in the Age of Networked Intelligence.* New York: McGraw-Hill.

About the League for Innovation

The League is an international association dedicated to catalyzing the potential of the community college movement. Since 1968, the League has been making a difference in community college education and in the lives of millions of educators and students. Twenty CEOs from the most influential, resourceful, and dynamic community colleges and districts in the world comprise the League's board of directors and provide strategic direction for its ongoing activities. These community colleges and their leaders are joined by more than 700 institutions that hold membership in the League's Alliance. The League–with this core of powerful and innovative community colleges and more than 100 corporate partners–serves nationally and internationally as a catalyst, project incubator, and experimental laboratory for community colleges around the world. Current initiatives take shape in the publications, conferences, institutes, and other quality services associated with the League's internationally recognized Learning-Centered Education, Leadership, Information Technology, and Workforce programs. These current programs, along with the League's 32-year history of service to the community college world, explain why in 1998 *Change* magazine called the League "the most dynamic organization in the community college world."